Chasing Spring

Ernest Wertheim with Linda Hamilton

ISBN: 978-1-4834-1408-9 (sc)
ISBN: 978-1-4834-1409-6 (hc)
ISBN: 978-1-4834-1407-2 (e)

Library of Congress Control Number: 2014911620

Chasing Spring reflects the opinions, perceptions, and memories of
Ernest Wertheim. The stories and conclusions he expresses within these
pages are matters of personal opinion, not necessarily fact, and are
in no way intended to be hurtful to any individual or group.

Edited by Steven Zlotowski, MD
and Rachelle Latimer

Lulu Publishing Services rev. date: 03/26/2015

Chasing Spring

"Once in a lifetime you meet a person who exemplifies the greatness of the human spirit. In youth, overcoming the extreme horror of a brutal regime, in America, struggling alone on a shoestring to build a new life, Ernest, with his keen mind, bravely faced the realities of war and not only survived but also thrived. All his life, he has cherished the value of family and friends, finding beauty in nature and people. This book will strengthen your belief in our ability to overcome life's severe challenges."
—Brian Minter, author of Canadian Best Seller, *Brian Minter's New Gardening Guide: Fresh Approaches for Canadian Gardeners*

"Wertheim is an unsung hero of the times; a masterful teller of a real life story of escape, daring and hard-earned success in his new homeland. You will enjoy this intriguing read that is an ode to marvelous plants and an incredible adventure combined!"
—Bob Dolibois, Horticulture industry executive and avid reader

"The life stories in Ernest Wertheim's memoir, by turns lyrical and horrific, are all the more gripping for the quiet voice in which they are told. *Chasing Spring* invites rather than demands the reader's empathy, a gift from any writer."
—Jackie Pels, Editor/Publisher, Hardscratch Press

"If this story was fiction it would be unbelievable, but it is an incredible account of the life of a remarkable man. It swings from the peaceful beauty of plants and nature to the inhuman and brutal atrocities of the Second World War. Having known Ernest for over 30 years he has been an inspiration to me and to many others."
—Warren Haskins, Chairman, Haskins Garden Centres Ltd.

To Margrit, Andy, Rick, and Brian

To Jacquie Williams-Courtright and Tom
Courtright and all my many friends

Acknowledgments

From Ernest:

I credit Jacquie Williams-Courtright, owner of Alden Lane Nursery in Livermore, California, with the idea that someone should write a book about my life. Many thanks to Anne Marshall Homan, the author of several local history books about the Livermore and Mount Diablo area, who became interested in the project and, for several months, took copious notes while I told her my stories. Her effort resulted in 17 chapters written in the third person. Without her initial work we could have never accomplished the final draft.

Thanks to Sabrina Hicks (wife of Stephen Hicks, president of Hicks Nursery in Long Island, New York), for her support and suggestions throughout the process even while she was writing her own book and having a baby in addition to taking care of their two other children.

When author Linda Hamilton and I met for breakfast on a Sunday morning in January 2013, we were still at the restaurant for lunch and afternoon tea as I told her my tales. Linda enthusiastically took on the project of bringing my memoir to life and did a fantastic job. As with projects of this nature, it took more than twice the time estimated, but Linda kept on working diligently.

We couldn't have finished the project without Steven Zlotowski, MD from Redding, California, who researched and caringly edited the entire manuscript. He also provided many suggestions along the way. There have been too many emails to count between Linda, Steve, Jacquie, Sabrina, and myself.

Thanks goes to my daughter-in-law, Lin, who edited several of the first chapters and also to Arianne Geraldin, who also did some editing and worked with me to start choosing photographs for the book. A lot of encouragement came from Brian Minter, my friend in Canada, the owner of the Minter Gardens and an author of several books and many articles, who is a great horticulturist, lecturer, and photographer.

A big thank you to the Latimer family, with whom I shared my stories as we drove to and from Alpine Meadows and the Bay Area. I appreciate their full support of this project, and, in particular, Ann and Rachelle's willingness to provide a final edit.

I would like to mention the names of my many friends in the horticultural and nursery industry who helped our office to get known, my friends on the ski hill, as well as the many architecture and landscape architecture clients I have worked with who became close friends. All these wonderful persons have influenced my life and should be mentioned, but there is just not enough room.

My gratitude goes to Tom Courtright, owner of Orchard Nursery and a very longtime friend who was supportive of his wife spending many hours reading e-mails and chapters, which meant she had less time to devote to her husband.

A word of thanks to my partner Jack Klemeyer, who tolerated my spending so much time on this book, and to our administrative assistant, Carole Haan, who has been with us for the past forty-three years and has looked out for me for all those years. I am deeply grateful to each of you for your partnership and friendship.

I want to acknowledge our sons, Andy and Rick, their wives, and our grandson, Brian, because they all received a lot less attention than they deserve. My love to you all!

Last but not least, I want to thank my wife, Margrit, for her love and support for more than seventy years. It is our partnership that has truly nurtured me and allowed me to grow and thrive. I am honored to be your husband. I continue to love you with all my heart!

From Linda:

Like Ernest, I want to thank Sabrina Hicks and Jacquie Williams-Courtright for encouraging Ernest to write his story and being supportive and providing needed opinions throughout the entire process. Thank you to Peter Turner, one of Ernest's skiing friends, for introducing me to this remarkable man.

I am very grateful to Steve Zlotowski who devoted so much time and effort to honing and polishing this story. He also guided some of the harder decisions about what to omit and was a cornerstone in the final phase of this project.

More love than can be expressed on this two-dimensional page goes to my husband, Doug, and my boys, Ben and Max, who heard Ernest's stories on many occasions, always curious and supportive, and to my parents, Bob and Nancy, who read early chapters, and kept saying they couldn't wait to read the rest.

Firstly and lastly, I am so very thankful to Ernest for the opportunity and his trust in me to write his story. I just couldn't help but pour my heart into this book, and I was continually humbled and inspired by his strength of character, kindness, his sense of humor and his ability to see beauty around him even in the darkest moment. What a pleasure to learn so much history in order to more fully understand and vividly portray his experiences. I thank him for making me a budding horticulturalist too. (My overgrown garden awaits!) Knowing Ernest (née Ernst) Wertheim has truly enriched my life. I know this is true for his many friends as well and hope the same will be true for you, the reader, as you ride along with him on his life's journey.

Table of Contents

Foreword

I first met Ernest Wertheim in February 2012. We had been in email communication for several months, but now we sat together for a late lunch in my hometown just hours before our initial interview would reveal his first twenty-five years and mesmerize a jam-packed community gathering. It's easy to interview Ernest, you just ask some questions and get out of his way.

Ernest was ninety-two years old then, still working full-time, and skiing on the weekends. Earlier that week, Florence Green had passed away just two weeks shy of her 111th birthday. She was the last known veteran of the First World War. Ernest's story begins on the heels of her military service. He was born in Berlin, on December 30, 1919, the second son of a German, Jewish family.

One of his earliest memories is watching French troops withdraw from Germany's Ruhr Valley, their march home one of the last tangible vestiges of the Great War. He would gather connections to many more historical events, places, and people.

As you join Ernest in his life's journey, you'll be there when Hitler comes to power and you are a freshly minted teenager, thrust into the role of protecting your mother and younger brother in a world turned upside down. You'll see Hitler's bunker get built and somehow turn an association with Heinrich Himmler to your advantage. You'll go away to college as a fourteen year old Jew in Nazi Germany. You'll listen to the 1936 Berlin Olympics on the radio while trying to reconcile which country's athletes you should cheer. You'll risk your life to help others ski out of Germany. You'll be a target on *Kristallnacht* in November of 1938. Eventually, you'll make your own narrow escape, carrying the fate of your family on your young shoulders.

You'll wash ashore in America and join a struggling but astonishingly talented immigrant community. Then you'll drop everything you've just built to fight for your new home even though you are an enemy alien. Army life will catapult you across the world to the most unpredictable encounters with General Douglas MacArthur, New Guinea headhunters, and the liberation of Manila.

And as if this abridged, *Forest Gump* sample isn't enough, you'll feel and see all of this through the eyes and soul of one who can't help but process everything in the context of the plants and landscapes that inhabit these great human dramas of the twentieth century. You'll discover the horticulturist and landscape architect within, always seeing beauty in even the most dark and heartbreaking of circumstances.

As you read *Chasing Spring*, it's hard to resist the temptation of wishing that, somehow, this could be your life. That your story and all of its emotional ups and downs could be played on such a grand stage, and that you, too, could always see the majesty in the world around you.

Or perhaps, we can just hope we have the courage and pluck and passion to live such a life. Beyond the sweeping adventures that span the globe, the orbit of Ernest's journey always spins around the enduring themes of how we treat each other and how we fail or succeed in resolving our differences. His experiences with bigotry, hatred, immigration, war, and career have something to teach us. Finally, his life is a reminder that hard work, frugality, humility, and integrity hold a cherished place in our past and, hopefully, in our future.

This is a book for history lovers and hobby gardeners, for veterans and immigrants and their families, for war buffs and horticulturalists, for Californians and for skiers. This is a book for anyone who has struggled with injustice and tried to put a best foot forward. This is a book for the romantics whose marriages might not tally seventy-two years and counting.

As you turn the page, it's my great pleasure to introduce you to Ernest Wertheim. He still works full-time as a horticulturist and landscape architect, and although you might not have met him yet, he's also changed the way you buy plants for your home or business. He's ninety-four years old and darn hard to keep up with, so you best not dawdle. Ernest is already writing another chapter of his extraordinary life.

—On behalf of my adopted grandfather,
Steven Zlotowski, MD in the spring of 2014
Editor, *Chasing Spring*

Part I

CHAPTER 1

The Crocus in the Snow

Crocus vernus (crocus)
Photo by Christian Pourre, www.hautesavoiephoto.com

During my youth, in the Germany of the 1920s, my country was in chaos, defeated by war, and in economic crisis. But all I could see was the crocus, the lavender and golden flower, poking its way above the snow after a long and colorless winter. The sight was exhilarating to my young eyes. How brave the crocus was withstanding the cold to announce springtime had come to Hamburg.

Equally exciting was the march of soldiers down Bendlerstrasse, the street in Berlin where my grandparents lived. In tight formation and pressed uniforms, the men paraded to the crisp tempo of fife and drum. I held my mother's hand, waving at them as they passed the American ambassador's private residence on their way to the German Army headquarters.

For the adults around me this parade was a reminder of Germany's former glory, when there were plenty of jobs and people ate well and lived well. A time when Germany had Europe's most powerful economy and military, second in the world only to the United States.

Near the end of the Great Empire in 1914, Robert Wertheim, a poised, serious young man in spectacles, fell in love with my mother, Martha Guttman, a beautiful, round-faced young woman full of optimism and vitality. Both came from metropolitan, well-educated Jewish families in Berlin. They attended the opera or strolled in the Tiergarten, always accompanied by a chaperon insisted upon by my grandparents. My mother was very unhappy about this custom because she felt she was mature enough to handle herself. The chaperon did not impede their courtship, however, as they were soon married.

My mother, Martha Guttman, as a young woman

Newly married and with the Great War raging, my father was recruited into the German Army to serve his country. Because of his poor eyesight, he did not become an infantryman, luckily for him. Instead, he headed up a government department in Berlin that collected iron and steel for recycling. This enabled my father and mother to live their newlywed years together in Berlin. Thus my older brother, Werner, came into the world on January 1, 1916.

I was "manufactured" when the war was over. Though it was peacetime, the people of Germany were still battling to rebuild their lives. During the war, resources and food had been diverted to the war effort. Afterward, Germany had to pay huge sums in reparations to the Allies. It was in this bleak time that I was born, December 30, 1919, in my parents' small apartment in Berlin.

In 1920, my father found a job with a large company that recycled steel. This meant leaving Berlin and moving to Hamburg. Mother did not like leaving her family but being well employed was important.

Three years after the war, hyperinflation gripped the country and wiped out the value of savings. Still, people clung to their optimism even as the situation in Germany worsened, much the same way a nurseryman looks forward to the spring when business will surely improve after winter. It wasn't until 1924 that things started to look up, just after I had seen my first crocus. As part of the Dawes Plan, the United States lent Germany huge sums of money. The economy started to improve, unemployment was reduced, and people began to feel more secure again. Germany was becoming increasingly prosperous and peaceful. My parents lived a quiet, stable, upper-middle class lifestyle. Thus began my remembered life, a childhood of reliable seasons. That is until my father was kidnapped one cold winter morning in 1933, changing the course of my life forever.

Before then winter meant ice skating and sledding with my neighborhood friends. Weekends promised a movie matinee, laughing at Charlie Chaplin falling or mugging at the camera in *Gold Rush* or being mesmerized by Greta Garbo's eyes. Winter vases in the apartment were filled with acacia branches, imported from the warm parts of Italy. While snow flurried outside, Werner and I slid down the U-shaped banister along the stairs leading from our second-floor apartment to the foyer of the building. It made for great fun, although we had to be careful not to laugh too loudly. Mother was not to know.

During the Christmas holiday, we played together all day long with our model train set carefully laid out all the way down the apartment's long hallway to the door of the maid's room, before curving into the living room and winding through the music room. The set included a turntable and could run several engines at once. After we were put to bed, we could hear my father and his friends, including my best friend George's father, running the engines and modeling for us that we all have an inner child in us.

Our home was never without flowers. In the spring, our neighbor's large lilac shrub hung over the fence into the garden, and I had permission to pick some blossoms to give to Mother. She loved the smell of lilacs. She had a natural talent for arranging flowers, and as I grew older, she often let me help with the arrangements. Along with the lilacs, bulb flowers like daffodils, tulips, and hyacinths replaced the acacia branches of winter in her vases. In March, Fräulein Liesel, our maid, brought forsythia branches in from a friend's garden. She would place them near the coal oven, the warmth encouraging the yellow flowers to open up long before they would out in the cool of spring. In May, Fräulein Liesel brought sweet peas back from the Hamburg farmers' market, abloom with purple, white, pink, and red flowers.

In late spring and throughout the summer, Fräulein Liesel returned from the market with baskets of plump, colorful fruit and vegetables for our daily meals and for my mother to can for the winter. The jars were stored in the basement along with wooden trays of apples and pears that lasted through most of the cold months. We also had a wine cellar. Wine was regularly served to the adults, and we children were allowed to drink it, too. I was very excited when, at a summer party for my paternal grandmother's seventieth birthday, I was allowed to drink champagne for the first time. This was a real occasion, and I can still feel the bubbles tickling my nose.

In summer, the geraniums on our balconies burst open, red and pink and white. The most beautiful were the ones placed on the largest balcony off the dining room, which overlooked Parkallee, the wide street below lined with broadleaved chestnut trees. When the weather was warm, our family ate out on the balcony around a table under a colorful umbrella shading us from the sun. My favorite meals, especially on hot days, included my mother's *Kirschsuppe,* a delicious, cold cherry soup, and my favorite dessert, *Rote Grütze,* a molded blancmange made with strawberries and raspberries, topped with real whipped cream.

With my Opa and older brother, Werner, in the summer of 1925

In autumn, the dahlias of late summer that my mother cut for our vases were replaced with autumn's chrysanthemums while Werner and I collected chestnuts from the trees along Parkallee. We shelled and cleaned them, working for several days to accumulate a wagonload. These chestnuts were not the variety humans eat; rather they were for animals. We pulled the wagon for two hours to the Hamburg Zoo to sell the chestnuts as feed for the animals in return for some spending money. Although we lived in a lovely, well-furnished apartment with a maid, we were trained to work for our pocket money. The words "loan" and "credit" were not in our vocabulary.

Even with all these flowers in the house it was my grandfather Guttman, my Opa, who firmly planted my interest in horticulture when I was just five years old. Throughout my childhood we visited Opa and Oma Guttman in Berlin, in their three-story apartment house my mother's family had built in 1865. When I was very young, my mother's grandparents, the Mendelsohns, lived on the first floor, Opa and Oma lived on the second level, and the family rented out the top floor to other tenants. In the summer of 1925, my parents went on a six-week vacation and left me with my grandparents in Berlin.

Opa had planted many flowers in large pots and flower boxes on the balconies, mostly geraniums, petunias and begonias. His fuchsia would hang over the edge of the balcony boxes, and as summer went along, they would create a beautiful sight to see from the street. Opa carefully tended to his plants each day. He made me his little helper and taught me the science of watering. I was too short to reach over the edge of the bigger pots, so Opa furnished me a stool to climb on. His watering can was much too heavy for me. He gave me my own small one, and I would gently pour the water onto the soil around the base of the flowers, according to his instructions. I especially liked my job on hot days when the poor flowers were close to wilting. A little while after I would make my watering rounds, I would run back to check on my flower-friends, and I was delighted to see how the plants had responded, straightening up their stems, and lifting their buds as if to say, "Thank you!"

Opa also taught me how to deadhead and how fertilizer works. After trimming the dying flowers and leaves, I helped carry them all to the compost bin. Inside the galvanized steel tub the leaves decomposed to become rich, new soil.

Inside the apartment, my grandfather had a special garden room where he kept a large collection of cacti. He taught me all their correct botanical names. When my parents returned to pick me up, my grandfather sent me home with several cuttings to start my own collection. I cared for them at home and would watch their buds form, waiting for weeks until they finally opened up into beautiful flowers, each species a different color and shape.

When I was about nine years old, Opa took me to a meeting of the Berlin Cactus Society. The society sponsored lectures by men who traveled to other countries searching for rare plants. Along with the cacti and succulents the members kept, these explorers collected: tulips from Turkey; clivias from South Africa; rhododendrons from Nepal; many different plants from China, Japan, Australia, and New Zealand; and orchids, lilies, and medicinal herbs from all over the world. The plants went either to their own collections or to botanical gardens or to research centers for breeding. The stories they told of their adventures were fascinating to me. I decided I wanted to become a plant collector, and I became the youngest member of the Hamburg Cactus Society. It was perhaps then I also decided I wanted to see the world.

As the years passed, whenever I was in Berlin I continued to work with Opa, nurturing his balcony gardens. After the early morning watering and a delicious breakfast, I often accompanied Opa to see my great uncle Wilhelm Wertheim in his store on Leipziger Platz. Uncle Wilhelm and his brothers were the owners of the renowned Wertheim Department Stores, a chain of big stores in four German cities, which were much like today's Nordstrom or Neiman Marcus. Wilhelm was my great uncle through marriage, having married Oma's sister, Martha Mendelsohn. It was just by coincidence that we shared the same last name.

Uncle Wilhem and Aunt Martha Wertheim

Opa Guttman sold gloves to the Wertheim Department Store. Even before they became related through marriage, Wertheim had always been one of Opa's best customers. I didn't know much about

Opa's business, except that he had a small office inside the main Wertheim store on Leipziger Platz. As a child, I was more interested in the treats in his pockets than how he accumulated the money to buy them.

We would walk from the apartment on Bendlerstrasse along Tiergartenstrasse, bordering Berlin's largest park, home of the Berlin Zoo. Then we turned up the Esplanade to Potsdamer Platz and the adjacent Leipziger Platz. This was always exciting. The Potsdamer and Leipziger plazas were the hub of Berlin. At the time, Potsdamer was the busiest traffic center in all of Europe and even had one of the first traffic lights. Besides the motorcars and many streetcars, the plaza was home to wide sidewalks filled with shoppers and travelers. It was constant motion with men and women getting on and off the streetcars, descending into the subway station, and going in and out of stores, hotels, and cafés.

Busy Leipziger Platz with Wertheim Department Store on the left, circa 1925

Here, too, was the heart of Berlin's nightlife, often compared to Piccadilly Circus in London and New York's Times Square. The Grand

Hotel Esplanade was on one corner, where Charlie Chaplin and Greta Garbo were regulars. The architecture was rich. In front of the hotel was a Doric temple designed by Prussian neoclassical architect Karl Schinkel. Its columns extended to the street curb, and we often walked inside this open shrine. In 1932, across Potsdamer Platz, they built the first modernist structure in the area, a nine-story office and shopping building called the Columbushaus, nicknamed "little skyscraper." I didn't care for its big, boxy feel, but it was one of the first of its kind in Germany. In contrast were the stately neo-Gothic apartment houses in the area belonging to the very wealthy. Uncle Wilhelm's brother, George Wertheim, and his wife, Ursula, lived in one.

Leipziger Platz was an octagonal park of grass and trees surrounded by walkways, which hosted a daily flower market with at least twenty stands. Opa knew the names of all the vendors, especially the ladies, and bargained with them as they frowned and giggled intermittently. He would always buy flowers to decorate his office or to take home. It was my job to carry back the single rose he regularly purchased for Oma.

The Wertheim Department Store was the most elegant of all the buildings in Leipziger Platz. Designed by the famous architect Alfred Messel in 1896, it had street frontage totaling well over three hundred meters and was made of granite and plate glass with a renowned and breathtaking glass-topped atrium. Inside, it had eighty-three elevators, three escalators, a thousand telephones, and ten thousand lamps. At the store's main entrance, a large uniformed doorman would open the door for Opa and me, greeting my grandfather by name. It made me feel very important.

Wertheim Department Store with the flower vendors in the square near the entrance, Leipziger Platz, Berlin, 1920

In the atrium of Wertheim Department Store, 1900

The grand entrance of Wertheim Department Store in Berlin, circa 1905

While Opa conducted his business, I would sit in one of the great leather chairs in Uncle Wilhelm's office and look out the window. Years later, after both my Opa and uncle had passed away, I would still visit the office with Aunt Martha. I recall standing at the window, just as I had as a young child, looking across the road behind the store where I could see the construction of the large basement and addition during the Reich Chancellery's renovation that began in 1935. Over the next decade, the actions that would take place inside that building would dramatically change the course of human history. It was in this basement where Hitler would take his own life at the end of World War II. I am glad I did not know then the phosphorous bombs and fire released from the sky onto Hitler's headquarters would also destroy most of the area's architectural beauty, including the magnificent Wertheim Department Store.

On Sundays, Opa and Oma often had guests for *Mittagessen*, our noon meal which was the main meal of the day. *Abendessen* was our lighter evening meal. Breads, sausages and cheese were served along with similar items, and maybe some fruit. My Oma was famous among their social circle for her cooking and her graciousness as a hostess. Several of the guests were Germany's top generals and their wives, my grandparents' neighbors and friends on Bendlerstrasse. One of the generals lived right next door. The couples would arrive at the general's house and enter through a door connecting his courtyard to that of my grandparents. This became increasingly important with the rise of the Nazi Party in Germany. If the generals were being observed, no one knew they were our guests. There were times when only the wives came over because their husbands were in the field. Even so, they always entered the same way.

After the meal, the ladies went into another room for coffee or tea and conversation. The men would stay to smoke and play cards. Opa usually smoked a pipe because he did not care for cigarettes. Filling the pipe with tobacco was always quite an operation to watch. I got to sit on Opa's lap, taking in the sweet, pungent aroma of his pipe while listening to the men talk about important things I did not understand.

As the afternoon stretched into evening, Opa would always pull out his beautiful, gold pocket watch, click open its shiny cover, look at the time and say, "I think I will go to bed now." That was the cue for all the guests to take their leave. They would thank my grandmother, leave money on a plate in the vestibule as a tip for the maid, put on their hats and coats, and bid farewell.

My Opa

Mother and I also spent time on the large estate of my great aunt Martha and uncle Wilhelm in Dahlem, an affluent district southwest of central Berlin. Aunt Martha and Uncle Wilhelm had a mansion with forty-five rooms and extensive grounds. I became good friends with the head gardener. When he saw my interest in plants, he let me follow him around, pointing out the various species, and telling me the plants' names. He introduced me to citrus trees that he kept in containers and transported to a large atrium in winter to protect them from freezing. I loved the sharp, fresh smell of the lemons and sweet oranges.

Of course most of my childhood days were spent in and around our apartment in Hamburg, mostly with my mother. My father wasn't home much. With the economy being what it was, he took a second job working as the estate manager for Duke Karl Rudolf, the 13th Duke of Cröy. This work meant leaving home early in the morning and returning after we were in bed, or sometimes even being gone many days in a row.

The noble House of Cröy dates back to 1486. In the 1920s, the family had branches in Belgium and France, as well as Germany. Duke Karl caused a scandal in 1931 when he married American Nancy Leishman, the daughter of industrialist John George Alexander Leishman, the United States ambassador to Germany and former president of Carnegie Steel. The marriage didn't last, but Duke Karl gained a reputation for his progressive ways.

Father oversaw the Duke's entire estate: his buildings, gardens, all the workers, and what used to be the Duke's extensive forests along the Rhine River. With the Treaty of Versailles at the end of the Great War (later to be known as World War I), the forestland had been transferred to the Belgian government. However, Germany was obliged to reimburse the Duke for the confiscation of his woodlands. One of my father's duties was to participate in the annual negotiations for this payment. He spent many hours in the majestic woods, making records of the tree growth, and assessing the value of the land. He became very knowledgeable about forestry, and the bookshelf in our library at home was filled with forestry and horticulture books. I often browsed the books with great pleasure.

My mother looked after us and managed the affairs at home. She was never a society climber. She volunteered for a peacekeeping organization in Hamburg, regularly attended the theatre and opera, read a lot, and enjoyed shopping downtown. After the noon meal she almost always took a nap, lying on the living room couch covered with a soft gray blanket of deep pile. We would be very quiet so she could sleep.

I admired my father, but it was my mother with whom I felt very close.

In the afternoons she occasionally hosted others for coffee and tea, but more often, she would go out to meet her lady friends at the local *Konditorei* (bakery) and have *Kaffee* and *Kuchen* (coffee and cake), chat and read magazines or foreign newspapers.

My father provided well for our family. Our apartment was very pleasant, with eight rooms and two baths. One of the rooms was for Fräulein Liesel. Besides the balconies and long hallways where we set up our trains, we had a big kitchen with a wood stove and an icebox. I spent time there after school and during summer holidays with Fräulein Liesel as she went about her chores. Daily she emptied the icebox water tray, and twice a week she ushered in a deliveryman with new ice blocks. Every Tuesday, she took care of putting away the dairy products brought by a lady farmer who arrived on her horse-drawn wagon from a farm outside of Hamburg: fresh butter, milk, eggs, and cream like I have never tasted since. Even though Fräulein Liesel was quite young, just in her early 20s, she was like a second mother to me.

She and her boyfriend had a small plot of land in a victory garden on the outskirts of the city, and they sometimes took me there on the streetcar. Her boyfriend, a policeman studying to become a detective, was very nice to me. Even though the Great War had ended, people kept up their efforts in the victory gardens. The only difference was since the gardens were on public land they now had to pay the government a small rent for the space. Water and electricity were furnished as part of the cost.

This was where I first witnessed how people could garden successfully in small spaces. They started their seedlings in what Fräulein Liesel called a cold-frame. It was a box topped with framed glass like a window, the bottom of which was filled with manure to create heat with planting soil added on top. At night they put the window over the box to keep the plants warm, removing it again during the daytime. In this way, they could continue to grow produce during the winter. It was like a miniature greenhouse.

They could not grow apple or pear trees normally on these small sites so they pruned and tied the branches to frames and trellises to make them grow into a flat plane. This was the first time I saw espaliered fruit trees, and Fräulein Liesel showed me how to prune them in this manner. After picking the fruit and vegetables and working in the garden, Fräulein Liesel and her boyfriend would bring home their colorful bounty dangling from shoulder poles.

My life wasn't only an informal study of plants. Most of the year, of course, I went to school. My parents enrolled me in a private school in Hamburg when I was five-and-a-half. I was very good in arithmetic and enjoyed our many field trips. I often had to memorize poetry for my classes. My mother quizzed me backwards and forwards on lines from famous poets like Schiller and Goethe until I could recite them perfectly. But when the time came to stand in front of the class and recite them, a funny thing happened. I made the required bow and when my head came up every line of poetry had retreated from it.

I planned to never speak in front of an audience again. Since I never showed any talent for music, performing in a recital would not be an issue, either. My music teacher once told me, "You'd do me a great favor if you would not sing."

In school we were taught to hate the French, and I shared this with my parents one day. A week later my father invited a business associate over for *Abendessen*. He was very nice, asked me questions, and even shared a joke. I enjoyed talking to him and getting to know him. As the meal wound down, he invited me to come visit him in Paris; he was French. I would have never known it because he spoke German perfectly.

After he had gone, my father told me he purposely had not shared the guest was a Frenchman. "I wanted you to learn that many French people are good people — no one should automatically hate an entire group of people."

With what was soon to happen to us, to everyone in Europe, my father's lesson that day would become an intricately woven thread in the broad fabric of my long life.

My good friend, George Salomon, attended the same school I did and lived only two blocks away, so George and I often played together. George's father, a professor, taught at the University of Hamburg and occasionally took us on adventures. We traveled on public transportation to places where we would then walk around and learn new things. I was fascinated by the oldest part of Hamburg, where the streets were very narrow and some of the houses had a second story that extended farther over the street than the lower floor. Once in a while, we went across the Elbe River into farmland and hiked on walkways along the roads. When our trip was a long one I entertained George, his sister, Edith, and his father with stories of my own invention. This was the beginning of my storytelling.

The first major change in my life occurred on the morning of January 17, 1927, when my father came into my room and told me he had a surprise for me.

"Did you bring me a dog?" I asked excitedly.

"No," my father laughed, "you have a new little brother."

I was invited to my mother's bedroom to meet my younger brother, Günther George, whom we simply called George. As was the tradition in those days he was born at home. I was seven years old and fascinated watching Mother breastfeed baby George. Once he was big enough to sit up and crawl, I occasionally looked after him while my mother was busy. As his big brother, I naturally felt very protective of him.

The mild prosperity of those few years following 1924 came to a devastating end when the American stock market crashed in 1929. It plunged Germany and all of Europe into an immediate recession. Many people were soon out of work again, particularly young people.

Unemployment doubled from three million to six million by 1932. Germany had become so fragile severe poverty overtook working class families very quickly. People were homeless. Tensions grew, both on the street and in parliament. The existing "Great Coalition" government, a combination of left wing and conservative parties, collapsed while arguing about the rising cost of unemployment benefits. In an attempt to restore order, Paul von Hindenburg, Reich president, established a new government, appointing a chancellor and cabinet ministers to rule by emergency decree instead of by laws passed by the Reichstag. Unfortunately this reorganized government did not restore order, rather it led to the destruction of the Weimar Republic.

During the Depression my father's employment at the recycling company came to an end. He found a position in Berlin with the Hinz Fabrik Company, which manufactured office furniture. He got my older brother a job there as well. Werner had only one more year of high school until he graduated, but he left school for this apprenticeship. This was a perfectly acceptable option in Germany; at fourteen years old it was legal to leave school to get a job or go to a trade school, and many people chose this path.

In 1933, at thirteen years of age and despite the worsening economy, I was still relatively carefree, except that my best friend, George Salomon, and his family announced they were moving to Blankenese, a suburb of Hamburg. What a terrible disappointment this was until I realized the adventure awaiting me. To visit George, my parents allowed me to ride the *stadtbahn* (local train), on my own. I felt very grown up. At George's new house we developed all sorts of new games. One of our favorites was hiding in the enormous old rhododendron grove on the property. The space under the plants was large enough for both of us to crouch beneath, pretending it was our fort and we were knights or soldiers under siege. Frequently, we walked down to the beach along the Elbe River and watched the riverboat traffic. I loved watching the large passenger liners arriving in Hamburg's harbor.

What felt like the greatest injustice of my childhood was the fact my older brother had been given a bicycle and I had not. One evening,

I was riding a friend's bike and was accidentally hit by a pickup truck and thrown underneath it. Miraculously, when the truck ran over me, I was almost completely clear of the tires. The driver slammed on his breaks and rushed out of the cab to check on me.

"I am fine," I told him, "but could you please move the truck forward so I can rescue my thumb?"

My thumb was fine, and even the bike escaped without much damage. But as I hurried home, I became increasingly concerned about what my father would say. Luckily he was working at the Duke's estate for the week. By the time he returned home, not much was said about the accident. However, as a consequence of the accident I became afraid of the dark.

In the summer of 1932, I spent four weeks away from home at a co-ed camp near Kiel, along the Baltic Sea. George was five at the time and came along with me. I looked out for him when I wasn't busy boating and playing on the beach with my new friends. I even met my first girlfriend.

During the second week of camp I received a very upsetting letter from home. My mother wrote that Opa had died, and there would be a service in Berlin. But she insisted I stay at camp, enjoy myself, and continue to look after George. This was my first experience with death. I didn't feel comfortable sharing the news with my cabinmates, so I tried to hide my grief except with my girlfriend, who made her best effort to comfort me. Opa's passing was a huge loss that even young love could not soothe.

As is the case with summer romances, camp ended with a heartbreaking farewell. My girlfriend lived in Berlin, and I lived in Hamburg. The distance seemed unbearable. We promised to write to one another, and I told her I would call her when I next visited Oma in Berlin. I kept both of those promises, and she became my "long distance girlfriend" for several years.

In 1933, my carefree childhood came to an abrupt end. On January 30, President Hindenburg appointed Adolf Hitler the Chancellor of Germany. On the following Saturday evening, February 4, my father took a night train as usual from Hamburg to Münster to work for several days on the Duke of Cröy's estate. Father's routine was to sleep on the train, arriving early in the morning at the station in Münster. The Duke's chauffeur was always there to pick him up in a limousine and drive him to the *schloss* (main house) in Dülmen. My father was reliable and punctual; however, the next morning we received a call from the Duke informing us that Father had not arrived. Mother was confused but not terribly concerned. She thought there must be some logical explanation.

After we finished our *Mittagessen*, Duke Karl called again. Several employees of the estate had kidnapped my father, but the Duke knew few details.

"I advise you to leave your home immediately," he told my mother. "Disappear for a while and make sure you are not followed. I will look into the matter. Contact me in a day or two."

After returning the telephone receiver to its base my mother stood there, stunned for a moment, and then took a long deep breath before speaking. "Go pack an overnight bag, Ernst." Then she took me by both shoulders, looking directly into my eyes as she said, "You are the head of the family now." I was just thirteen years old.

CHAPTER 2
A Change of Seasons

Forsythia viridissima (forsythia)

What do you take with you when you need to disappear? Clothing? Money? Toys? Books? Photographs? What had just happened? Who knew when — or even if — we would return to our apartment?

It was as if I were watching some other boy fold pants and shirts into a small suitcase, hiding a billfold with a little cash underneath his clothes. Werner was not around since he was in Berlin working for the furniture company. The responsibility was on my shoulders to take care of Mother and George. I was no longer a boy as I carried my bag downstairs, put on my winter coat and hat, and waited uncertainly by the door for my mother and baby brother.

When you are in a rush to disappear, where do you go? After weighing different possibilities, Mother thought we should set off for the Salomons' house outside of Hamburg. We promptly took a streetcar to the train station. During the train ride exiting the city, I tried to think clearly to understand what was happening to us and to my father. Why was Father kidnapped? Where was he now? The Duke had mentioned it might have something to do with being Jewish but we really did not understand the implications of this, even though we already knew of Hitler's anti-Semitic rhetoric. Of course we had heard conversations about Hitler, the popular new chancellor. He was certainly a powerful and engaging speaker on the radio. Just a couple of days earlier, Mother had read in the paper that Hitler had passed a new law officially banning political demonstrations, most likely due to the rapid growth of the Communist Party. At thirteen years old, I was more concerned with my studies and friends, not government and politics. But after I heard part of Chancellor Hitler's "Proclamation to the German Nation" on the radio a few days after my father's kidnapping, I decided to start reading the newspaper regularly in an effort to understand what was going on.

The Salomons greeted us kindly and offered drinks and cake in the library just like any other social visit. When my mother explained what had happened, they were incredulous and a bit scared. Professor Salomon announced he would call some colleagues for advice. He spoke with a couple of friends from the university, who were also Jewish, as well as some people in Berlin. All responded they were aware of arrests by the Nazis but not of rogue crimes like this one.

As Professor Salomon left the room to place one more call and Mrs. Salomon went to check on something in the kitchen, Mother commented on their kind-hearted assistance. Then we suddenly realized our presence might be putting the family in danger since they were also Jewish. We decided we needed more advice from the Duke and called him next. He suggested we head back to Hamburg, get a hotel for a few days, then change to another one, and try to stay out of sight. We thanked the Salomons as we left, trying not to take in their worried expressions.

Arriving back in Hamburg, we checked into a familiar hotel near the central train station. By this time, the three of us were pretty hungry but going to a restaurant was not an option. I thought of the *Wiener Würstchen* man, walking along the platform of the train station selling Vienna sausages to passengers through the open windows of the train cars. I ran to find him and ordered ten sausages along with small containers of German potato salad. He raised his eyebrows and asked to see my money, but I was not offended as I opened my billfold. I was proud I successfully provided my family with a reasonable meal for that evening.

On Monday morning, I called my school and George's school to report we were ill. My pocket money had been enough to pay for our previous meal but we didn't have enough to pay for our room. Mother felt it was unsafe for her to go to the bank based on Duke Karl's warnings, so she told me to go and ask to see the bank manager in order to withdraw money from our family's account. As you can imagine this was not a simple task for a thirteen-year old boy.

I walked to the bank from our hotel wondering how, exactly, I was going to persuade the banker to hand over a large sum of money bearing only a note from my mother.

The bank lobby was very impressive with marble columns, a granite floor, and dark hardwood furniture. I walked over to a teller station and asked to speak with the manager. She directed me to a desk where the manager's secretary sat in front of his office. She instructed me to sit and wait.

The manager, a tall, well-dressed gentleman, saw a thirteen-year old boy standing in front of him and grinned. He must have thought it was a joke until I told him why I was there. He ushered me into his office, polite yet guarded. I explained my mother was ill and had sent me on this errand to withdraw five hundred *Reichsmarks* from our account. He asked a lot of questions: the full names of Mother, Father, and my grandparents, along with their addresses. He asked me what I intended to do with the money. I did not have a planned reply to that question. I simply told him most likely Mother had to pay bills, including rent, while Father was out of town. Fortunately the manager decided I was being honest and authorized the funds.

I hurried back to the hotel so we could pay our bill, and we then set out to find a less expensive hotel. Afterwards we decided to take George for a steamboat tour of Outer Alster Lake in the heart of the city. We all needed a day of normalcy, a day of fun. From the boat we enjoyed the sights of picturesque Hamburg: the Neoclassical apartment houses, Neo-Renaissance city buildings, stately hotels, and tall church spires, like that of St. Nicholas' Church, one of the tallest in the world. The Hamburg Rathaus, our city hall, reflected its stately image on the water. In the plaza on the other side of the building was where the Nazi Party held most of its demonstrations.

We admired the woodlands and parks along the shore, marinas full of bobbing skiffs and yachts, and several of the many bridges in our riverside city. The Alsters are actually two artificial lakes created in the thirteenth century by damming up the Alster River, a tributary of the Elbe, to flood the moats of the city's fortifications and to power watermills. Waterways connected the Outer Alster to the Inner Alster to the Elbe River. The steamer stopped at various piers to drop off and let on passengers. It was an enjoyable way to spend a few hours forgetting our troubles.

The next day we went for a long walk in Stadtpark, passing the planetarium, and the city pool. When we rested on park benches, I told George stories while Mother read a newspaper. Back in the hotel room we listened to the radio, played games with George, and, sometimes, Mother and I played chess. After George went to sleep, we had some serious discussions. Should I quit school and learn a trade? Should I try to get a job at the local grocery store? Mother had proficient typing skills and thought she could get a position as an administrative assistant. If we both were working who would care for George? We considered moving to a smaller apartment or leaving Germany for either Switzerland or England, but only she had a passport.

Mother always looked at the bright side of things. Despite the uncertainty and seriousness of our situation, she somehow managed to frame these conversations with optimism. She finally declared Father would be back soon so we should enjoy this short vacation and be grateful to be together.

Five days after Father's kidnapping, the Duke had garnered enough information to relay to us. Some employees from his estate had aligned with the Nazi Party. Resentful of my father's position, they had kidnapped him for ransom and were holding him in a nearby town, probably Münster where he had been seized. Duke Karl felt it was now safe for us to return to our apartment. He would negotiate with the kidnappers to get my father released and back home.

Upon opening the door to our apartment, it didn't look like the same home we had hastily left behind just a few days earlier. It was very cold and musty. The fading winter sunlight through the gaps in the partially drawn drapes gave it a surreal quality. Our maid, Fräulein Liesel, was gone. She would have been in danger had she continued working for a Jewish family. To this day I wonder whether Mother told her to leave or whether she left on her own. All I knew at the time was that we would have to assume all her chores.

After unpacking our bags, I lit the fires. I helped my mother dust the house, make dinner, and wash the dishes. We worked as a team. I went down to the basement to see what had happened to the forsythia we had cut and placed by the boiler before we left. Sure enough, the branches were covered with pretty yellow flowers. I brought them up and carefully arranged them in one of my mother's large vases. For a moment, we both stopped to stare at the burst of color.

The next week, George and I returned to school as we tried to get back to a regular schedule. The grocery stores still delivered our food to the house, the iceman our blocks of ice. Mother put the food away. I emptied the water tray in the icebox. No one at school was aware of Father's kidnapping. In order to stop sadness from overwhelming me, I concentrated on my studies, sports, and new household chores.

Finally, three weeks after his disappearance, we heard a knock on the front door. My father was standing on the landing. I had only a moment to register the bruises and scratches on his face as my mother pulled him inside, closed the door, and swept him tenderly into her arms. Her embrace seemed to release everything inside of him. He put his hands on her back, buried his face in her shoulder, and began to cry deep, loud sobs.

My father had always been a serious, undemonstrative man. He was the pillar of our family, and it was just unbelievable to watch him cry uncontrollably. I took a mental picture of my father's streaming tears, his weary embrace, and broken look. That image has lived in my mind ever since, vivid as the world around me.

I suddenly realized I should leave my parents alone so I went to the kitchen to make some tea. I took our best cookies out of the cabinet, arranged everything on a tray, and brought it out to the living room.

By then Father had composed himself. He began telling us about his ordeal of the last three weeks. At first he was just surprised to see employees from the estate at the train station. When they grabbed his arms, forced him into a car, and blindfolded him, he was confused and, of course, afraid. He had not been held in Münster but rather on the Duke's estate in one of the agricultural warehouses in the countryside where no one would think to look. They gave him little to eat, mostly bread and water. My father had lost fifteen pounds.

He mentioned nothing about the bruises and scratches we could clearly see on his face. Occasionally, though, he winced as if they were still painful. His story skipped ahead to how he was driven to the train station where the Duke's chauffeur was waiting to give him some money and a train ticket.

My mother called our longtime family doctor who came to the apartment early that evening. Two of Father's ribs were broken. Mother applied bandages and massaged balm into my father's wounds based on the doctor's instructions. The emotional damage, however, was not so simple to treat, let alone cure.

During the next few days, Father mostly slept while his physical injuries began to heal. Once he felt a little better, he watched as I did my chores around the apartment and took care of George. I think he recognized how quickly I had grown up in the three weeks he'd been gone. He spoke to me differently. His tone was more matter-of-fact, his words less censored. It was as if he was talking to an adult.

A few days after my father's return, I read in the newspaper an arsonist had set fire to the Berlin Reichstag building where the German Parliament assembled. The next day civil liberties were suspended, and the government instituted mass arrests of the communists assumed guilty of the crime. After learning of this news combined with the weak economy and the new sight of Nazi gangs in brown shirts roaming the streets, not to mention my father's kidnapping, an idea solidified into a plan for my future. At supper the following evening, I told the family, "I want to go to the United States of America and start a new life."

Keep in mind Hitler had been in power for just one month, so no one realized where Germany was headed. My family had deep roots in Germany, and my parents would scarcely consider leaving their home. We assumed the incident with my father was an isolated one. Perhaps some understood Hitler had been trying to plant a seed for change by declaring the Jewish people "the enemy" since the 1920s. However, no one foresaw the absolute power he was acquiring or the atrocities he would mandate in the future. Basic humanity doesn't lead us to such evil thoughts or actions. Most people operate on the assumption that the situation cannot get worse. The storm will pass, spring will arrive, and the flowers will bloom again.

The desire to go to America was nothing new for me. It was born out of watching western movies and feeling curious about the world. But now I had a responsibility to earn money for my family, to help take care of them. I could not envision accomplishing this in Germany. I had no idea how I was going to get myself to the United States, but my decision was firm.

My father listened thoughtfully and then asked very seriously, "Son, what are you going to do in the United States? How are you going to make a living with no profession?"

Deciding to go to America meant it was time to choose a vocation and train in it. Father knew I enjoyed looking at his forestry books, and I constantly questioned him about his work on the Duke's woodlands. He asked if I was interested in forestry.

Family vacations on the island of Rügen came to mind. After long, hot days on the beach, to cool off we would go for walks in a lovely birch forest. I marveled at the zebra-like bark and the drooping catkins like little caterpillars. There in the forest I was introduced to my first wildflowers, along with wild strawberries and blueberries, and ferns and tall grasses swaying in a gentle breeze. Yes, I realized, forestry definitely interested me.

Vacation in Rügen with Oma, Opa, and Werner, 1927

The next Saturday, Father arranged for a meeting with a forester who oversaw the woodlands just outside of Hamburg. He and my father had become acquainted through Father's work on the Duke's estate. We took the local train out of town. I noticed new flags were now raised on the flagpoles outside the station. The Weimar Republic flag with its horizontal stripes of black, red, and yellow had been replaced with two new flags flying side by side. The government had reintroduced the flag of the old German Empire, a tricolor flag of black, white and red. Along side it was a new flag, the flag of the Nazi Party with a red background, a white disk, and a black swastika in the middle.

Arriving at our destination, and after introductions, my Father left me for the day to shadow the forester. The man asked me questions as he inspected the woods and took measurements. When Father returned to pick me up, he asked his friend if I had a future in forestry.

The man smiled and shook his head. "He will not be satisfied with just forestry. He needs to study the wider field of horticulture."

After that weekend my father returned to his office to work for the furniture factory. I noticed he was still in pain, but he had to start earning for the family again. He never returned to the Duke's estate although he spoke to the Duke on occasion by phone. Under the circumstances, I think the Duke had to protect himself and discontinue his public relationship with my father.

A few weeks later an even longer train ride took us to the village of Ahlem near Hannover. My father had arranged for me to take the entrance exam to a college called the *Israelitische Gartenbauschule Ahlem,* a Jewish horticultural school, and the first of its type in Germany. Originally, it had been developed to train young Germans to work as agriculturalists. It offered a three-year program with study of general subjects along with specific classes such as horticulture. The Nazis, now in complete power, authorized the school as a center of vocational training specifically for Jewish youth intending to emigrate to Palestine, specifically the area that what would become Israel.

My father explained the Duke of Cröy had donated money to the *Gartenbauschule.* Several graduates from the school had worked for Father on the estate. This connection enabled him to secure an interview with the school director, Leo Rosenblatt. Herr Rosenblatt didn't want to admit me since I had not yet graduated from high school. He felt I was too young, but Father was firm in his belief that I could compete with the other applicants. "Let him take the entrance exam and then decide whether to admit him."

Father had called my school in Hamburg to have me excused for a few days so we could visit the *Gartenbauschule.*

I was excited and scared. Other than a few weeks with my grandparents, I had never lived away from home. I had only ever attended my private school in Hamburg. What would this place be like?

The train ride was delightful. We rode first class and ate in the dining car on pristine tablecloths while attentive waiters wearing white gloves served our meal and poured our drinks. Father talked about the gardens and the greenhouses at the *Gartenbauschule*. He surprised me with how much he knew about horticulture. He had never discussed such things with me before.

He told me about a time on the Duke's estate when they were looking for oil. They made a dowsing rod out of a forked branch from a tree and walked with it over the land. When it pointed down toward the earth they knew there was oil underneath. The practice of dowsing or using a divining rod to find oil or water originated in Germany in the fifteenth century. My father grinned at the memory. They never drilled, he said, because this required big expensive equipment, and they were not certain how much oil they would really find.

I rarely spent so much time with my father. He didn't tend to share much, so I soaked in his words and kept asking him questions to keep him talking. He told me about the big royal parties the Duke hosted and about all the various dignitaries and celebrities invited to such events. I felt so proud of my Father, something I had never felt before.

From the train station we took a taxi to the school. The first thing I saw was a soccer pitch, an encouraging sight. Looming over it was a stately four-story building with a high roof and many arched windows. Students, all much bigger than me, were having a game on the field. In another building, we signed in for a tour later in the day and the exam on the next day.

My first view of the *Israelitisches Gartenbauschule* in Ahlem

A young man in his final year was our tour guide. We gathered with other parents and applicants and followed him as he showed us his living quarters, a study hall, and one of the classrooms. He pointed out the orchards and the fields, some full of budding plants, others containing evenly spaced furrows of dark soil waiting to be planted. He also took us into one of the greenhouses where I saw students caring for plants. In the fields off in the distance, I saw others studying tree saplings. It was exciting to see all this activity.

After the tour we took a taxi into Hannover to a hotel where my father secured us a fine room, and we ate well in the hotel restaurant. Despite the comfort of the bed, I did not sleep well that night.

The next morning we returned to the school, and I filed into a meeting hall full of long tables and chairs. I had no idea how I would do with no preparation whatsoever, no formal study in agriculture or horticulture. I read the questions carefully and did my best to answer them. Miraculously, I found I could answer many of the questions, but I was still nervous about the results. We thanked the director and headed for home.

It turned out that some knowledge seeped in over the years when I watered flowers with my Opa, followed the gardener around at

Aunt Martha's, and propagated cacti in the greenhouse. About two weeks later a letter arrived from the school. I placed tenth out of three hundred and fifty applicants. It wasn't because I was a genius. It was because I had concentrated on those things throughout my childhood.

I was accepted into the *Gartenbauschule* and would start in a year's time, in the spring of 1934. I would be fourteen years old then, and the plan to get to the United States was officially in the works.

On April 1, 1933, the Nazis organized a one-day boycott of all Jewish-owned businesses in Germany. The headline on the front page of the *Hamburger Tageblatt* newspaper read: "*Die Judenboykott beginnt — Morgen Schlag 10 Uhr!*" ("The Jewish Boycott begins — this morning at the stroke of 10!") The Hamburg department stores Hermann Tietz, Karstadt, and Woolworth had already been boycotted by Nazi picket lines in March, but the movement on April 1st was more widespread and coordinated.

Sturmabteilung (Storm Troopers) or SA threateningly stood in front of Jewish-owned stores and professional offices. The Star of David was painted in yellow and black across thousands of doors and windows. Signs with accompanying anti-Semitic slogans such as, "Don't Buy from Jews" and "The Jews Are Our Misfortune," were plastered just about everywhere.

April 1st was a Saturday, the Sabbath, so many of the businesses were closed. It was easy for us to stay home that day, but on Monday, this was not so simple. George and I had to walk to school, and my mother had to do some shopping. It was becoming increasingly unnerving on the streets. During that period there were no arrests, to the best of my knowledge, but there were beatings of shopkeepers and customers. I was very worried. Many nights I woke up asking myself if I wanted to go to school or stay home.

Even before Hitler came to power there had been incidents in public, and we made it a habit never to walk alone in what used to be good neighborhoods. At first it was not primarily a "Jewish thing." More often the thugs were communists, young men out of work and hungry, who targeted anyone who looked to be upper middle class. More than once I was rushed by such a youth who demanded my lunch money. I stopped carrying money in hopes that they would not come after me if I had nothing to steal. While antisemitism wasn't exactly new in Germany, I had never experienced anything negative on account of being Jewish until 1933. I was lucky, I suppose, that I was never beaten up on the street. I saw it happen, though.

A week later the new government passed something called the Law for the Restoration of the Professional Civil Service, which restricted employment in the civil service to "Aryans." We didn't exactly understand this term, except it clearly excluded Jews. We heard it on the radio and read the announcement in the papers. The new law declared Jews could not serve as teachers, professors, judges or in other government positions; doctors followed closely behind. Jews were barred from claiming any rights as war veterans. In the Great War, over one hundred thousand Jews, about twenty percent of Germany's total Jewish population, had served in the military. Twelve thousand Jews had perished, and roughly three times that number had been decorated for bravery.

The new law didn't seem to take effect right away. Professor Salomon, George's father, kept his position, and we knew some judges who did as well. In fact, we had one family member who was a judge in Magdeburg and kept his position until around 1937. My dear uncle, Alfred Traube, was an attorney and was active until *Kristallnacht*.

Though my father worked for a privately owned furniture company, the leaders must have gotten scared or had Nazi sympathizers among them because they let him go.

Not long thereafter, school let out for the summer break as usual. There was no camp for me this summer. I continued my household chores earning a *Pfennig* each time I washed the dishes. I went to the market with my mother, helped her can fruit for winter, and spent time with boys in the neighborhood. Shortly after the summer holiday began, my father announced he was leaving for Belgium. Though he did not share all the details with me, I knew he was out of work. Given the kidnapping, my father could not return to his previous position with the Duke. However, the House of Cröy originated in Belgium, and my father spoke French. I guessed the Duke must have referred my father to family members or perhaps he could still oversee the forests from the safety of Belgium. Traveling to Belgium with my father was his secretary. She had been a part of our lives for several years, sometimes working in my father's office at home and enjoying a coffee with my mother during her afternoon breaks.

Mother had taken George and gone to visit Oma in Berlin for a long weekend. My father asked me to come along and help him carry luggage to the ship that would take him and the secretary to Belgium. It was, already, becoming difficult for citizens, especially Jewish citizens, to leave Germany. I took care of the secretary's luggage and she flashed me a pretty smile. We rode by taxi to an assembly place downtown. There you could catch a bus, for a forty-five minute ride, to the harbor on the Elbe River where all the big ships were anchored. Porters met us at the bus station and checked the bags, loading them onto a cart. The three of us then made our way up the gangplank and onto the ship.

It was such a treat to be onboard. We went to the elegant dining room and had lunch overlooking the pier, and I could feel the slow rolling of the ship in the water. Then a crewman announced that guests needed to disembark. My father gave me cash for the bus and taxi ride home, along with a characteristically unceremonious farewell. I was anxious to get back and see my friend, Kyle, and tell him about the ship.

Kyle was one of my closest friends. He lived across the street, and we had been friends for nearly seven years. We played together in the nearby park, and his parents occasionally came over for dinner. We even tried our first cigarette together on the back balcony of my apartment. My father, who did not smoke, was aware of this and told me, "If you start smoking, you will buy your own cigarettes. I will not pay for them." It was the only cigarette I ever smoked.

We had always attended the same private school, usually walking to and from school together. When Kyle got a fancy new bicycle, I was finally allowed to ride my brother's old one, and we rode to school together. After the summer break, we were both advancing to the same *Oberrealschule*, the public school.

I knocked on Kyle's door upon returning from the harbor. The maid answered, but instead of letting me in, she went to fetch Kyle. Something was wrong. When he appeared in the doorway he had the strangest expression on his face. After one glance at me, he spoke to the ground. "I can't be friends anymore," he said. My stomach lurched. What had I just heard?

He went on quickly, perhaps while he still had the courage. "My father said his son cannot be friends with a Jew. He said it might jeopardize his career." Kyle's father was a U-boat captain, and I could hear these words in his father's stern voice. Kyle's cheeks were red in embarrassment or perhaps shame, and after he had finished this pronouncement there was really nothing else to say. Without a goodbye, Kyle closed the door.

I was devastated.

The rest of the break was just a blur until I started at the *Oberrealschule.*

The public school was different from the protective environment of my private school where the coed students were from wealthy and educated families. My new school was an all-boys school that admitted students from all walks of life.

The first day was terrible. Some of the teachers remembered my brother, who did not have the best reputation and thus prejudiced them against me. Being Jewish did not help because they taught Christian-based religion at school. When it was time for religion class I was excused, and my teacher was not particularly polite about sending me to the library along with four other Jewish boys, where we sat reading in silence until the period was over.

At the new school I didn't build friendships that quickly. I knew a few other boys who had also transferred from the private school, but they were not necessarily friends, just acquaintances, except for Kyle. I guess he was neither anymore.

"*Exschnelz!*" ("Pipsqueak!") someone called me. I had always been on the short side, and it didn't help that I was younger than most of the boys in my class. It was a tough day, but it was okay. I was not a child anymore. All the recent events had matured me. Since the end of

January, the world had looked different. I learned not to let the name calling or belittling bother me. I had bigger things to worry about.

Things got better when the sports program began. I may have been small but I was good at sports, especially soccer. I was agile and quick and played hard, and I was a good team player. In the first contest of the year, I scored the first goal. We were playing another class, and this was a big event. I earned the respect of both students and teachers. I made the team representing our school as did Kyle. We played together as we always had, passing and dribbling in precision down the field, but we never spoke to each other. The desire to win and beat our competition was strong. In order to do this, we had to work together as teammates, so around soccer there was at least a certain amount of warmth and camaraderie. It was nice, even though it existed only on the field.

Every Friday we had military instruction. Two teachers with swastika armbands taught us how to march in formation and how to carry guns. They spoke to us about having pride in our government, and how we would have a new and better way of life. We had to show respect for the flag. We were lectured on the evils of communism, too. It was a lot of brainwashing.

The instructors led us on *Ausflugs* (field trips), to different destinations that we reached by marching with our rifles on our shoulders. On one of these outings, we came to a pond that was frozen over, where we were allowed to take a little rest. We started playing a game of hockey on the ice with branches for sticks and a stone for the puck. Suddenly, I slipped and fell. I felt an intense, sharp pain around my shoulders as I hit the hard ice; something was broken. I told the teachers, but they refused any sort of medical treatment for me. "Boys should be tough" was their creed. The pain intensified as they forced me to hike and carry my rifle on the hurt shoulder all the way back to school. It was difficult to hold back the tears that came with the pain. When I finally arrived home at the end of the day, my mother called the doctor. He came to the house right away. I had broken my collarbone. He set it right, but the recovery was rough.

Around us the Nazi fury was intensifying. The brown-shirted gangs with their arrogant, gangster-like behavior taunted passersby. We saw them driving around, often drunk and showing off in fancy new cars. We heard rumors of them extorting money from local shop owners, beating up and even murdering innocent civilians. It was especially scary to be on the street at night.

Each weekday morning, I biked to school. While George Salomon took Greek and Latin at his *Gymnasium*, we were required to take *Plattdeutsch* (Low German), Hitler's dialect of choice. "Low" refers to the flat plains and coastal area of the northern European lowlands, in contrast to the mountainous areas of central and southern Germany. Besides playing soccer I also ran track, training intensely to compete in the 100, 200, and 400-meter races. It was a terrific distraction and made me feel strong. I finished first in the 100-meter event at our first meet.

After practice, I biked home with my pedaling powering the dynamo electric lantern clipped to my handlebars. With the increasing Nazi presence, I was always glad to arrive home and shut the door of our apartment building behind me. I spent most evenings doing homework.

On a sunny, brisk day in the early spring of 1934, when the crocuses were in bloom, I found myself packing my suitcase for the *Gartenbauschule* in Ahlem. I had a wonderful relationship with my mother, and I had to fight back the sadness of being separated from her and my baby brother. I felt I took good care of them, so I felt guilty that I was abandoning them to an unknown fate since my father was still abroad. I had not spoken to him since we were on the ship, and I don't know if my mother had.

The fact that Mother and George would be with Grandmother Guttman provided some comfort. Mother had decided to move in with Oma. Within a few days after seeing me off, she and George would be on the train for Berlin. She had already cancelled the lease and had hired a firm to move her nice furniture.

I had no sad feelings about leaving the *Oberrealschule*, that's for sure. Although I had learned to navigate my way around, the longer I stayed in the school the more difficult it had become. There was increased urgency in our military training and even my classes started to feel more like boot camp. The Nazi mindset was increasing. Others more frequently called me names. I would hear a group of students talking about the Jews, and then they would stop and stare at me. Since it was very early into the Third Reich, school textbooks were still being rewritten to include Nazi ideology and eugenics as well as the Nazi version of German history. We weren't taught history or much science, just mathematics and grammar. My injury on the ice didn't endear me to anyone either because it was considered a weakness. Endurance was the most prized characteristic at our school. The injury had meant weeks during which I could not play soccer and without my sports participation my stature and reputation quickly suffered.

But even before my broken collarbone, there had been increasing jealousy of my athletic achievements. When I was chosen to represent the school in races against other schools, those not chosen would call out, "Here comes the Jew!" They might not have understood what they were doing, as children are prone to say cruel things, but in this case the Nazis encouraged them.

In one soccer game I scored two goals in the last five minutes giving us the win. This was a very important game for my school. As soon as the final whistle blew students from the stands ran onto the field to congratulate the players, but no one approached me. I was left out until the captain of our team came over. He looked at me with a grin, hunched down, and lifted me up onto his shoulders to carry me out while the rest of the team jumped up and down around us and cried their bravos for me. My team still respected me, but most of the other students just sang along with the Nazi tune. Our team captain took a real chance that day. In later years, he would have been in big trouble for doing what he did.

The tension at the *Oberrealschule* never ceased. I never knew if or when someone might lash out at me or start a riot against a Jewish person. It was like this every day. No, I was not sad to leave that school even though I was quite anxious about going away to college.

The *Gartenbauschule* had sent a list of required clothing, and my mother had purchased what I needed. As I put the clothes in my suitcase, I imagined myself gardening in the new work shirts and socks. I packed stationery so I could write to Mother and my girlfriend in Berlin, with whom I had been writing letters now for almost two years. I also packed a photograph of her, a pleasant reminder of her pretty face.

I had very mixed feelings as I prepared to go to college in Ahlem. I knew I was younger than most of the students there. What if they did not accept me? Would I make it for three whole years? I had never been separated from my mother for more than a few weeks, when at camp or staying with Opa and Oma. But I was excited to learn and excited about my new adventure. However, I really did not know for sure if this schooling was going to help me when I finally made it to the United States. I told myself most people who start college go through such uncertainty. This couldn't be that unusual.

And what about the Nazi developments around me? Would it invade this school like it did the *Oberrealschule* and transform it into a soldier factory? What else might happen to a college for Jewish youth?

Then there was the matter of money. Until Hitler came to power we did not worry about our finances. Now, however, my father was in Belgium, no longer working for Hinz Fabrik or the Duke and money had suddenly stopped coming in. I didn't know exactly what was happening with him; although I often wondered, there was no time to dwell on it. I didn't know what my mother knew or how much she was really sharing with me. How was she going to manage? It helped that she did have some money of her own, which I think she had inherited when her grandparents died. Then there was my tuition for the college. It was substantial. I felt terrible I was taking money from her. Mother must have seen the worry on my face. She had been full of good humor in the days before my departure.

Other than her and my brother, George, there was no one really to say goodbye to in my neighborhood anymore. I took a short walk and bid a quiet farewell to my favorite trees, the horse chestnuts on Parkallee, rubbing a palm along the ribbed gray-green bark and staring up into the foliage of the wide spreading branches. Because it was spring, the large, finger-like leaves were plentiful and held spikes of dense white flowers. In the courtyard, I bent my nose to the lilac shrub that hung over the wall from our neighbor's garden, taking in the sweet smell as deeply as I could.

My last night at home, Fräulein Liesel and her boyfriend came to say goodbye. My mother must have told them of my departure the next day. They came after dark, when no one on the street could recognize them. Fräulein Liesel gave me a big hug and a kiss. They brought me a cake to take along on the train. The policeman boyfriend asked me to write to Fräulein Liesel and just sign my letters with a very "German name." He told me that way, they could learn more about plants. Their presence that night demonstrated to me there were many people who did care and had the courage to show it.

The next morning the taxi arrived. My mother and George came down to the sidewalk and watched me load my suitcase and cake box into the trunk. I ruffled George's hair then pulled him up off his feet and into my arms. My heart ached. I was his protector. I flashed to the summer a couple years earlier when we were at camp together. George did something the counselors did not like, and I felt they were too strict in their punishment. I stood up to them and said, "Leave him alone!" I remembered when he was a baby and I watched my mother breastfeed him, naïve as to where the milk came from, let alone how my mother produced this hungry infant. I remembered the day he learned to walk.

For the last six months with Father gone, I was the only man George had, even if I was just fourteen. What would he think, with all the men in his life always leaving? I could barely look at him again after I put him down. I turned to my mother who smiled and pulled me to her in a very warm hug. I can still feel it. She will be with Oma, her sisters, and Aunt Martha I reminded myself. There were many people in Berlin who loved her. Still, it was about all I could bear without crying. I climbed into the taxi and closed the door. "To the railroad station, please," I said, as we pulled away from the curb.

My mother, circa 1937

CHAPTER 3
A Spade Is Not a Spade

Philadelphus 'Belle Étoile' (mock orange 'Belle Étoile')

This time my father wasn't with me to keep me company on the train. I didn't ride first class or eat in the dining car. The seat beside me was unoccupied, and I ate a sandwich and Fräulein Liesel's cake as the train sped away from Hamburg.

At the station I hired a taxi to take me to Ahlem. The driver dropped me off on a dirt road by a greenhouse. I watched him drive off and looked around. I couldn't remember where anything was from my tour the previous year. I had no idea where to check in.

A postcard of Ahlem

A much older boy, I assumed a student, was striding toward the greenhouse. He was wearing tall black, very well polished boots, Nazi-like boots. With my suitcase in hand I hurried toward him. When I asked him where I might check in, he merely pointed across a field toward a two-story building and said, "Administration," then he moved on.

I found the office and told a secretary my name. She wasn't much friendlier but was at least polite. She found my name on a list of incoming students.

"Please wait here," she said and left the room. She returned with another student trailing behind her. He was taller than she was, definitely an upperclassman, looking annoyed at the assignment he was just given. He eyed me doubtfully then nodded his head toward the door.

"Follow me."

We walked along paths between buildings and past fields until we reached the largest building on the grounds. I was starting to work up a sweat. At that time we did not have rollers on our suitcases.

"This is the student building," he said as we approached. As we moved around the corner of the shrub-lined, four-story building, I suddenly remembered it. This is where I had taken my exam. The entrance was on the other side of building from us and upslope of the soccer pitch.

Up two flights of stairs and down a hallway, my reluctant guide opened a door to reveal a big room with eight single beds. Next to each bed was a side table and a narrow wooden wardrobe. There were no other students around. I guessed they were all in their afternoon classes, or if they were new, they hadn't yet arrived.

"That's yours, *Knirps* ("Little Squirt")," said my guide. I put my suitcase on top of the bed.

"Follow me." He took me down the hall and pointed into a shower room, where the floor and walls were made of white tiles and there were eight showerheads with no partitions between them.

"When you've unpacked, you can wash up. When it's dinnertime, head down the hall that way, and turn left. You'll find the cafeteria."

He turned on his heels and left.

I unpacked my clothes into the wardrobe, my stationery and pictures into the nightstand drawer just to the right of the bed, threw my toiletry bag and a towel on the pillow, stashed my suitcase under the bed, and went to the shower room and washed my face. Back in the room, I felt very lonely. I wrote my mother a letter letting her know I had arrived safely. I would have to find out how to mail it later.

After an hour — what seemed like an eternity — my dorm mates, evidently all first-years, who had started a quarter or two ahead of me, returned from their classes to shower and eat. Some arrived in clean clothes with books in hand; others looked like they'd been out in the fields, pants dull with dust, and shirts crumpled with the sleeves rolled up. All had those tall, black boots. A few boys introduced themselves. They seemed curious as they sized me up. I was by far the youngest of them all.

I followed them to the cafeteria. I had never before eaten cafeteria-style. I could not tell what was being cooked by the smell. I imitated the other students, standing in line to get a plate of food. It was *sauerbraten* (sour roast) overcooked and a bit tough in a thick brown sauce with sticky potato dumplings on the side. It certainly wasn't my mother's cooking. The vegetables, however, were very fresh: carrots and steamed cabbage that must have been grown and stored on the grounds. I again imitated the rest of the boys as they bussed their plates.

I asked a student from my dorm where I should go next. "Boot polishing," he said, "In the basement. Do you have any yet?"

I shook my head.

"They'll issue you some. Go down the hall that way," he pointed, "until you see some stairs."

It was all so new, and for someone used to privacy the openness of the dorms, showers, and cafeteria was shocking. During my previous tour of the school, I had seen only the upperclassmen's dorms, with just two students to a room. The hardest part by far was being so much younger and shorter than everyone else. It seemed like most people looked at me either inquisitively or dismissively, which made me feel as if I didn't belong. But I was determined to belong. This was my ticket to the United States and my future.

The basement was lit with many ceiling lamps. There were rows of benches and tables where students used buckets, rags, brushes, and polish to clean and shine their boots. An instructor saw me. "You're new?" he asked. I nodded. "What is your shoe size?"

He returned from some shelves with my new black boots, which reminded me of Nazi boots. He showed me how to clean them and warned me that it was very important to keep my clothes and boots clean.

"There is an inspection every morning," he said.

I chose an available spot near an older boy, almost a man, concentrating intently on cleaning his boots over a bucket of water. He had black hair and was quite slender. When he was satisfied that he had removed all the soil from them he wiped down the boots until they were dry. He applied some polish in circles. I watched him for a while and then started on mine, which having never been worn, washed and shined up pretty quickly.

"That looks good." It was the young man. He was looking at my boots and at me. "Are you new?" he asked.

"Yes," I said. "I just arrived today."

He studied me for a moment longer then he extended a hand and smiled. It was a warm smile, the first I had seen at the *Gartenbauschule.* "I'm Friedel Weiss."

"Ernst Wertheim," I said shaking his hand.

"Do you know much about fruit trees?" he asked me.

"A little," I replied, thinking of my mornings with the gardener at Aunt Martha's estate learning about the citrus trees.

"Nothing to study or do tonight, right? No laundry on your first day?"

I shook my head.

"Listen, I have to study for my final exam. I have only four months to go before graduation. Want to come with me to the library? Maybe you can help me study." His voice was kind.

"Sure," I answered. If I were a puppy, I would have been wagging my tail. I followed him outside.

By then it was dark and quite cold. I shivered without a coat. He led me to yet another building, a wonderful one: the library. I had never seen a true library. Germany had no public libraries while I was growing up. Families with the means kept their own private collections. Our study at home had been full of books. Otherwise, libraries existed primarily on university campuses.

Of course, during the previous year, the Nazis had taken control of most of the country's libraries. They were state-funded now, guarded by the SA, and full of propaganda. I wouldn't get near one, especially after the book burnings of May 1933. At that time, all across the nation the German Student Association, in an "Action Against the Un-German Spirit," threw books — mostly written by Jewish writers — into bonfires.

The *Gartenbauschule* library smelled of parchment and aged leather. I admired the wall-to-wall books on evenly spaced shelves, the majority about horticulture and agriculture. There were many tables and chairs at which students studied by lamplight. It was warm and inviting, with an air of knowledge. I was very impressed. Friedel demonstrated how to look up a book by its title, subject, or author in a card catalogue, which was housed in a wooden cabinet with many tiny drawers. I watched him check out a book with the librarian. It was a reference book about fruit trees, which he told me could not be removed from the library.

"I am doing my thesis on identifying the different varieties of fruit trees," he said.

Showing me pictures in his book, he spoke quietly about how each variety has its own growth habit. "I have to be able to recognize the varieties in the winter when there are no leaves at all, no flowers or fruit. I have to show I can tell a pear tree from an apple tree and even, say, a Red Delicious from a Gravenstein."

"How do you do that?" I asked.

"Well, some characteristics are easy to spot. If I have to tell an apple tree from a pear tree, for example, I can look at the growth of the branches." He turned to a page and pointed at an illustration of a bare tree. "See, apple trees spread their branches wide while pear trees," he pointed at another drawing, "tend to grow their branches more upward in a U-shape."

I looked and listened intently, absorbing it all.

"But how do you tell one variety of apple tree from another?" I asked.

"Here, I'll show you," he said. Undoing his book bag, he pulled out two small sections of branches. Friedel showed me how the shape of the shoot and the feel and tint of the bark were different depending on the kind of apple. This took keen observation. I was amazed. He could identify the apple and pear varieties of both young stems and older wood without foliage.

"This is important," he explained, "because when you are handling trees a label may disappear. Or say a new owner buys an old grove during winter and doesn't know what he has. Someone must be able to identify the trees. This is what I will be tested on."

After a while he glanced up at a clock on the wall.

"You better get a move on," he said. "First years have to be in bed by ten. You only have about fifteen minutes."

I asked him about his curfew and he laughed. It turned out that seniors were allowed to stay up as late as needed to study. They were encouraged to do so since they had to finish their theses before graduation. Friedel invited me to meet him the next afternoon to go out in the fields and orchards to look at the trees. He was pretty sure I would have an orientation in the morning, which I was relieved to hear. I bid Friedel goodnight and rushed back to the dorms.

As I lay in bed, the unfamiliar sound of other boys breathing and snoring around me reverberated throughout the large room. I felt uncomfortable and very alone. I didn't sleep much. At the same time, I thought of Friedel. He had made a difficult first day into something good, and when I reviewed all that I had learned from him, I was excited to learn more.

The next morning, I dressed in the trousers and new work shirt my mother had bought for me, slipped on my new boots, and went with my classmates to the dining hall. Afterwards, the dormitory supervisor, who was also a professor at the school, went over dorm and school rules and led those of us who were brand new on a tour of the grounds. Though we didn't march, the teacher spoke like a sergeant to his infantrymen. I didn't expect such a military tone at a horticultural school.

The professor handed out class schedules and described some of the different things we would have to do to meet our requirements. We had to pick a thesis after our first three months and that would guide the focus of our studies for the next three years.

After lunch, I found Friedel at the edge of the fields behind the student center. He pointed out the rows of young fruit trees, identifying them as one year, two years, or three years old. The students were growing them to sell to the public or to other nurseries. All shrubs and trees were grown in long rows similar to any other farm product. Then we walked to the orchard. It contained rows of healthy mature trees: apple, pear, peach, plum, and cherry. Friedel pointed out the different ones at a distance and up close, highlighting the details of each.

"When they blossom," said Friedel, "it's easy to identify the trees by the color of the blooms and the number of petals in each flower. And of course, they all have their seasons. But identifying them when they are bare, that's the trick!" He nodded with pride and excitement.

On Monday morning, the new students were instructed to meet at the same place I had met Friedel, on the edge of the field behind the student building. It was good to see the other new students looking nervous, too, even though they were older. An instructor met us, led us to a storage shed, and then issued each of us a spade. These weren't the nice long shovels that I would later become accustomed to in the United States. The spades were three feet long, the heads nearly flat. The professor demonstrated how he wanted us to hold them on our shoulders, just like the rifles at my prior school. Then, in two lines, he marched us like little soldiers out into the fields.

We walked until we came to a rhubarb field one hundred meters long. He assembled us so we each stood facing a row of the plants that were low to the ground with their very early spring foliage.

"Now, your job for the day is to cultivate the area between the rhubarb plants. Each one of you will have one row. Spading does not only mean turning the soil to a certain depth. It also means breaking the soil into small pieces. The better the cultivation, the more air can get to the root system. Use your spades to turn over the soil and break it up," he commanded. "Understand? Get to work!"

I couldn't believe it. I came here to learn about horticulture and on my first day I was to spade a field? I stooped low, dug in and then stood up to empty the shovel of its soil. With the short spade I had to really bend over. Stoop, dig, and stand. Stoop, dig, and stand. I repeated this about five times before the professor was by my side telling me to stop.

"I guess you don't know how to spade," he said.

I didn't know what to say to that.

"Where did you grow up, in the city?"

"Yes, Hamburg," I replied.

He chuckled. "Oh, you really don't know."

"Well," I said, "I really didn't come here to learn how to spade. I came for an education."

His smile immediately disappeared as he glared at me.

"Well, young man, the boys who graduate from this school often get positions in management." He pointed his finger at me, moved it close to my face and while shaking it for emphasis added, "and this means they will tell others how and what to do. In order to do this a person has to learn each task, and the first one will be how to spade. Before you can ask others to do it, you need to know how it feels to do this all day long." He walked away angrily.

What he was really saying was, "Young man, you don't have a chance at graduating with that attitude!" Eighty years later, I can still see that pointing finger trying to penetrate into my brain.

With that I asked the boy in the next row to show me how to spade properly. He showed me how you waste energy if you stand up so you stay bent over your spade while digging.

We turned the soil of that entire rhubarb field, taking most of the day to do so. I was in fairly good shape but I wasn't prepared for such continuous physical labor. My muscles ached. By the time I was in bed after cleaning my boots I was bushed, but boy, did I know how to spade.

Ahlem students with spades on their shoulders, 1938

The *Gartenbauschule* emphasized practical training along with traditional learning. We studied agriculture and horticulture, as well as math, composition, and science. The physical labor continued. Days later I was out spading again, learning the three-spade system, digging to a depth that was three spades deep. This method was used in landscaping because the deeper cultivation creates a much better environment for new plants to grow and thrive. We had no rototillers in the 1930s.

The first few evenings we did not have any evening study, but as soon as regular classes began that immediately changed. It really helped that I got to study beside Friedel. We spent many evenings together in the library or study hall, which was in a separate building. There were study halls for each year of students, but because I accompanied Friedel I was allowed to go to the seniors' study hall. This exposed me to very serious students in more advanced classes. I felt because I was so young and small I needed to accelerate my learning to prove myself. The professors did not seem to like me very much. Maybe they thought I was just too young to keep up or perhaps even that I had bought my way in. Since the seizure of power by the Nazis the previous year, the number of applications for admission to the *Gartenbauschule* had doubled, perhaps even tripled. In 1935, more than five hundred applicants would apply for only one hundred positions, with even more applying in the years to follow. The *Gartenbauschule* offered the learning of a trade and the hope of emigration, a rare safe haven for a Jew in Hitler's Germany, at least for a while.

Though Friedel was a good-looking young man, perhaps 5'8", strong even in his slender frame, he was not outgoing. He did not let others get close to him. However, because he was very intelligent, his classmates looked up to him. He was very perceptive and saw things others did not. I guess he saw something in me. I think he enjoyed teaching me because I absorbed things quickly. With my learning expedited by Friedel, I did well and began to feel I was gaining the respect of my teachers.

Since most of our time together was spent learning there was not much time for socializing. We had some discussions about Palestine because he wanted to go there. Friedel said he was a Zionist, an idea with which I had little acquaintance. Many students at the *Gartenbauschule* planned to emigrate to Palestine after graduation. Friedel had learned from our instructors that a horticultural and agricultural education would be of great value there, and he felt his thesis would help him show his expertise to potential employers. He also felt it was safer in Palestine, away from the growing Nazi violence in Germany.

In one of my first lessons an instructor asked me to come over and water a geranium in a pot. I walked over with my silver watering can and poured some water in the container.

"Ernst," he said, "you did not water this plant."

"But I did," I said.

"No, you did not. Come see."

I peered into the pot and then looked at him questioningly.

"Do you see all the water standing in the saucer below the pot?"

I nodded.

"A root ball shrinks to a smaller size when dry. This means that if the plant is in a container, most of the water will flow through the small separation between the root ball and the sides of the container and end up in the bottom, draining out through the holes in the pot. See it now?"

"I see," I said, "What do I do to correct this?"

He smiled. By then it was clear to him I wanted to learn and learn well. "You use warm water. It will penetrate the dry soil more easily than cold water. Make certain some water falls on the root ball. Apply it slowly and watch it sink into the soil. Repeat this two or three times."

There were many great lessons, such as this, I have never forgotten. Today, we have wetting agents to do the same thing, but without them, this method still applies.

I couldn't wait to write to Fräulein Liesel to tell her about the extensive cold frames at Ahlem and all the plants we grew in them. Nurturing the plants throughout the cold months was very labor intensive but rewarding.

The seedlings included lettuce and other leafy greens as well as flowers such as petunias, begonias, impatiens, and marigolds. In spring, we transplanted the lettuce to the fields. When the flowers were well sprouted, they were moved to the greenhouses. The frames gave us a chance to start these plants early without taking up valuable greenhouse space. Some students helped open and close the frames while others brought in the manure and prepared the base. At those times my boots required extra scrubbing!

Students caring for the coldframes at *Israelitische Gartenbauschule* Ahlem, 1938

In May, strawberry season began.

"Tomorrow," bellowed a professor one afternoon after we had inspected the strawberries to find them ripe for picking, "you will need to get up at 0400. Dress quickly, look sharp, and promptly meet here."

We all set out clothes the night before. While it was still dark, the hammered bell of an alarm clock rang. The first hint of morning light was illuminating the sky as we gathered in the fields.

"While picking," said the professor, "you may eat as many as you wish."

We began stuffing the juicy berries into our mouths, while loading others into the baskets. They were delicious. Those first few days we ate berries until our stomachs ached, but quickly the novelty wore off. We found out we could not live on strawberries alone.

At 0600, the teacher showed us how to carefully load the berries into a horse-drawn wagon. He then chose a few of us to go to the wholesale market. It was important to get to the wholesale market as quickly as possible. We climbed into the wagon with the berries and were off, the professor working the reigns to move the horses. We munched on sandwiches on the way since it would be midmorning before we returned.

It was fun, a terrific change from regular classes.

"Your assignment is to sell all of your berries. You are not allowed to bring any back to the school, understand?" A few boys raised eyebrows. Then the professor explained, in case we did not understand such a simple concept, these berries could not be sold tomorrow because they would no longer be fresh. It was very exciting, and a different kind of challenge than the physical labor and academic study at school. We had to deal with people, which was incredibly valuable.

After the first three months, I was ready to choose my thesis topic. At the time there was a great deal of research developing around the rootstock, which is a plant or small shrub with an established, healthy root system. By taking a cutting or a bud from another plant and grafting it onto the healthy-rooted plant, one could propagate a variety of fruits that normally wouldn't grow well in a specific soil type. The plant part grafted onto the rootstock has the fruit or decorative properties desired, while the chosen rootstock obtains the necessary soil, water, and minerals, and resists pests and diseases. I found this interesting and decided to choose it for my thesis. I had been exposed to orchard culture during my visits to Fräulein Liesel's victory garden, by visiting orchards near Hamburg to buy fruit directly from farmers, and by walking around with the head gardener at Aunt Martha's estate. I was not an expert, but I knew a bit about pruning, irrigation, and fertilization. Learning to manipulate rootstock would significantly add to my abilities.

By this time Friedel had finished his thesis, passed his exams, and graduated. During that entire first quarter, as I adjusted to being away from home for the first time and to the regimen of college, he had taken me under his wing. I was very happy for him but very sorry he was leaving.

For whatever reason — I never found out — Friedel had no family to attend his graduation. After the formal graduation exercise, the director, Herr Rosenblatt, and his wife hosted a special dinner for the top graduates and their families. Friedel asked that I be invited as his guest. It was a wonderful, memorable evening. After dinner Herr Rosenblatt invited each student to talk about his experiences during his time at *Israelitische Gartenbauschule Ahlem*, both pleasant and unpleasant, and make suggestions on how to improve the program. Guests were also invited to make a comment. When my turn came around, I expressed that I felt the school was too army-like. The director's wife laughed. It turned out Herr Rosenblatt was a lieutenant in the Great War. No wonder he made top sergeants out of his teachers.

It was obvious the staff greatly respected him, and he had chosen dedicated men with significant expertise. Most of the teachers were not Jewish. This was fine when I started at the college in 1934. By my last year, however, some of the instructors started suffering psychological trauma as they tried to make sense of the conflicting Nazi propaganda and the immense respect they had for Herr Rosenblatt and the school. They became increasingly concerned for their own safety, as well as that of their students. The stress was very apparent to me, but not because of anything in particular they said or did. You could just feel it, at least I could. It's amazing how sensitive you become to people's emotions and intentions when you must navigate your way through danger and violence, when you witness cruelties you never thought you would see, and when you become accustomed to listening for footsteps running toward you from behind.

Friedel and I exchanged addresses but the graduation dinner was the last time we spoke to each other during my time at Ahlem. Though I missed him, I became tremendously busy at the beginning of the summer season. I joined the track team and started training for the 100, 800, and 3,000-meter races as well as relay races. Our coach, a professor at the school, taught us how to train properly. We competed against other schools. Meets on other school grounds were not attended by anyone except the students involved. Maybe this had something to do with us being Jewish.

It was considered a duty to win for the school, so I trained very hard. I had made several friends by then, including my good friend, Dieter Nassau. Dieter helped me keep time and made certain I trained regularly. My preference was to rise early, and Dieter was always by my side.

By then, summer flowers were everywhere, and the shrubs alongside the student center were full of cascading little white blossoms, so thick you could barely see the leaves. I learned it was called bridal wreath *Spiraea vanhouttei* (bridal white spirea). I would run alongside the hedge until it was nothing but a streak of white in my periphery.

The training paid off. I did well, winning races for my school. Winning also helped my ego and it earned me a certain amount of respect from other students and faculty, just like soccer had at the *Oberrealschule*.

That summer it was my turn to do one of the least pleasant chores at Ahlem. Ahlem had no sewers, and everything in the kitchen sinks, the showers, and latrines went into cesspool tanks. As they started to get full, the *Jauche* (liquid manure), was pumped into big tank wagons horses would pull out into the fields. We had to help with this process, siphoning the jauche into the wagon's tank until it was full, and plugging it carefully. Upon reaching the fields you had to use a kind of sledgehammer to knock the cork out of the tank. Every undergraduate living in the dorms had to do it at least once a year.

The first time I was assigned to do this job, I was really nervous. I had once seen and smelled a student as he rushed to the showers afterwards. If you didn't get the cork out properly, the jauche would pour all over you. When I found out my turn was coming to fertilize the fields, I went out the day before to practice removing the stopper while the tank was empty. That night I dreamt about doing it incorrectly and the horrible mess that would ensue.

The next day, there I was facing the tank and the cork with my sledgehammer. I focused on the task and swung the hammer with force. Luckily, the cork fell away just right. I had to repeat this several times that day and for the next three days. My swing wasn't perfect every time, but fortunately, only my boots ever needed extra cleaning.

One day in midsummer, I was on a long distance run passing by the administration building when I smelled the most intoxicating fragrance. It brought me to a halt. It was the most sensuous thing I had ever smelled, both sweet and sultry, a mixture of citrus and honey and spice, of orange blossoms and sandalwood.

I followed my nose until I came to a large shrub with abundant flowers of creamy white with maroon blotches at their centers. I closed my eyes and breathed in the scent again. If you have ever experienced the effect of just the right perfume on a woman you love – the satisfaction and pleasure of the smell – then you know what it was like for me every time I passed the *Philadelphus* ('Belle Etoile' or mock orange).

With the smell of fertilizer in the air and the all-boy student population of the *Gartenbauschule* sweating in the fields all day, this was a nice contrast. From then on, I made sure my long distance runs always passed the 'Belle Etoile'.

The school allowed us to apply for research oriented field trips to illustrate something we had been learning or to access plants and/or agricultural concepts we didn't have on campus. If granted, they paid for all our travel expenses. My first trip happened in July 1934, when I traveled to a horticulture institution in Münster, affiliated with the university. I had written to the horticulturalists who were involved in rootstock research to ask if I could come to study for a few days. Some of the trials I would visit were conducted on property owned by the Duke of Cröy.

As I arrived at the Duke's estate, I became anxious as I gazed at the agricultural warehouses dotting the countryside. I had never been to the estate before so I wondered if these were the buildings where my father had been starved and beaten. I thought of the Duke, too, and how he had kept my mother, George, and me safe and paid for my father's freedom.

I wondered what my father was doing at that moment. Where was he? In Belgium? Or was he in Paris staying with his brother, Erick Wertheim, and his wife, Erna? I hoped he was safe. I decided to write my mother when I was back at school to find out. I was used to not seeing him for long periods of time, but being in this place made me wonder about him. I was relieved when I found the researcher, who welcomed me and led me to the fields where he and others conducted their work.

A few days later, on August 2, 1934, President Hindenburg died. Power was consolidated, and Adolf Hitler became the head of state in Germany, with the new title, *Führer und Reichskanzler*. In the dormitory we listened on the radio to Hitler's speech at a rally in Nuremberg. He promised prosperity and that the Third Reich would last for a thousand years. My companions and I just looked at each other.

We had a retail site on campus open to the public on weekends. We organized the greenhouse and prepared the display area by raking the fine pea gravel and arranging bales of hay and a few display tables. We had to be mindful to allow several people at a time enough room to view the plants. This was my first introduction to setting up an area for retail. How very handy this experience would be twenty years later, when I was asked to design a nursery for the first time.

We didn't have containers for our trees and shrubs as we do today, so we carefully wrapped and secured the roots in burlap. They would remain in the burlap until they were placed in soil in their new locations.

We moved this inventory to a main assembly area, then quickly into a large warehouse that had temperature and moisture controls. It was very important to keep the place cool and the shrubs and trees watered until it was time either for a weekend sale or until we took them to the railroad for shipment to non-retail customers. When the trees and shrubs were sent out to the various nurseries within Germany, we would assemble the orders and load them onto horse-drawn wagons to transport them to the trains.

At the station, we placed all the plants into boxcars. It was an art to stack them properly, keeping the varieties separated and unharmed, while packing in as many as possible. To keep down the costs of transportation, you didn't want to waste space. Only a few years later, the Nazis loaded people into the very same boxcars, taking into account the same economy of space.

We had only one vacation a year, three weeks at Christmas. I packed my bag for Berlin. I was lucky because not everyone went home during the holiday break. Some students didn't have a home to go to.

The industrial sounds at the Berlin train station were startling. It was such a contrast to the quiet of the fields and study halls. But the noise disappeared when I saw my mother hurrying towards me.

We were so pleased to see each other. During the taxi ride, I asked about George. He was at a Jewish boarding school and had a different break schedule, so I was not going to see him. I was very disappointed, but Mother said he was doing well and promised to show me his letters. She said this with a smile, but I felt her sadness. At the Bendlerstrasse apartment, Oma greeted me with a great big hug and said I was just in time for Shabbat dinner. Every Friday night she had at least one guest for Shabbat. She also kept up the habit of hosting friends on Sunday afternoon, just as she and Opa had done when I was a child. Shabbat at *Gartenbauschule* was optional, and I usually spent the time studying. My parents never made a tradition of it in our home. However, I enjoyed Shabbat with Oma. She always made it festive with good food and wine.

The next day, I accompanied her to the graveyard where Opa was buried. His grave was covered with ivy, as were most graves in Germany. In front of his tombstone were three vases we filled with flowers from the market. I missed Opa very much.

On Sunday afternoon, my mother had tickets to the matinee opera. We spent Saturday reading the novel from which the opera was based so we could follow the performance. Later during the holiday break we went to a number of plays, one of which was Shakespeare's *Hamlet*. The plays were in Jewish theaters and were performed by Jewish actors. There was more than enough entertainment during that visit.

We also read some Thomas Mann, one of the newly banned authors in Germany. This became a delightful habit, reading and discussing the same books. Mother had so much enthusiasm for art, literature, and culture.

On Monday, Mother had to return to work, and I decided to go with her. She was doing social work for a Jewish organization in Berlin. I watched her interview people in her office, many of whom were crying or trying not to cry. She helped them find work and helped wives whose husbands had been arrested. Others had their stores destroyed or confiscated. There were many people who needed housing or even basic meals.

I already had great respect for my mother. But seeing her earn money for our family, working hard with so much responsibility, communicating and working with people who were distraught, scared, embarrassed, hungry, and grateful for her efforts — well, I saw her through an even wider lens.

Oma also worked at the non-profit. She specialized in managing several *Altersheim* (elderly homes), and securing financial support for them. Grandmother Wertheim lived in one of them, and I visited her twice during my vacation. We played card games and walked through the gardens together.

A few afternoons I spent in the company of my girlfriend. We mostly had afternoon coffee and cake at her house or mine. A couple times we put on our winter coats for a walk in the Tiergarten. We strolled holding hands, which was a wonderful new experience for me.

I worked very hard my first year at the *Gartenbauschule* and as a result earned a scholarship that would cover my tuition for the next two years. I couldn't wait to write my mother to let her know she no longer had to pay for my education. With this scholastic achievement, the professors treated me with much respect, and they gave me special opportunities to learn. Most students were not offered such opportunities. I was also asked to work with new students to help them understand the purpose of the school and how to make the most of their education. It was very gratifying.

One of those special opportunities took place in August 1935. This trip was to Munich to learn more about the understock or rootstock of stone fruits. At first, the head researcher talked to me like I was a little boy and only shared the most rudimentary things. I only had one day with him and wanted to get the most out of the experience. Though I had gained respect at school, to the rest of the world, I still looked like a child. So I started peppering him with questions heavily laden with botanical language, and he quickly became enthusiastic to talk with me. By day's end he gave me understock I could take back to Ahlem for my research.

I was allowed to stay an extra day to tour the Munich Botanical Gardens, twenty-two hectares of gardens on the city's outskirts, bordering the Nymphenburg Palace. Many new understock seedlings were grown in the Botanical Garden's propagating house. Once they were large enough they were planted on a farm outside Munich, and a year later they would be grafted with many different varieties. It took a minimum of fifteen years to reach suitable conclusions about the grafting. The trees had to be bearing fruit for a number of years in order to determine which rootstock was most successful.

Near the end of summer, I received a letter from my mother with sad news. Great Uncle Wilhelm Wertheim had passed away. My mother encouraged me to stay in Ahlem. Because I would have to travel at her expense, I agreed, but I wrote to Aunt Martha with my condolences. I had often stayed with her and my uncle in Dahlem. She reserved a guest room for me that had a bed in a golden frame. Aunt Martha had always treated me like a son, and Mother was by far her favorite person in the family. I had to grieve in solitude as I watered the plants in the greenhouses.

My uncle passed away just before the enactment of the Nuremberg Laws in September 1935. The new "Laws for the Protection of German Blood and German Honor" were posted everywhere. Our own country now considered us Jews and not German citizens, if we had three or more Jewish grandparents. It banned sexual intercourse between people defined as Jews and Germans, and it prevented Jews from participating in German civic life. It meant that Jewish people could be barred from employment as lawyers, doctors or journalists. We were prohibited from using state hospitals and could not be educated by the state past the age of fourteen. Because the *Gartenbauschule* was private, we could stay in operation, but even still, a hushed dread fell upon the school for a few weeks. When nothing changed on campus, the dread was replaced with tentative relief.

One of the laws stated that, "Jews will not be permitted to employ female citizens under the age of forty-five, of German or kindred blood, as domestic workers." Though Fräulein Liesel had not worked for our family since 1933, I decided I better not write to her anymore. I was afraid this might somehow endanger both of us.

In November, these decrees were expanded to include "members of other races whose blood is not related to German blood, as, for example, Gypsies and Negroes," as well as Germans with mental illness and genetic deformities. War memorials were to have Jewish names expunged. Even the lottery could not award winnings to Jews. Public parks, libraries, and beaches were closed to Jews. The punishment for defying these laws included imprisonment, fines and hard labor. I felt lucky that I had already seen Munich's Botanical Gardens. I wondered where I would walk with my girlfriend during the next winter holiday in Berlin.

During the holiday break, I visited my late Uncle Wilhelm's office and sat in the same leather armchair I had as a child. I watched the construction of a new addition to the Reich Chancellery across the street for what was to be Hitler's new office. I didn't know it at the time, but part of this large new building was on property the Nazis had appropriated from the Wertheim Department Store family. Like any new construction, it was interesting to watch. But in this case, it embedded something in my memory that would prove quite significant years later. On the street level was Hitler's new domicile. Some of the concrete work I witnessed was for his *Vorbunker*, protected by one-and-a-half meters of a thick concrete roof that supported the weight of the large reception hall overhead. I had no idea the details of what I saw that day would be of future value to the U.S. military, and that

I would be recalling it to my superiors during special training while serving in the United States Army.

I also spent time with friends during the break. One day, I introduced my girlfriend to another of my friends, and the three of us spent an afternoon together talking and laughing. I knew we had a good time together, but I didn't realize the extent of it until a few months later. I received a "Dear Ernst" letter. My girlfriend not only broke up with me, she announced she was dating my friend. I was very naïve and inexperienced when it came to the opposite sex so this was a difficult part of my education.

Back at Ahlem, just as I began my final year in 1936, the school changed its rules about what topics were permissible for our theses. When I initially selected rootstock for fruit trees as my thesis focus, the school's policy allowed for a thirty-year window between theses written on the same subject. The new ruling, however, stated any subject previously studied for a thesis — regardless of how long ago — could not be selected again. After two years of studying rootstock, my work was no longer eligible. This was a bitter disappointment. I had studied it very intensively and was most interested in the subject. I thought it might become my life's work, but I had no choice but to find another topic.

I was taking my first class in landscape design at the time. I discovered nothing had been written about landscape architecture in relationship to contemporary architecture and suggested this to my advisor. He heartily approved this topic.

With her husband gone, my Aunt Martha had decided to build a smaller one-story house on her Dahlem estate. Because of the Nuremburg decree, I think she lost some of her best housekeepers, and the estate was too much for her to manage. She engaged the services of a Bauhaus architect to design her new house. I wrote to my aunt explaining my new focus and asked if I could design a garden to complement her new home. She welcomed the idea and arranged for me to meet with the architect and walk through his plans. I then started corresponding with him during the project. The more I engaged and learned, the more I enjoyed the work in landscape design and construction. Designing a garden for someone I loved so dearly made it all the more exciting.

The majority of my classes the rest of the year were related to landscape architecture, which was still called landscape engineering at the time. On top of the course work we were provided with practical experience, as we were in everything we learned at the *Gartenbauschule*.

Clients came to the school for garden designs. One potential client was invited to speak to our class. We listened to him talk about what he wanted for his gardens and looked at site drawings and photographs.

After the client left, the professor created teams of students and put us in competition with one another to create the best landscape design using the client's requirements. The professors evaluated our designs and presentations and selected three to exhibit to the client. It was very exciting when my team's design was chosen as one of the three finalists. We met the client again in a conference room when all three plans were presented. The client selected my team's design!

The next day we went to the client's property to take measurements and look at the soil. Over several long days and nights, we created the concept, drafted the construction drawings, and estimated the cost of the project. The instructors checked on our progress and approved the specifications and estimate. Then we began project construction.

I dug in my spade for the first time on site and — clang — hit something hard. I dug again a foot away. Clang! Kneeling down, I brushed the soil away. I couldn't believe it. The two visible inches of good soil lay on top of six inches of broken pieces of brick.

I reported this to our supervising professor. He simply told me it was too bad and I should have checked it before I started the design. All the brick had to be removed and the planting soil returned to its original place after additional soil had filled the space of the excavated brick. This meant many additional hours of labor and the additional cost of more topsoil. My estimation was thrown completely out of whack. I had to work evenings and weekends to correct the problem, grateful for the additional labor offered by some of my classmates. It was a lesson I would never forget.

In the summer of 1936, my older brother, Werner, made a surprise visit to see me at the *Gartenbauschule*, riding his bicycle all the way from Berlin. I hadn't seen him since I had started at the *Oberrealschule* over two years earlier. It was strange to see him now as a man. Perhaps he felt the same of me as a teenager.

Werner had come to say goodbye. He was leaving for Valparaiso, Chile, in a matter of days. His friends, the Putzrath family, had arranged for their fifteen year old son to go to Chile to study, and they asked Werner to accompany him. They helped him obtain a visitor's visa and paid for his round trip ticket on the ship. Werner would help the son get settled during his first year and then return. While we had never been great friends, he was my brother, and I was touched by his visit.

I showed him around the school and arranged for him to stay in the visitor's quarters. He had a train ticket back to Berlin the next day. After breakfast, he called for a taxi to take him to the station in Hannover.

When the taxi arrived outside the greenhouses, he pushed his bike towards me.

"Here, you have it."

"Thank you, Werner," I said, and I happily took the handlebars. I would cling to that memory of my brother until I would see him again, nearly twenty years later.

He got in the taxi and waved goodbye.

I waved after him and then mounted the bicycle to try it out. It was a glorious feeling, the warm air rushing past me as I pedaled.

That bike was a big deal for me. My friends at school admired my fancy new bike, and I was very proud of it. It allowed me more freedom of movement. From then on, when I had a free weekend, I rode my bike around to explore. I rode to the Herrenhäuser Gärten in Hannover where the main avenue was planted with one hundred year old sycamores. They were fantastic trees, providing wonderful shade over the spacious street. A few of my friends had bicycles, and a favorite activity of ours was to ride to a small lake in Hannover where we rented a rowboat and spent a few glorious hours on the water. We had so little free time, this was a real treat.

Once, we rode to the nearby town of Hildesheim. Standing on a slope above the town center was an ancient church, St. Michael's. It was constructed between the years 1010 and 1031. Ever since my childhood trips to the older neighborhoods in Hamburg with George Salomon and his family, I had admired architecture. Now, as a horticulture student, I was also able to appreciate a climbing rose on the church's stone exterior, which we were told was a thousand years old.

The church was destroyed by an air raid in March 1945, and later rebuilt to the former glory that stood before me that day. Still, I am glad I got to see the original. Since 1985, it's been on the UNESCO World Cultural Heritage list.

That same summer, Berlin hosted the 1936 Olympics. We followed it as much as possible, listening to the events on the crystal radio with mixed feelings. Despite all that was happening in our country – the restrictions and fear we faced as Jews – it was a wonderful thing to have the games in Germany. They built a huge stadium and designed beautiful gardens that made a fine impression on the international community. Hitler was showcasing the "new Germany" to the world. We saw pictures of the gardens in a magazine. As Jews, we weren't allowed to see them in person.

My classmates and I weren't pulling for the German athletes, so it certainly didn't bother me when I listened to the crackling radio broadcast as American Jesse Owens won the 100-meter final. We had become detached and indifferent to our country. Our government had ostracized us and was taking away money and means from our families. Feelings ranged regularly from anger to fear to confusion when it came to our homeland.

For Christmas 1936, I rode my bike home to Berlin. My time with my mother and grandmother was a bit shorter because of the two-day travel time each way, but the ride was invigorating. I also spent time with my aunt and uncle, Hilde and Alfred Traube, and their family. Hilde Traube was my mother's younger sister. I felt very close to my aunt and uncle. Alfred was a good attorney and handled all of Aunt Martha's legal matters. They had two daughters a little younger than me, and I had often spent time at their house in Hallensee during my childhood.

It must have been shortly after the holiday break that my father was arrested or detained, whatever word might best suit the Nazis, as he attempted to come back to Berlin after being out of the country for three-and-a-half years. As best as I know, he was taken away as soon as he stepped off the train. Mother's letter offered few details. I don't remember if it really registered emotionally, certainly not like his disappearance just after Hitler came to power.

In March 1937, I received my graduation certificate at the age of seventeen. My mother was very pleased at how well I had done at Ahlem. Unlike Friedel's graduation, no one threw a party for my graduating class. We had a simple ceremony in which my name was called, and I walked up to receive my diploma. Herr Rosenblatt shook my hand and congratulated me, then I sat back down. No parents were invited; no one from the outside attended. The important thing for German Jews in 1937 was not to draw any attention to ourselves.

I packed my bag and said goodbye to the *Gartenbauschule*. I would miss the safety, the learning, my teachers, and friends, but I was ready for the next challenge. I would focus on getting a job and securing my immigration to the United States.

CHAPTER 4

White Asparagus

Asparagus officinalis (white asparagus)
Photo by Cora Mueller © 123RF.com

The U.S. visa required that two people sponsor me, to vouch for my character, and promise to provide for me financially if I could not provide for myself. The American government would not allow anyone to enter the country who might easily become a burden to the system. If you didn't know anybody, a way around it, normally, was to declare you were bringing a large sum of money with you. But as a Jew, I was not allowed to take Reichsmarks out of Germany.

My mother had a distant relative and friend named Hanna Hellinger, who had already settled in the United States as a refugee. We wrote to Hanna asking her to provide my affidavit. In 1937, overseas letters traveled by ship back and forth across the Atlantic, and we could not expect a reply for at least six weeks. With the worsening situation in Germany, time was of the essence, but I had no choice but to wait for her reply.

In the meantime, I was eager to start contributing financially for my family and saving the money necessary to pay my way overseas. Oma helped me secure my first horticultural job. I was to remove the large stump of an old pine tree from the garden at a Jewish *Altersheim*, where Grandmother Wertheirm lived. Since Oma was on the board, she had influence on the acceptance of my bid. I called my friend, Dieter, to help me as he had also moved back in with his family in Berlin.

Grandmother Wertheim waved to me proudly from the porch as Dieter and I arrived early one morning with spades and enthusiasm. Hours later we stood sweating over a deep ditch and piles of soil and wood, nowhere near the base of the roots. They went much deeper than I expected. Instead of one day, the job took three. Again I missed estimated the project, but it was a good learning experience. Next time we did a much better job of estimating the cost.

Aunt Martha also engaged me to oversee the gardens on her estate. The head gardener and several other workers had left. The law made it dangerous for them to work for a Jewish woman. Aunt Martha did retain two maids and Herr Glaubitz, her longtime chauffeur, whose loyalty overshadowed the risk of working for a Jewish family. As a child, I loved riding around in her large, black, Chrysler passenger car with Herr Glaubitz at the wheel. He treated me like a little king. Sometimes I'd go along when Aunt Martha and Uncle Wilhelm had an event to attend, such as the opera. I'd hang out with Herr Glaubitz, who would introduce me to all the other chauffeurs in Dahlem. They were all friends, and they would talk; share news and stories and jokes; and smoke cigarettes. They were very kind to me.

With Uncle Wilhelm gone, my great aunt lived in the smaller, contemporary house she had built on the property for which I had designed the garden as my college thesis. Along with this garden the entire ten-acre estate needed regular maintenance. Three acres contained an orchard and a vegetable garden. There was also the large conservatory where, as a child, I had been introduced to citrus, camellias, hibiscus, palm trees, and other tropical plants that needed protection from the cold winters. Brown wicker chairs with deep cushions and coffee tables invited one to sit and feel, for a moment, as if one was in the tropics. The conservatory was a wondrous place.

Aunt Martha's smaller house with the garden I designed, circa 1937

In the early morning hours, I rode my bike from Bendlerstrasse in Berlin out to Dahlem, inspected the conservatory and gardens, and gave instructions to my small crew. At precisely eight-thirty, I went inside to have breakfast with Aunt Martha. These morning meals became sacred to both of us. Over eggs and toast we discussed the estate as well as our private affairs and thoughts. Aunt Martha treated me like a trusted son.

A few weeks into this routine, Herr Glaubitz offered to give me driving lessons. It was a real privilege and a great thrill to cruise in the Chrysler through the streets of Dahlem. Under his tutelage I was able to pass my driver's license test just prior to my eighteenth birthday. That day felt bigger than my graduation from Ahlem. From then on, I drove Aunt Martha whenever Herr Glaubitz was sick. This included excursions to the lake, where she swam almost daily.

Occasionally, Aunt Martha hosted meetings and parties for social organizations. When they were especially large, I would stay overnight. She felt better if I was around to help her with some of the social aspects. I had my own bedroom in Aunt Martha's new house, simply furnished and warm with morning light.

At the urging of my mother I also took a night class to learn how to be a butler. "In order to survive in America, you need to be employable in a number of areas," she told me. "You can be a gardener, a chauffeur and a butler."

I complained. I was going to be a landscape architect, a horticulturalist.

"What are you going to do?" she said. "Climb up on a stepladder in Times Square and announce, 'Here I am, give me a job'?"

Of course, she was right, so I enrolled. Two nights a week I went to the school in what used to be a large home owned by a wealthy family on Kurfürsten Damm, the broad avenue considered the Champs-Élysée of Berlin. The instructors were well seasoned in the hospitality industry. Learning in an actual home made it feel very real.

It was not a Jewish school, and at first the others stared at me, keeping a distance as if I had a disease. Most students were learning hotel management or cooking. There was a huge kitchen with a large pantry where the students learned to be chefs. The kitchen doors opened onto a formal dining room with a large table, where the butler students gathered. It was our job to set the table properly, to carry the food out from the kitchen, to serve each dish in just the right manner, to pour wine the right way, and then to clear the dishes. I stayed quiet and precisely followed the teacher's directions so that after a few sessions the others seemed to forget about me. In about six weeks, I could stand, serve and walk like a butler.

I had more good fortune with employment. Aunt Martha had a couple of renters adjacent to the garage. It turned out that one was a lady landscape architect named Fräulein Fischer. She had an office as well as living quarters in an addition next to the garage. One day I told my mother excitedly over *Abendessen* that I was going to ask her for work. "Be good to the woman," she said.

At Aunt Martha's with Oma, George on my shoulders, my mother,
and the landscape architect, Fräulein Fischer, circa 1937

I had no idea what that meant, but I guess I was good enough. She
hired me, and I worked for a real landscape architect for the first time.
As her site inspector and supervisor, I checked on the progress of each
job: how well the laborers installed the water lines, the drain lines, the
walkways, terraces, and retaining walls; or how they conditioned the
soil and planted the trees and flowers. I wasn't supposed to speak to
the laborers but rather report my findings to the foremen. Privately,
however, I often talked to the landscape crew. I found this helpful.

When not sleeping at Aunt Martha's, I settled into life on
Bendlerstrasse. My mother and Oma continued their work for the
Jewish welfare association. Oma still hid her best cookies high in the
dining room's antique cupboards. She was convinced that if you held
the handle of the teakettle, it boiled faster. She was a wonderful person
and her home was an incredibly loving place.

Occasionally, I accompanied Oma to the synagogue on Saturday.
Afterwards we would visit Opa's grave and place fresh begonias I had
cut from Aunt Martha's gardens into the vases now held captive by
tangled English ivy.

The New Synagogue of Berlin where Oma and the
Wertheims worshipped, illust. 1866

With all the work and classes, my days were full. Other than Dieter,
I had no friends in Berlin, which was just as well. I had little time for
leisure. There was no chance to sit and worry about things. Otherwise,

there would have been a lot to worry about. The number of Gestapo on the streets was increasing. Over the winter, Hitler fired and replaced many political and military leaders. In March 1938, Germany annexed Austria creating the *Anschluss*, which had been forbidden by the Treaty of Versailles. The Nazis were routinely imprisoning people like my father so this concern came up more and more among my relatives.

Because Father had traveled for work throughout my life, I was used to him being gone. And for four years — since late 1933 when he'd left the country — I hadn't been in contact with him whatsoever, not even a letter. My mother rarely spoke of him, and she had already declared me the "man of the house." It was as if I didn't have a father at all. His arrest by the Gestapo had been disturbing, but I had been so deeply focused on my studies at Ahlem, so sequestered from the rest of the world, that I hadn't thought much about the situation, let alone what to do about it. It was horrible to think of him imprisoned. But I didn't fully comprehend it, not until I returned to Berlin after graduating. Now, living where all these strange and horrible incidents happened regularly, my father's imprisonment suddenly became a reality.

Father was being held in *Sachsenhausen* in the town of Oranienburg, just a bit more than twenty miles north of Berlin. When would Father be released? Was there anything to be done? Trying to imagine his situation did me no good. I had no idea what he was experiencing. Mother referred to *Sachsenhausen* as the "concentration camp." What was this *camp*? We had never heard of such a thing (it was established in 1936).

At Aunt Martha's Bendlerstrasse apartment and while visiting with Uncle Alfred and Aunt Hilde, Father's imprisonment was spoken of in whispers. Through the Jewish welfare society we learned that a hefty bribe might get Father out of *Sachsenhausen*. But who would accept such payment, and how would we get it to him? People wanted to help us but did not wish to become involved. And it wasn't easy to get information. We learned the government was tapping phones, censoring mail, and following people they suspected as enemies of the state. We needed information we could trust. Friends of my uncle and father, many non-Jews, offered money but otherwise could not risk association with this operation. In order to safely collect funds from those wishing to help, I spent time at Wannsee Lake in West Berlin where there was a beach full of swimmers and sunbathers, even in the late spring. It was all prearranged. I would go for a swim, and when I returned, I would find money or notes with useful information under my towel.

One day I found Herr Glaubitz alone in the garage and told him what we wanted to do. He leaned back on the car and looked at me for a moment with great concern before nodding.

"Fritz is coming tomorrow. I will talk to him. Do you have some white asparagus in your garden?"

Fritz was a fellow chauffeur. He and Herr Glaubitz had been friends for a long time. Until the previous year, Fritz had worked for a family who lived a couple of blocks away. Then the family left suddenly, and Heinrich Himmler, chief of the SS and Gestapo, moved in. The government gave Himmler the estate free of charge as an official residence. Fritz had little choice but to work for this new family, though he was in no way a Nazi sympathizer.

He and several of the other chauffeurs came regularly for cherries, apples, and seasonal vegetables from Aunt Martha's gardens. She had always shared these with her neighbors. The drivers took some for themselves and delivered the rest to their employers. When I took over the estate, they came to me for these gifts. The favorite of Fritz's boss was white asparagus.

White asparagus takes great care to harvest, making it a delicacy. A perennial, asparagus remains dormant all winter. In the spring months the stalks grow literally overnight. Ours were planted in mounds of rich soil. Early in the morning, before sunrise, I would search in the faint light for the tips of spears, just cresting the mound, and carefully cut them. Devoid of sunlight, the plant can't develop the chlorophyll that turns it green.

The next day I had a basket of beautiful white asparagus ready. Fritz was in the garage with Herr Glaubitz, and I could hear them speaking in muted tones as I approached. Usually their conversation was animated.

"Hello," I called out before entering the garage. I asked Fritz how he was and handed him the basket of white asparagus. "Beautiful," he graciously replied before his face took on a taut seriousness. "I will help arrange things. It might take a while."

We had no idea Himmler had set up Dachau Concentration Camp as early as 1933, creating this work-death camp as a model for more to come. Or that Himmler would go on to be the principal architect of the Final Solution, the systematic genocide of Europe's Jews. Of course we knew the Gestapo and SS were violent and dangerous and that military action seemed imminent. But not many of us could have fully fathomed the plans of Hitler and his cronies in 1937.

With what I was about to do, it was better I didn't know. It was good I was so young, too naïve about my own safety or lack thereof. I decided I would go inside the prison to fetch Father. My mother's face was pale and somber when I told her. I knew I could never let her or Oma go. Who else was there to do the task? She was scared for me but did not try to dissuade me.

Summer came and along with it, the big wedding. My cousin Elsa Wertheim, Aunt Martha's adopted daughter, was getting married in June and the reception would take place on the Dahlem Estate. Aunt Martha was very pleased. From almost the moment I arrived home from Ahlem, preparations had begun and we often discussed plans for the reception over breakfast. It was going to be a major society affair. Elsa was not of Jewish descent, nor was her betrothed, Herr Jurgen Ziehm, a music teacher at the famous *Berliner Dome* (Berlin Cathedral), where the wedding ceremony would take place. This removed some apprehension about throwing a big party. Aunt Martha arranged for a thorough cleaning of the large villa in which many of the guests would be staying. She put me in charge of the flowers, giving me a blank check for expenses.

Martha Wertheim und ihre Adoptivtochter Elsa, ca. 1919.

Aunt Martha and her adopted daughter, Elsa, 1919

Several days before the first guests arrived, I set out early in the morning, driving the estate pickup truck to the wholesale market to purchase flowers, many of them roses. I then drove to a few small farms to pick up more flowers. With the help of some of Aunt Martha's house staff, I spent two-and-a-half days arranging the flowers in beautiful large vases, placing them in all the different rooms of the villa. Each room required a different color scheme to complement the furnishings. It was great fun. We set up large pots on the front veranda and down the front steps and planted them with flowering shrubs and tree roses in full bloom. A corridor of roses indicated the pathway for the young couple to walk through after they returned from the wedding ceremony at the *Berliner Dome*. Also visible from the villa's entrance was the main garden, which the workers and I had meticulously manicured and to which we added many bright annual and perennial colors. It was lovely, and I couldn't help but feel a bit of pride when viewing the finished product.

Jurgen and Else, circa 1937

The wedding took place on a perfect summer day. As the guests arrived from the church, Elsa and Jurgen greeted them, along with Aunt Martha and my mother. During the reception, light food was served while the guests toured the villa and the gardens. After an hour a maid rang a big bell, and the guests sat down where their name cards had been placed on big tables with white cloths and fine china. It was a magnificent wedding feast, with each course requiring a different wine. The meal lasted two hours. The young newlyweds performed the first dance while a quintet played lovely music. Everybody applauded and then joined them on the dance floor. I didn't dance. I had never learned.

I watched for a while until Aunt Martha waved me over and introduced me to Pastor Martin Niemöller. I was pleased to meet him, having heard him preach. He was the minister of the Lutheran church in Dahlem. Aunt Martha had often spoken of him over breakfast. He was openly critical of the Nazis' restriction of religion and the persecution of baptized Christians, who happened to have Jewish ancestry. He protested when members of his church were arrested, and my mother, through her work, heard he was helping the families of Nazi protestors escape. After Herr Glaubitz described his sermons to me, I had decided to go hear him for myself. On a Sunday morning, I quietly slipped in through the back of the church and sat in the pews to listen. He was very impassioned and articulate, calling for the right for all to worship God. These were dangerous words in 1937. I feared for the pastor, who was certainly under surveillance by the Nazis.

Pastor Niemöller complimented me on the roses and gardens and asked me if I wouldn't mind taking him for a guided tour among the garden's flowerbeds.

"I'd be delighted," I replied, and we walked out together into the sun-filled gardens. Everyone else was inside dancing. The pastor had an expressive face: eyes that could be at one moment sad, serious, or childlike; and a mouth that could go from a thin line into a broad smile in a moment. He had rather large ears and receding dark hair. He was very cordial, complimenting me on how neatly the boxwood was trimmed and asking what several plants were, pointing at the fibrous and tuberous begonias in their warm blooms of red, orange, and yellow. As we strolled farther into the garden, the pastor looked around to see if anyone was near us and then said, "I understand your father is in Sachsenhausen."

"Yes," I replied.

"Many good people are." He paused, "Do you like to ski?"

This seemed like an odd question. "Yes, I have only been once. I need lessons to learn properly, but I like it very much."

"You know," he continued, "there are many young people like yourself that need to get out of Germany. Their parents are in the same camp as your father or other camps like it. There is a way one can cross the border into Czechoslovakia without papers, through the Sudetenland."

"Yes?" My heart raced.

As the pastor spoke, he leaned out over the white phlox bush beside the path to gently touch the petals of the tall dark blue delphiniums in full bloom.

"In the Riesengebirge in winter, they can ski across the border if well guided. Have you been?"

My last winter at the *Gartenbauschule*, I had gone with friends to the Harz Mountains to ski for the first time. My friends had equipped me with borrowed skis and poles and we climbed the Brocken Mountain's serpentine trail to the top — 3,743 feet. There were few lifts in those days and walking up the mountain was considered part of the sport. We trekked up with climbing skins, which looked like socks on each ski to keep them from sliding backwards. At the top we took off the skins and wrapped them around our waists like belts.

Walking up was easy but coming down was another matter. I had no idea how to turn. Finally, I just skied across the mountain and then sat down, pointed my skis in the opposite direction, got up, and did it again until I made a very slow, stop-and-start, zigzag down to the bottom.

Pastor Niemöller told me the name of a ski instructor in Riesengebirge, who knew the route and ran a bed and breakfast at the foot of the mountain. "He can be well trusted, and I have heard he is a very good teacher, too," he smiled.

We walked silently a few paces before he said, "Many innocent people could die — children — because their parents have spoken out."

I nodded. We turned and walked back. The pastor resumed his compliments and questions about the flowers as we neared the villa.

"Thank you for the tour, Ernst. You have a great eye for beauty in God's garden."

I walked back into the celebration with a lot to think about.

Less than a month later, the Gestapo took Pastor Niemöller into custody and held him for eight months before giving him a trial. Released after the trial, he was walking down the steps of the Reichstag when the Gestapo arrested him again. That time they held him without a trial, indefinitely. History has questioned some of his early motivations and seemingly anti-Semitic statements before he openly rejected Nazi ideals. But at the wedding, he was most impressive, and I can understand how, in the postwar years, he became credited with perhaps the most powerful distillation of what was at stake in Nazi Germany:

"First they came for the communists, and I did not speak out —
because I was not a communist;
Then they came for the socialists, and I did not speak out —
because I was not a socialist;
Then they came for the trade unionists, and I did not speak out —
because I was not a trade unionist;
Then they came for the Jews, and I did not speak out —
because I was not a Jew;
Then they came for me —
and there was no one left to speak out for me."

During the days before I was to go to the *Sachsenhausen* concentration camp to bring my father home, I could not sleep. The August nights were very warm.

"You don't have to go," my mother said to me the evening before the big day.

"But I do," I replied.

The following morning I rode my bike to Aunt Martha's in a daze. I had nearly five thousand Reichsmarks in an unmarked envelope under my newly pressed shirt when I got into the Chrysler with Herr Glaubitz, my stomach was tight, adrenaline fueling me after many sleepless nights. I had provided some of the money myself. We barely spoke as we drove north for nearly thirty minutes. Herr Glaubitz turned off onto a side road where Fritz was parked and waiting. I changed cars and Fritz drove me the last few miles to Oranienburg, where the camp was located.

As we turned down the driveway, everything abruptly turned gray — gray stone, gray steel. Beside the road was a stone wall, about ten feet tall, outside of which was an electrified wire fence that was even taller. We passed a guard tower in which a soldier stood in front of a menacing machine gun. At the front entrance gate, Fritz stopped to show our IDs to a guard. They recognized him and his car as belonging to Himmler, so they made short work of it. I stared ahead at the metal work of the black gate that contained the words: *Arbeit Macht Frei* (Work makes you free).

The gates of *Sachsenhausen*

The guard waved us through, and we drove inside. I would not let my mind ask, "Will I make it back out?" So much could go wrong.

After that day, I knew what a concentration camp was. There was a huge parade ground. I had never seen so many SS officers or so many guns. Barrack huts sprawled out beyond the parade ground. Prisoners, some very old, all thin and lifeless and wearing gray, striped uniforms, marched somberly across the square as several Nazi soldiers walked beside them, holding guns and yelling horrible insults. On each prisoner's uniform were numbers and upside-down triangles of different colors: red, pink, and yellow. I could see the look in their eyes for many nights afterwards, the vacant stares of weariness, lifelessness, fear, and exhaustion. I blinked at a scene in the distance, not believing it to be real. A prisoner standing alone against a wall, a soldier raising a pistol and firing, and the prisoner crumpling to the ground. I began to shake. There was more, much more: a gallows, the smell of decay, and soldiers joking and laughing in contrast. I tried not to see anymore. I still don't want to remember.

Fritz led me to the camp administration office just inside the gate and held the door open for me to pass. "I will wait for you in the car," he said quietly.

Inside, I tried to make my voice calm and low as I told a Nazi soldier sitting behind a desk I had an appointment and told him the name of the officer. "Follow me," he said. He ushered me to another office, where another assistant sat at a desk and closed the door behind me. This man pulled an envelope from out of the desk drawer, a replica of the one under my shirt. I took out my envelope full of money and exchanged it for his, as planned. Then he led me back out the door and into the yard. He pointed at a building about sixty feet away. "Go in there to receive the prisoner."

What choice did I have? Every step farther away from the safety of Fritz's car felt heavier, every footfall louder on the gravel. I entered a green building. It was not well lit inside. There were many tables and chairs and an empty bar against one wall. It smelled of cigarettes and stale beer. No one was inside. I stood waiting for what seemed like an immeasurably long time. I didn't even think of sitting down. Much later, I learned this building was nicknamed the "Green Monster" and at night became a makeshift casino for the drunken Nazi soldiers.

Finally, a door swung open with bright light spilling in and silhouetting a guard who shoved in another man. Clear of the light, I saw my father. His head had been shaved, and his face was rough with whiskers. He was in work clothes that didn't fit him, smeared with dirt and oil, his shirttail out. He looked at me, and it took a moment for him to understand what he was seeing. Stunned, he began to sway. I took his elbow as his knees buckled.

"Go on then," said the guard. Back outside, I saw Fritz's car. I wanted to run to it, but my father moved slowly by my side as I supported him. Tears ran down his cheeks as he stared sideways at me.

Fritz opened the door for us, but my father just stood there not comprehending.

"Let's get into the car now," I said. We sat silently in the back as Fritz closed the door behind us, put the car in gear, and drove us out the gates of *Sachsenhausen*. We had made it.

It was so hard to see my father like this, beaten and broken, much worse than before. What must he be thinking? Did he expect to live? He certainly didn't expect this to happen nor to see me in that terrible place. I'm sure he hardly recognized me. I was a young man now, four years older than when he'd seen me last, dining on the ship that would take him to Belgium..

Fritz drove us to a different meeting place a few miles from the first. Herr Glaubitz was there waiting.

"Hello Herr Wertheim," he said, bowing slightly to my father as he held the door of the Chrysler open, and I helped my father sit inside. Father nodded. He couldn't seem to find his voice.

"I'm off to Berlin to get Himmler later today," said Fritz. I shook his hand.

"Thank you," I said.

He nodded, got back into his car, and drove off.

Herr Glaubitz took us to Bendlerstrasse.

Father was not in good shape. He had trouble walking up stairs and was exhausted. He slept for a very long time in the room Mother had prepared for him.

All I knew was in the act of bringing him home that day, I left a great deal of innocence back inside those terrible gates. I became ever more conscious of footfalls behind me. Horrible dreams filled my nights for weeks afterward, awakening me in the dark, thrashing, and sweating. I became fearful of the night, just as I had been as a child after the truck hit me on my borrowed bike.

Fortunately, I could not let fear make me paralyzed because I received a letter from America. Hanna Hellinger had agreed to sponsor me. It was a very positive step toward my goal. Because she was a refugee and didn't have much money, I still had to find another sponsor. My mother learned of a Jewish-American organization, and we wrote to them for help in finding me a second sponsor. Another letter across the sea and another long wait. I refocused my efforts on my work.

CHAPTER 5

A Farewell With No Flowers

Photo by ALIAKSANDR KAZANTSAU © 123RF.com

By January 1938, I decided I had saved enough money for a one-week ski vacation in Riesengebirge. This was my first vacation paid for with my own earned money, a big event for me. I contacted the ski instructor Pastor Niemöller had recommended and asked if he was available for ski lessons. When I received a positive answer, I arranged for the four-hour train ride from Berlin, feeling very proud that I was able to treat myself. I was still considering the pastor's suggestion of assisting citizens in their escape from Germany, but had not yet committed to the task.

The ski vacation package included bed, breakfast, ski lessons and equipment. The instructor was a very personable, athletic man in his thirties, whom I liked immediately. His lodging was located at the base of Schneekoppe, the highest peak in Riesengebirge range, at over 5,200 feet. Equipment was quite basic back then: bindings were leather and ski boots were just like hiking boots. The skis were carved and waxed wood. My instructor was a very skilled teacher and I learned quickly. After spending the first two days practicing on the beginner hill, we rode the single-seat chairlift part way up the mountain to practice turns, carving our skis down the hill. The rest of the week we walked up the mountain beyond the end of the chairlift to have a longer run. Once I became more proficient, we climbed even further up the mountain to a ridge, which divided Germany from its neighbor, Czechoslovakia. At the eastern end of this ridge was the top of Schneekoppe, a cone-shaped pinnacle, similar to Mount Shasta in California, although much lower in elevation. The cone rose just above the ridge and on top there was a small *hütte* (basic lodge). The *hütte* contained a restaurant with a fireplace and cots for sleeping.

Arriving at the hütte after the vigorous trek up the mountain, my ski instructor and I sat at a corner table with a lovely view of the scenery and the village below. We both ordered a beverage, a mug of beer for him and *Mit Schlag* (hot chocolate with whipped cream) for me. Since our table was a bit private we felt we could safely discuss the escape route. My instructor spread out a detailed map of the area, pointing out the course to ski down to arrive at the meeting place in Czechoslovakia.

Since Pastor Niemöller had mentioned the border crossing, I had learned my mother had been helpful in a couple of similar missions through her work at the Jewish organization. Evidently, people went to Switzerland and Austria via a ski route, until Hitler marched into Austria.

The *hütte* on the Schneekoppe was right next to the border between Germany and Czechoslovakia, almost precisely at the top of the mountain. German border patrol guards stood in a line every fifty feet or so, checking passports of those skiing down the Czech slope. In the afternoon a fog often rolled in, making for poor visibility that got even worse when it was snowing. Obviously, this was the best time to attempt to cross the border. With a cold, thick fog or snowstorm outside, the guards often left their posts for the comfort of the *hütte*. On my visit it was a clear day, and I was able to see the top of the route quite easily.

Upon returning to Berlin, I decided to help with an escape mission. A group of us met a few times, in different shops and offices, to discuss the plan. We studied maps, photos, and weather forecasts. I met the boys and girls I would be escorting out of Germany, and I met a few of the parents not yet imprisoned in the camps. It took about three weeks to formalize our plan. Before I knew it, I found myself back in the *hütte* on Schneekoppe.

There were nine young adults — men and women — that I would be escorting across the border. Half of them were the children of non-Jewish Nazi resisters. Everyone traveled to the ski resort independently.

The plan was that I would relax in the *hütte*, drink my hot chocolate, and wait for the fog to come in. The others would hike up the mountain on their own or in pairs. Slowly, they started to trickle in. One small group pretended to be getting a ski lesson. They arrived carrying all their belongings in small rucksacks.

As the weather worsened, I signaled it was time for the crossing by standing and putting on my hat and coat. Most of the guards were inside the *hütte* by then, waiting out the weather.

It started snowing as I put on my skis, and I could see that the first members of the group were just getting ready. I took a deep breath and pushed off downhill. I skied down the German side of the mountain, to fool the guards that had stayed outside. After a few hundred feet down the hill I made an abrupt, almost 180 degree turn taking me to a very steep part of the mountain on the Czechoslovak side. It was a difficult turn even for a more experienced skier. When skiing in fog and snow, it's hard to tell whether you are going uphill or downhill. You can't see very far ahead. Obstacles, like boulders and trees, can suddenly appear right in front of you. We planned to use some of the trees as guideposts, but they were very difficult to see. The group wouldn't be able to linger. They needed to follow my tracks in the snow before the wind erased them.

Once I had skied about three hundred feet down the mountain, I stopped in a grove of trees and waited. I felt this was far enough that bullets couldn't reach us.

The others were to exit the *hütte*, in staggered intervals, and take the same path. Though it was less than ten minutes before the first two arrived, it felt like forever. Then the others showed up a few at a time until the whole group of nine was present. I was able to breathe a little easier. We skied together the rest of the way, more slowly, so no one would get hurt or lost. We still feared a German border patrol guard might follow us into Czechoslovakia. This of course, would have ruined everything, since none in the group had a legitimate visa or passport to enter the country.

We made it down the mountain undetected and walked on through a valley to our destination, a sheepherder's hut in a snowy meadow. We passed a couple of barns and could hear the animals inside. In winter, the herders' huts were normally empty. But inside one of them, a group of Quakers waited for us. They took care of the group from there. Everyone in the group was ecstatic to be out of Germany, but also weary of their uncertain future. It didn't help that the Quakers were British and did not speak German very well. However, most of us spoke some English and so we managed.

After a few quick "thank-yous," everyone left except for two Quaker men assigned to help me get back to Germany. They were expert skiers and had a car. We drove to another part of the mountain, put skins on our skis, and walked up to the German border. We all had our passports but were thankful no one stopped us. I said goodbye and skied down the mountain back to the instructor's bed and breakfast.

I collapsed onto my bed. I was exhausted and at the same time exhilarated to have helped nine young adults, many my age, who might otherwise have ended up in concentration camps. They did not have the opportunity I had of acquiring a visa to go to the United States, or for that matter, to any other country. I was fortunate to have sponsors who could assist me, if need be, in my new country.

The next morning, I found myself back on the train to Berlin.

After a few days back home I was still amazed at what I had accomplished. It was a dangerous mission to take on, and yet, I hadn't really felt afraid, except when I was worried the guards on top of the mountain might follow us downhill.

I repeated such an escort two more times, helping eight people on each journey. Only when I was safely back on the train to Berlin did I let myself feel the stress and danger of these missions.

When a representative of the church asked me to take another group, I refused. After three successes, I didn't want to push my luck. It was time to focus on my own plans for leaving Germany.

That spring, my father was finally well enough to go back to work at the old furniture company. To earn additional income, Oma decided to rent out the two front rooms of our apartment. The tenant was an American, Gladys Wells, who was employed as the private secretary of the new American Ambassador, Hugh Wilson. She worked primarily at the ambassador's home, which was within walking distance of our apartment and very close to the Tiergarten.

Gladys immediately became a part of our family. She was nearly six feet tall, slender and attractive, in her late thirties and highly educated. She had a delightful sense of humor and often helped me practice my English. Though she wasn't Jewish, Gladys almost always joined us for Shabbat on Friday evening. We lit the candles at sundown, sung the blessings, and enjoyed one of Oma's special meals. Gladys was a warm addition to the household.

In April, my father surprised me with a gift: my own car. It was a glossy gray Hanomag with a large chrome grill up front and a rounded boot in back. I couldn't believe it, my own car! I had to restrict my driving to weekends because petrol was so expensive. Nonetheless, it gave me a great sense of independence.

A 1938 Hanomag, my first car was a gift from my father

Soon after he gave me the car, my father asked me to take him for a Sunday drive. He didn't like traveling by car, so this was another surprise. For a short time thereafter, Sunday outings with Father became a routine. We drove out into the country. On one such excursion we drove to Potsdam to see *Schloss Sanssouci*, the former summer palace of Frederick the Great, King of Prussia. Germans felt this palace rivaled Versailles. Not far from the palace there was a well-known and very large nursery. It specialized in perennials and alpine plants. While we walked through the nursery, Father asked many questions about growth habits, where the plants originated, and how to care for them. As I answered him I think he was very proud of my accomplishment at the *Gartenbauschule*.

On these drives we didn't talk too much because Father didn't want to distract me. However, we always stopped somewhere to have *Mittagessen*. He would have a beer while I drank apple cider. We made small talk about things we saw along the way and about our jobs, but nothing too personal. During one trip, I mentioned my frustration with the lack of progress in securing my visa.

"Son," he said, "you were very successful in Ahlem, but you do not know much about life. For example, what do you know about girls?"

Since I really had no romantic experience, I had to agree with him. After all, I attended a predominately male college with all male instructors. There hadn't been much opportunity to get to know the opposite sex. I was completely focused on getting the most out of my education. This one-on-one time together was the closest relationship I had with my father.

In May 1938, I took an extended drive to Essen for the annual National Flower Show. Several of my friends from college came along, including Dieter. We drove all night long to save money on accommodations and arrived on opening day. The flower show was a significant national event; horticulturalists prepared for it with the same seriousness that athletes train for the Olympics. Nurserymen and women, park department personnel, and other horticulturists competed to make beautiful, exotic, or unique landscapes and flower arrangements. Nationally renowned horticulturalists were on hand to explain the newest techniques on the production of various plants. We saw many unusual plants we had previously only seen in books. It was an exciting, memorable weekend, and an escape from the tormenting reality of our changing country.

Dieter was planning on going to Argentina. Shortly after the flower show, he started taking a Spanish language class at night. I decided to take the class with him, both to keep him company and fill the gap of having close to no social life. The teacher was very encouraging and patient. Some years later, I would put this class to good use when I was with the U.S. Army in the Philippines and needed to communicate with people who only spoke Spanish.

Meanwhile, I pressed on with the process for my emigration. As bad as the political and police situation had become, friends and some family members were surprised I wanted to leave Germany. Many Germans still hoped for the best and were comfortable with their known world, but I had seen the inside of *Sachsenhausen*. I had experienced my father's imprisonment and torture and the deadening effect it had on his psyche and spirit. I had helped refugees up and down a snowy mountain to flee. Nothing could persuade me to remain in Germany.

Early in 1938, I secured my second U.S. sponsorship. However, fulfilling the requirements of the German authorities proved to be just as complicated and time-consuming. I was required to collect my records from the *Oberrealschule* in Hamburg. I also needed clearance papers from the local police department proving I had no traffic tickets or arrests. Lastly, I was required to show documentation releasing me from serving in the German armed services. Even though as a Jew I was barred from military service, these forms were the most difficult to acquire.

Oma asked one of our neighbors for assistance. She was the wife of a general, who had been a good friend of Opa's. I arranged an exam with a Jewish doctor who falsified my medical report declaring me unfit to serve due to bad hearing. Then the general's wife arranged the final release document through her husband. In exchange, she was interested in learning about the process I was going through and all its details. She had many practical questions. This didn't surprise me since I knew a number of high-ranking army officers did not want to serve under Hitler; however, they were not given a choice.

Once I collected all the paperwork for my emigration application, I was given a number and had to wait for my appointment date. I was forced to be patient since I had no control over the system.

During this time, transatlantic passenger liners were still sailing from Hamburg to New York. They left only once a month and were filling to capacity. I discovered I could buy a ticket with cancellation insurance in case I still wasn't authorized to leave Germany. I booked a second-class ticket on the König line, departing in late August.

The persecution of the Jewish population in Germany was becoming increasingly egregious. In July, we read about a law that would go into effect January 1, 1939, requiring Jews to carry cards identifying them as such. An additional requirement for the identity card was that all male Jews were going to have to precede their name with Israel, females with Sara. I would become Israel Ernst Wertheim. Also in July, the government revoked the medical certification of all Jewish physicians, effective September 30. After that date, Jewish doctors could only function as nurses for Jewish patients. In August, the main synagogue in Nuremberg was confiscated and then demolished.

Later in August, I received a letter from my good friend, George Salomon, announcing his father had secured a job teaching at Swarthmore College outside of Philadelphia. I wrote him back immediately and told him I was coming to join him in America.

Time both crawled and flew by, and my number had not been called. My brother, George, had returned to boarding school in Berlin. In response to my frustration, my mother suggested we spend a week hiking in the Harz Mountains. She offered to pay for the vacation. Before Hitler, money was never an issue. Now, we carefully budgeted our trip for petrol, food, and accommodations. I cancelled my ship's passage for August, rescheduled it for October, and wrote to George Salomon about the new date.

Mother and I drove nearly four hours to the mountains in my car. We stayed in a pleasant bed and breakfast owned by a Jewish couple and took walks everyday. There was a footpath up to the Rosstrappe and a chairlift that ran in the summer to catch magnificent views of the Bode Valley as far out into the Harz foreland as Halberstadt and Quedlinburg. We walked through the valley, where rock meadows and gorges hosted pink-petaled dianthus, lavender alpine aster, and starry white heather.

In the fir wood forests we found wild blueberries, moss, and ferns growing beside creeks or in the shade of granite boulders. We heard black woodpeckers drumming at dead wood. We hiked on trails through forests filled with dense groundcover. It was all very green and smelled wonderful. Then, one day, cresting a hill, we heard distant cracking noises and voices echoing off the mountainsides. Over a ledge, down in a canyon, we saw many tents and soldiers with rucksacks and rifles training in an obstacle course. We watched nervously for a few minutes before turning back down the mountain towards the village.

It was very obvious to us the Nazis were preparing for an invasion of the Sudetenland and a takeover of Czechoslovakia.

The week that Mother and I spent together was just lovely. We very much enjoyed each other's company. Every afternoon during our retreat we would stop at a café or bakery for some *Apfel Kuchen* (apple cake) with *Schlagsahne* (whipped cream). Sometimes it was *Kirschkuchen* (cherry cake).

By September, I started to worry I would never leave Germany. Neville Chamberlain, British Prime Minister, came to Munich to meet with Hitler to negotiate the Sudetenland, which the *Führer* wanted to reclaim as part of Germany. During a speech in Nuremburg, Hermann Göring called the Czech people a "miserable pygmy race," that was, "harassing the human race." Hitler had raised his demands to include occupation of all German Sudeten territories by October 1, 1938. We all feared war would start at any moment and then no one would be able to leave Germany.

In the last days of September, the German, Italian, British, and French leaders agreed to Germany's demands for annexation of Czechoslovakia's Sudetenland. The Czechoslovakian government was excluded from the negotiations. Nazi troops marched in and occupied the area by the middle of October. War was temporarily averted with this concession.

On October 5, the Nazis had declared a passport decree, confiscating all passports held by Jews. I now had to get issued a new passport, which could take up to three weeks to receive. Once again, I was forced to cancel my ship passage to New York. In the meantime, transatlantic ships had been banned from German ports. My new route now involved a train ride to Holland, a ferry to Dover, and ship passage from England to New York on December 17.

Keeping myself busy working on the estate was the best way to curb my anxiety. I removed the annuals from the garden and oversaw the raking of leaves dropped by the elm trees along the lane.

One day in October, Mother mentioned that a childhood friend of mine, Lore, and her cousin were coming to stay with us for a few days. I had not seen Lore since we were children, but I had fond memories of her. We had met in a sandbox in 1925, when my family had lived in Dusseldorf for about six months. We rented the upstairs of a villa while her family lived downstairs. We shared a small backyard along with its sandbox, where we played together almost every day.

To provide Lore and her male cousin with their own rooms while they stayed with us, I cleared some of my things out of my room and set up a cot for myself in Mother's room. This way one would sleep in my room and the other in George's. I looked forward to their visit and the diversion, as Mother asked me to show Lore and her cousin around Berlin.

At the station, I watched their train slow to a halt and kept an eye out for two young passengers. Finally, I saw a lovely, young lady disembark. It was Lore, and with her was a handsome young man, who I knew must be her cousin. I greeted them warmly. We packed all their baggage into my small car and drove to the house on Bendlerstrasse.

Back in the apartment, we settled in for a coffee with Oma and Mother.

During their visit, I took Lore and her cousin to dinner and the opera as well as to the theatre. As I had carefully been saving money, I had not indulged in such entertainment for quite some time. I also showed them the grounds at Aunt Martha's and drove them to the lake. I invited Dieter to the apartment, and we all spent time together talking, just young people having a good time. Dieter was leaving for Argentina in just a few days. For one glorious week I forgot about visas and ships, concentration camps and Nazis. It was so invigorating to just relax and enjoy being young and alive.

While Lore was with us, my new passport arrived with a "J" stamped across the identification information. Finally, after months of waiting and much uncertainty, it appeared I had everything I needed. I simply had to wait a bit longer for my departure date. Oma cooked a celebratory dinner that night. Lore and her cousin left for Dusseldorf the following day. Lore promised to keep in touch, which I was very happy about.

Less than a week later, on November 7, we heard that a young Jewish man in Paris had shot a German embassy official in retaliation for the forced expulsion, at the end of October, of almost sixteen thousand Polish Jews. All had been rounded up in one night, forced from their homes with a restriction of one suitcase per person for all their belongings. They were put on trains to the border where they were refused entry by Polish border guards. They spent days starving and without shelter from the heavy rains as neither country wanted them. The young man's parents were among those stranded at the border.

Two days later, on November 9, 1938, Oma's phone began ringing early in the morning. The first call was from a distant relative in Munich, who said the Gestapo had arrested her husband and the synagogue was in flames. Oma tried her best to calm her and had no sooner hung up when the phone rang again. It was Lore's mother in Dusseldorf. Her husband had been arrested, too. Calls came from friends in Hamburg and other cities with similar news.

Soon after that first phone call we heard shouting in the street, distant gunshots, and the shattering of glass. We could smell smoke. We had no idea what was going on, and we were afraid.

The manager of our apartment, neither a Jew nor a Nazi sympathizer, knocked on our door with a plan, "If I see the Gestapo in the street coming and ring the bell, you will see a red light in the hallway so you know. Okay?"

We sat waiting for the red light. That evening there was a radio announcement declaring that the German diplomat in Paris, Ernst vom Rath, had died. At about eight o'clock that evening, the red light came on.

My father turned to me and said sternly, "Disappear and fast. Go. Just disappear."

As I ran down the backstairs towards the rear garden, I heard the doorbell ring repeatedly. I climbed over the neighbor's fence, crossed through his garden and out a side gate that opened onto a quiet street. A few people hurriedly shuffled past me. I walked briskly, trying to avoid the main boulevards. I headed for the subway, thinking the best place to disappear would be Dahlem.

On the way to the station, I walked past horrific scenes. Young Nazi boys were herding Jewish men at gunpoint through the streets.

They marched them into a plaza. One older man couldn't keep up the pace, so they beat him with clubs and left him lying in the middle of the road. A car came down the street and ran over him. I saw the Gestapo push men and women to the ground and hit them with the butts of their rifles. A shop owner tried to stop some Nazis who were carrying sledgehammers and axes from destroying his shop. As he begged them to stop, they took a sledgehammer to his front window and then pushed him through another window. He fell to the ground bleeding. Oma's synagogue was in flames. Nazi troops were throwing wood, books, and rocks into the fire. The energy on the street was crazed.

The Berlin synagogue after *Kristallnacht*

There was nothing I could do for others without endangering my own life, so I just kept moving, trying to be invisible. I managed to get away from the central area and catch a bus. I transferred to the subway and had to change trains several times to avoid the Gestapo as they were taking people off the subway and herding them out onto the street. There appeared to be a competition among the Nazi troops to inflict the most damage possible onto these poor people. While walking from one bus stop to another, I saw one man hanging upside down from a lamppost. I hastily boarded a double-decker bus heading towards Dahlem. I tried to remain as inconspicuous as possible during the thirty-minute ride to the end of the line. I rode on the upper level from which I could observe the violence with stark clarity. As the bus drove out of the city center and into the suburbs, the violence gradually subsided.

Once in Dahlem, I walked to Aunt Martha's estate, arriving around two in the morning. Not wanting to wake anyone, I crept quietly to the conservatory to try and rest. Of course, no sleep would come. Just past sunrise, I walked over to Fräulein Fischer's apartment-office and knocked on her door. She greeted me as usual but quickly asked what was wrong after looking me over. She had heard nothing about the activities in Berlin. I told her that Jewish men were being rounded up and taken away from their families. I couldn't find words for the rest of what I had seen.

"Would you please walk over to Aunt Martha's and let her know that I am well? And could you check to see if there are any Gestapo around?"

She invited me in and told me to stay put; she'd be right back to make me something to eat.

I was too tired to protest and sat on her sofa and waited. She returned with very little news. Dahlem had been rather quiet, most likely because the majority of residents were not Jews, but instead, high-ranking government officials.

Fräulein Fischer called my mother and told her I was at work, our code meaning I had arrived safely. Fräulein Fisher insisted I stay with her that night even though she could be putting herself at risk.

The following night, November 11, I headed back to Oma's house. On the way I stopped to check on Aunt Hilde, Uncle Alfred, and my cousins. Uncle Alfred had been picked up by the Gestapo and was in prison. Aunt Hilde and her two daughters were shaken up but safe at home. Some thoughtful neighbors had provided them with food.

Upon returning to Bendlerstrasse, I learned eight members of my family had been arrested, including my father. One out of every four

Jewish men in Germany and Austria were taken to camps that night. The camps were not yet considered death camps; however, many of the men never saw home again. The last words I ever heard my father say were, "Just disappear."

The extent of the violence was not immediately known. Over the next few weeks we learned that the *Gauleiters* (Nazi party leaders), the SA paramilitary, the SS, the Hitler Youth, along with German civilians had destroyed as many Jewish properties as they could in pogroms all over Germany and Austria. German authorities encouraged these activities in retaliation for the death of the diplomat. The official number of Jews killed that night is ninety-one, but somewhere between thirteen hundred to two thousand actually died as a result of injuries sustained that evening. The Nazis arrested thirty thousand men and incarcerated them in *Dachau*, *Buchenwald*, and *Sachsenhausen*. The attackers burned, looted, and vandalized hundreds of synagogues. Nearly every Jewish place of worship in Germany and the Austrian capital of Vienna was damaged or destroyed. Jewish homes, hospitals, and schools were ransacked. Over seven thousand Jewish businesses were similarly devastated, a number that would otherwise have been much higher if not for five years of "voluntary" expropriation of Jewish businesses. Before that horrible night, about two-thirds of Jewish businesses had already been sold after years of relentless pressure. The events of November 9 and 10 became known as *Kristallnacht* (Night of Broken Glass), for all the shattered windows littering the streets.

Shortly thereafter, Hitler's government blamed the Jews for *Kristallnacht*. Jews were ordered to pay over one billion Reichsmarks as punishment for vom Rath's murder and damages to the nation. Back in April 1938, through the Decree of the Registration of the Property of Jews, all Jews had been required to register both domestic and foreign assets. Now, the *Suhneleistung* (atonement payment) was accomplished through the government's acquisition of twenty percent of all Jewish assets. What an unholy twist of words given that the most sacred day in Judaism, Yom Kippur, is also known as The Day of Atonement. In another cruel turn, many millions of Reichsmarks in insurance payouts due to the Jewish community for property damages were instead paid to the government. Hitler declared German Jews were forbidden from participating in economic activity. Jews were also prohibited from attending movies, concerts, and other cultural performances. There was a police decree for a Jewish dress code and restrictions on our freedom of movement. On November 15, Jewish children were expelled from German schools, and my brother, George, came home from boarding school.

Giving George a piggyback ride with my mother at Aunt Martha's, 1938

After *Kristallnacht*, Mother's sole concern was to save her youngest child and get George out of Germany. Werner was safe from the Nazis in Chile. I was soon going to America. George was eleven years old, had no passport or visa, and his father had been put in a camp. Mother was determined the Nazis would not touch her baby.

Through her social work she learned of the *Kindertransport*. On the day George's school closed, just five days after *Kristallnacht*, a delegation of British Jewish and Quaker leaders appealed to British Prime Minister Chamberlain. They requested that the British government permit the temporary admission of Jewish children to Great Britain. Within days a bill passed in parliament, stating the government would waive certain immigration requirements to allow the entry of unaccompanied minors, from infants up to the age of seventeen. The Jewish agencies set their target number at fifteen thousand children.

On November 21, various Jewish and non-Jewish groups working on behalf of refugees merged into a non-denominational organization called the Movement for the Care of Children from Germany. The British Home Secretary realized travel documents would need to be issued based on group lists rather than individual applications to speed up the immigration process. The agencies pledged to find homes for all the children and committed to financing the project, ensuring none of the refugees would become a burden on the British public. Every child would have £50 sterling to finance their eventual re-emigration, as it was expected the children would only stay temporarily. Soon thereafter, the Movement for the Care of Children from Germany, later known as the Refugee Children's Movement (RCM), sent representatives to Germany and Austria to establish the process for choosing and transporting these literal and figurative orphans.

A network of organizers was established in Germany, with volunteers working night and day to create priority lists of those most in danger: homeless children, children from impoverished homes, children with parents in concentration camps, Polish children threatened with deportation, or children in Jewish orphanages. My mother's welfare society became involved with some of the planning. Once the children were prioritized, their guardians were issued a travel date with departure details. The children could take only one small sealed suitcase with no valuables and a maximum of ten Reichsmarks.

George didn't quite qualify to be included on the list. Though our father was imprisoned, mother had a job and was capable of taking care of him. She had to be persistent, meeting with multiple people to have him included.

George left Berlin on December 1, 1938, as part of the first *Kindertransport*. I had gone to Aunt Martha's to work. My mother took George with his little suitcase to the train station. The Nazis had decreed the evacuations must not block ports in Germany. Transport parties had to travel by train to the Netherlands, then to the British port of Harwich by taking the cross-channel ferry from the Hook of Holland near Rotterdam. It was the same route I was scheduled to take a couple weeks later.

I don't know what my mother told George or even how he felt about leaving. I can only imagine Mother's amalgam of relief and sadness as she hugged him farewell and put him on the train, convinced he would be safe from then on.

My brother, George, never talks about his experience on the *Kindertransport* or his early days in Great Britain. I can only piece together his general experience from historical documents and hints in our conversations. Most of the almost two hundred children on his train were from a Berlin orphanage the Nazis burned during *Kristallnacht*. The other children were from Hamburg, and then there was George.

The lucky children who had prearranged sponsors waiting for them were sent to London to meet their foster families. The unsponsored children, like George, waited in Dovercourt, a summer holiday camp near Harwich, until individual families came forward to take one or two children into their homes. Hostels were readied to take larger groups of children.

Many families, Jewish and non-Jewish, opened their homes to take in these children. The last *Kindertransport* from Germany departed on September 1, 1939, just as World War II began. In all, the rescue operation brought approximately ninety-five hundred children to Britain. About seventy-five hundred of them were Jewish, from Germany, Austria, Czechoslovakia, and Poland. As adults, many

Kinder would go on to be leaders in their fields, including several Nobel Laureates.

Children usually can adapt to change much more easily than adults. Still, I will never know how hard this experience was for George. Mother believed it was the only way to protect her son, and she most likely saved his life. But I can imagine as an eleven year old child, George was confused about why he was being sent away to live with strangers in a different country. When I was speaking with George on the phone about writing my story, he kindly requested that I not write about him or his life in detail, so most of his story ends here. I can say although we were prematurely separated by life experiences and physical proximity, we are good friends today.

One of the last pictures taken of me with my mother
and little brother George, circa 1938.

After *Kristallnacht*, the decrees against Jews and other "undesirables" came even more frequently. On December 3, the government confiscated Jewish driver's licenses. The government also enacted the Decree on the Utilization of Jewish Property, requiring "aryanization" of all Jewish businesses. German authorities forced Jews to sell immovable property, businesses, and stocks to non-Jews, usually at prices far below market value. This was the fate of the Wertheim Department Stores. On December 8, Heinrich Himmler issued the Decree for Combating the Gypsy Plague. It defined gypsies as an inferior race and tasked the German police with establishing a nationwide database, identifying all gypsies residing in the territory of the Greater German Reich.

In the midst of all this craziness, it was time for me to leave. I bid farewell to Aunt Martha a week before my ship's departure date of December 17. She gave me Uncle Wilhelm's thick, warm, winter coat to wear in America. She had it tailored to fit me. As she cried and hugged me, I wondered whether I'd ever see her again.

The authorities allowed me one suitcase and sixty-five American dollars for my journey. My suitcase was packed primarily with clothing, plus a few photos and one truly valuable item, Opa's gold watch. The contents of the suitcase had to be documented down to the last handkerchief, and I had to pay the German government the total value of my belongings. I also had to pay the *Reichsfluchtsteur* (the escape tax) enacted after *Kristallnacht*. This would have been levied even if I were being deported to a concentration camp outside of Germany, another twisted idea devised by the Nazis. All this paperwork and payment involved yet another trip to the local police station, which was always an uncomfortable and time-consuming process. They documented everything. The Nazis later employed a similar sort of detailed tracking when they indexed the names of all the people put into gas chambers. What did their names matter to the Nazis? And yet, it was all written down: the name of the death camp, the date, everything chronological and alphabetized.

I had to pay a fortune to take Opa's watch. The police sealed my suitcase with knotted string so I could not add anything to it before my departure.

My mother offered to accompany me to our old home city of Hamburg, where I would catch a train to start my long journey.

On the morning of December 12, I looked around Oma's apartment for the last time. Both Oma and Gladys gave me long hugs. Gladys asked whether I had remembered the pair of American two-dollar bills she had given me for good luck. Of course I had; I needed all the luck I could get. It would be years before I allowed myself to spend those precious slips of paper.

"Ernst, you must remember to tell the Americans everything that is happening in Germany," Gladys said. I promised her I would. Gladys was very upset President Roosevelt and America did not seem to understand what was occurring in Germany and what would soon befall Europe as Hitler prepared for war. Gladys encouraged me to speak up about the concentration camps, *Kristallnacht*, and the German troop movements.

Mother and I took the express train to Hamburg. We had dinner and stayed overnight at the same hotel where we had first stayed when Father had been kidnapped by the Duke of Cröy's employees that cold February morning almost six years ago.

Waiting on the station platform, I felt many mixed emotions: excitement that I was on my way to America, fear that my future was so uncertain, guilt for leaving my mother alone in Germany, and a heavy responsibility to earn enough money to bring Mother to the United States.

As my train pulled up in front of us, Mother took me in her arms and hugged me for a long time.

"Please, take care of my little baby," she said in my ear.

I was just shy of nineteen years old. I did not know what would happen to me in America. I had only sixty-five dollars in my pocket to take me thousands of miles. And now, I carried the obligation to take care of my younger brother, who was in an entirely different country.

From my seat on the train I couldn't find Mother in the crowd, but then a mass of bodies parted and I saw her, wiping away tears. Despite all our time and trials together, I had never seen her cry. She always seemed so strong. It hadn't occurred to me until that moment that she did all her crying in solitude. The train rattled out of the station.

We were within a mile of the Dutch border when the train stopped. Two German border patrol officers entered my car. They wore the Nazi swastika and carried pistols in holsters on their belts.

"Identification please," they said to the passengers in the rows ahead of me. My stomach tightened as I readied my papers. Then one of them was standing over me.

"Identification please."

I handed him my passport with the "J" stamped on it. He looked at me.

"Come with me," he said. My heart sank. I didn't know what else to do. I grabbed my suitcase from the rack above my seat and followed the officers off the train.

My father came to mind, how he was taken off the train and sent to the concentration camp. I had heard the Nazis randomly selected Jewish people and then took them out and shot them.

Walking on either side of me, the two officers took me to their small headquarters building at the station. Inside, they cut the string sealing my suitcase and rummaged through it. They then asked for my overcoat and searched the pockets. They kept my passport and visa, putting them on a nearby desk. I looked at them longingly. The officers took a long time to look over Opa's watch. One of them looked at my passport again and whispered to the other, who nodded before approaching me.

"You owe ten thousand Reichsmarks to the German government for this watch."

"What? But I already paid for all my belongings in Berlin." They didn't like this.

"You need to pay now." All I could guess was that with the name Wertheim, because of the department stores, they thought my family was rich.

"I don't have that kind of money."

"Fine." The man grabbed my right arm and held me until the other had grabbed my left. They led me into another room toward a narrow wardrobe. With his other hand, one of the officers opened the door and they pushed me inside. Immediately, I felt stabbing pain and fought to get out.

"No, no!" I shouted.

It was too late. They locked the door and as they did so I retracted my hands quickly. There were nails protruding through the door. The same was true of the sides and back of the closet. There were even nails protruding from the low ceiling.

"When you are ready to pay what you owe, you can come out."

I made small movements but each one hurt. Something wet was trickling down my spine and the backs of my legs and I realized it was blood. If I stood completely upright, my head came up against the sharp points. If I slumped, my back scraped on them. I was forced to squat, my legs cramping and burning in this dark cage.

What was I to do? My mother was most likely still on the train back to Berlin. She wouldn't be home yet, and anyway, she didn't have that kind of money. Ten thousand Reichsmarks was a fantastic amount even for those not restricted by the new anti-Semitic regulations. It seemed out of the question. All the men in my family were in prison. All my relatives were struggling. Even going to Aunt Martha didn't seem like an option. To come up with such a large amount in an hour or two was simply not possible. Besides, I didn't want to give in to these people.

An hour passed as I crouched painfully in the closet. Then two more went by. The cramps in my legs became unbearable. My undershirt and shirt were soaked in blood. I tried to think of anything but the pain. My mother and father had done so much to get me out of the country. Everyone had done so much to help me. "Take care of my little baby," I heard my mother say. "Just disappear," came my father's voice. I refused to die in here, so close to freedom. What hope of getting out of Germany did my mother have if I were to die at this moment?

"Alright!" I called out to my captors, "I will pay. Let me out. I will get the money."

The light of day blinded me for a moment and the fresh air rushed at me, turning my wet shirt cold against my skin. One of the guards dragged me out of the closet, and he pulled me up as I stumbled while trying to straighten my stiff legs and back.

"I need to use your phone."

I dialed the number of the Bendlerstrasse apartment. Explaining the situation to Mother would not be simple. I could not tell her what actually was happening because I was under guard.

"Martha," I said when she answered. Mother and I had developed a language that enabled us to communicate cautiously.

"Ernesto? Ernesto, what is it?" She knew something was wrong.

"I need ten thousand Reichsmarks wired here." I told her to wire it to the station.

My mother was silent for only a moment. "I understand. I will find the money somehow."

"I know how difficult this task is. Please do not worry if you are not successful," I told her.

"By morning," said one of the guards. I repeated this into the phone.

"Don't worry," my mother said, "I will get it, Ernesto." This was typical of my mother, always optimistic and full of encouragement. I told her to contact her friends in London to tell them that I would not be on the train as expected.

I hung up the phone. It was the last time I ever heard my mother's voice.

The officers shut the station for the night, warning me I had better be back in the morning. They returned Uncle Wilhelm's warm dark blue overcoat and my money, but kept everything else as collateral. No more trains were coming through until the next day. In the station washroom I cleaned up and rinsed my shirt, then wringed out as much blood as I could before putting it back on. The wet shirt felt cool against my wounds. With my coat buttoned all the way up, you couldn't see the damage the nails had inflicted. I tried to reserve a hotel room for the night, but none of the local people would risk getting in trouble with the police. They would not even sell me food or drink.

It was dark. I walked around the small border town, feeling increasingly uneasy.

What would happen if Mother could not piece together the money by morning? It was so much money. I wondered if there was a chance of crossing the border without being seen. I wouldn't have my passport or my visa but perhaps I could still make it to London and then on to the United States somehow. At least I'd be out of Germany.

I walked to the railroad tracks, picturing the train I should have been on. I knew the border patrol kept German shepherds trained to catch people who tried to cross without permission. Unlike on Schneekoppe, I did not know the territory across the border. I looked over the area around the tracks. Maybe if I walked parallel to the tracks, a short distance away from them? I walked a ways but could hear the dogs barking. It was much too dangerous. I turned around and walked back into the small town.

In a park I sat on a bench to rest. Almost immediately, as if he had followed me there, a young man about my age sat down beside me.

"Do not try to attempt to cross the border," he whispered, not bothering with a greeting.

"How did you...?"

"Everyone has been put on alert that you might try, and if you do, they will simply shoot."

"Thank you," I said. "Why are you willing to volunteer this information? Doesn't it put you in danger?"

"My family does not believe in Hitler and what he is doing, but I need a job to feed my family. We simply cannot afford to resist." He looked away shamefully for a moment. "I do know a way to cross the border but it is several miles from where we are, and it would be too dangerous to go there now because," he stopped to glance around, "everybody is watching."

We both stopped to listen for a moment. All I heard was the wind through the bare branches of the trees in the park.

"How's your memory?"

"Okay," I replied. He told me his address so I could inform others who needed to be brought across. He quoted a price, which was very reasonable, and mentioned this would all go to food and clothing. He also gave me the passwords for him and his contacts in Holland. I committed it all to memory. I dared not write it down.

"I'm sorry I can't help you further," he said, "Do you think you will get the money the guards are asking for?"

I looked at him for a moment wondering how he knew.

"It's what they do," he said, shaking his head. I told him I didn't know but my mother was trying.

"Return to the station where you can be watched, and they will know you are not trying anything funny. Wait it out on the steps of the station until daylight."

"Okay," I replied, "I will. Thank you."

The young man rose and walked away.

I spent a freezing night on the cold concrete steps of the station.

In the morning the money had not come.

"The banks are not yet open," I reminded the officers when they approached me. They waited impatiently, and then at noon, I heard my name called at the ticket booth. The money had arrived by wire. I'll never know how my mother managed that sum. Even later, from the safety of America, I didn't want her to tell me. Letters were sometimes opened and read. I imagine she was up all night, contacting everyone she knew. I wondered what debt she incurred on my behalf or did others help out just because they could? Either way, I had been gifted another chance to flee Germany.

The officers arranged a seat for me on the next train. They had my luggage placed on the train and returned my passport to me. I felt like

I could breath again. In my coat pocket I had my passport, my visa for the United States, my tickets for the train and ferry, as well as my ticket for the ship to New York.

As I finally approached the train, I spotted the same two officers walking briskly toward me.

"There is another problem," one of them shouted through a sinister smile. "You cannot board the train."

The conductor blew the whistle. My back was to the train as I stared up at the two officers, their hands on their hips, greed in their eyes. I quickly looked back and saw the doors close and the train began to move. This couldn't be happening. I could not miss this train. I placed my hand next to my coat pocket to feel the passport and the other papers inside. Then I turned toward the retreating train, jumping onto the steps that protruded at the end of the last car.

Bang! Bang! The guards were shooting at me. The conductor opened the train door and took my arm, managing to quickly slip me inside. He shut the door behind me.

I leaned against the side of the car, breathing heavily, my heartbeat loud in my head. The conductor stood silently beside me for a minute as I caught my breath. I was only partially aware of him looking me over to see if I had been shot. "Let me take you to your seat."

I followed him forward through several cars.

I saw my luggage on the rack above as I sat down. The conductor nodded and walked on. Once seated, my whole body started to shake.

Only a couple minutes later the train stopped again. Panic overtook me. I looked around to see what was happening.

Uniformed officers were moving through the train again, but their uniforms were different, their expressions friendly. It was the Dutch police. We were over the border. I showed an officer my papers. He smiled and asked me where I was going.

"To America," I replied, my voice breaking slightly.

The man handed back my papers. "That's wonderful," he said, "The best of luck."

The train moved on towards the coastal town of Hoek, where I would catch a ferry to England. It took a while to feel like myself

again. Fear turned to anger. The German officers were acting on
their own behalves, making money on the side; I was sure of it. After
Kristallnacht, Hitler had given a blank check for such behavior.

As the time passed and after sitting, breathing, and looking out
over the calm Dutch countryside, a sense of security returned to me.
Hunger then took over. A British man in my cabin, who had been
observing my recovery, finally approached me and asked what had
happened. After I attempted to explain the incident, he invited me to
join him in the dining car. I ordered a meal, my first in more than a
day, and I ate while the train sped toward a new world.

CHAPTER 6
Trying to Grow Roots in Winter

Ilex aquifolium (English holly)

When we arrived at the Hook of Holland, our train was transferred onto a rail ferry to cross the English Channel to Harwich, England. On the ferry the cars were lined up side by side in such a way that as we motored over the water my view was limited to the windows and sides of other train cars. The water was choppy so I moved up to the deck, letting the cold wind dampen my seasickness.

A few hours later, after the train cars were maneuvered back onto the tracks and the couplings secured, British border agents asked for each passenger's passport and visa. Our train continued toward London. It took me a while to feel safe and at ease. I was still recovering from the ordeal at the German-Dutch border. Once I managed to calm myself a bit, I learned from conversations with fellow passengers they were just as excited to get out of Germany and just as worried about loved ones left behind.

We passed by many small villages full of old houses with tidy and dormant winter gardens. I saw many hollies covered with red berries. The *Ilex aquifolium* (English holly) I recalled from my studies, is highly adaptable to new conditions. I would do well, I thought, to imitate this resilient tree.

Since I arrived a day later than scheduled, I suspected no one would be waiting for me in London so I braced myself for a restless night at the station. The small amount of cash I carried had to be saved for room and board in New York until I found a job.

Luck, however, was on my side. Mother's friends, whose names have been lost in the hazy memory of this journey, were at the Liverpool Street Station to greet me with reassuring smiles. As I sat in the back of their car, I tried to listen as they pointed out the sights. We drove by Piccadilly Circus, pink and red neon signs breaking through the fog, theatergoers and tourists filling the sidewalks. They pointed out other landmarks but not much penetrated my fatigued consciousness. Though very grateful for their assistance, I was emotionally and physically exhausted, and I found it difficult to pay attention. I felt grateful for a bed and slept deeply that night.

After breakfast they drove me to the London Waterloo Station. As we said goodbye, they promised to write Mother that I was safe and continuing my journey.

Waterloo was a very large station with twenty-one platforms, kiosks, bookstores, and refreshment booths. It was teeming with travelers moving in every direction and porters rolling trolleys full of luggage and goods, all overseen by constables in their round-topped helmets. Some men tipped their fedoras as they walked past. I followed suit, tipping my new felt fedora that Mother insisted I purchase for the trip. Unaccustomed to wearing hats, I found it a bit awkward. While awaiting my train to Southampton, where I would board the ship, I had a light lunch in a small café.

Boarding the train this time was delightfully mundane. I took my seat by the window. After we cleared London, I saw green fields, grazing sheep, and lovely countryside. There were no grand mountains, but the rolling, green hills created a pastoral view onto which I could rest my eyes. For the first time on my journey, I was at peace. The image of grazing sheep still conjures a reassuring calm all these years later.

I thought of my brother, George, and wondered where in England he was at that moment. Had he found a loving family? Then I thought of Mother, wiping tears off her face at the train station in Hamburg. I recalled her words, "Please take care of my little baby." It is now over seventy-five years later, yet at times it seems like yesterday.

I do not remember much about the arrival in Southampton, even though I loved ports. In Hamburg, we often went to see the big German liners, such as the Europa and Bremen, as it was common to welcome back friends or bid them farewell. And I always admired the wonderfully large elm trees that lined the river.

The ocean liner RMS Aquitania, heading to New York City, was a big, beautiful ship with four mighty funnels. What a sight she was anchored in the harbor! I signed in on the passenger list, walked up the gangplank, found my second-class cabin, and then went back out to stand on the deck as the ship's horn bellowed. All of this, with the anticipation of sailing across the Atlantic, was absolutely exhilarating.

The ocean liner RMS Aquitania, my passage to America

The price of my passage included all meals, gratuities, and an allowance for shipboard services. During my voyage I ate very well, and even got myself a haircut. My one disappointment was discovering my command of the English language was terribly lacking. To improve my English, I decided that every day I would order something different on the menu until I had ordered everything. I brought a notepad with me to the dining room. When the waiter came I pointed to an item on the menu, and when it arrived and I saw what it was, I wrote down the translation.

I also forced myself to practice English by engaging people in conversations. Most were very patient with my attempts. The Aquitania became my classroom for a seven-day crash course in English.

The vast sea was relatively calm, white crests on the deep blue water. I felt the thrill of wanderlust as we made our way, day after day, with no land in sight. On the last night, I received an invitation to dine at the captain's table. I assumed it had something to do with my last name, and this was certainly a more welcome association than I had experienced at the hands of the German border patrol.

In second class our dining tables had clean, white tablecloths, which were very nice, but in first class everything was much more sumptuous. The first class dining room had marble columns and frescos on the ceiling. The chairs were made of rosewood with embroidered upholstery, and the china had a lovely and delicate pattern. There were tall bud vases on every table containing white and red roses. I reveled in this elegant meal, talking with several fascinating passengers, and of course, meeting the captain was quite a treat.

The following day I stood on the deck in the early morning light, grateful to be wearing my uncle's warm coat. I watched the distant Statue of Liberty grow larger off the bow. It was cold, below freezing, not much different from the German winter I had left behind. Lady Liberty's promise of freedom could hardly have been more appreciated. The Aquitania blew her horn as we came into the harbor. At that moment, I was overwhelmed by the joy and excitement of finally reaching America. In this new country I could carve out a successful life for myself and, most importantly, earn the money needed to get my mother out of Germany.

Lady Liberty from the water, circa 1938

I was fortunate to have all my papers in order and, therefore, didn't have to go through Ellis Island. The processing at the port was smooth as I went through passport control and customs. I presented my two affidavits, one from my relative, Hanna Hellinger, and one from Mr. Greenstein, a gentleman living in Baltimore. I had the opportunity to visit Hanna a couple years later, but Mr. Greenstein preferred not to meet with me. Maybe he thought I would ask him for money, or maybe he was being modest in the great mitzvah (worthy or kind deed) of facilitating my escape from Germany.

As I walked out of the controlled area of the dock, there stood my old friend, George Salomon. It had been nearly six years since I was last at his home — when Mother, my brother, George, and I had visited the Salomons in early February 1933 — after Father was kidnapped. We had not seen each other since I'd gone to school in Ahlem, now almost five years ago. Seeing my friend again, in this strange new land, had the peculiar feeling of a homecoming. George's father was a well-respected professor of Russian history, and the family's escape from Germany had been enabled by an invitation to teach at Swarthmore College outside of Philadelphia.

Standing on the dock at the port in New York, we looked much older, of course, but still easily recognizable. We grinned at each other and heartily shook hands. We had much to talk about.

We put my suitcase and George's travel bag into storage at the port. Then we walked from the waterfront into Manhattan, past brick warehouses and apartment buildings crisscrossed with fire escapes, until we reached a bus stop. Our first order of business was to find a place for me to live. Thinking ahead, George had bought a newspaper and found several inexpensive rooms for rent. Traveling by bus and on foot, we made our way around the city to look at potential rooms. It helped that George was pretty familiar with New York City.

We had plenty of time to talk on the bus rides. I asked George about his family. They lived in a comfortable home in Pennsylvania, and his father enjoyed teaching at Swarthmore. Now fluent in English, George was attending the college tuition-free, a benefit of his father's employment.

George asked what it was like back in Germany. I told him about *Kristallnacht*; the men taken to concentration camps, including my father and uncle; and the burning of the synagogues. I told him about how I had taken young refugees over the mountain across the Czechoslovak border and about the closet and bullets at the Dutch border. He listened quietly, all at once astonished, angry, and sad.

I chose the third room we looked at that day because it was cleaner than the other two and was managed by a woman with a kind disposition. It was also located closer to city central. Back at the port, we retrieved my suitcase and George's overnight bag. There were many people trying to get a taxi, so it took quite a while to get back to my new room. George was staying the night with me. After we both freshened up a bit, I realized I had left my brand new fedora hat on the ship. I never cared much for hats so it wasn't a great loss. From then on I never wore a hat again except while skiing. George asked whether I was ready to venture into the city. Since I had been thrifty aboard the ship, I received a refund on the unused portion of the prepaid shipboard allowance. My cash again totaled about sixty-five dollars. George gave me a quick lesson on American currency, going over each coin and bill before we went exploring.

The rest of the afternoon and evening was spent sightseeing, primarily on foot. I would not spend my meager funds on public transportation. We walked through the Garment District and along 34th Street. We took the elevator to the top of the Empire State Building. It was a breathtaking view, but more importantly, it was a great orientation to the city. George pointed out the various neighborhoods, parks, buildings, rivers, and bridges. We ate lunch in an automat diner, typical for that time. You would put coins in a slot to open a window and take out a sandwich or a piece of pie. I found it amusing.

The next morning, December 24, George left to catch a train home for the holiday. I had arrived in New York on a Friday, two days before Christmas. Job hunting would have to be postponed until Monday. I spent all day Saturday exploring the city on my own. I walked through Central Park and up to Harlem, then all the way to Madison Square and the West Village. I was young and full of vim and vigor.

Manhattan was very different from Berlin, Hamburg, and London. I loved the mixed backdrop of townhouses side by side with tall buildings; however, I noticed very few gardens and only some trees. Landscaping was almost nonexistent, except for the parks. I wondered how plants — living in small sidewalk planters — were able to survive in such a dense city with so many shadows cast by the tall, looming buildings. I also found it difficult to understand New Yorkers. On the ship, I had practiced British English. Now, I needed to fine-tune my listening skills to be able to communicate in New York. It was another unexpected hurdle to jump over, but this did not discourage me. I was finally realizing my dream, living in a country where I did not have to be on the lookout for SS troopers or the Gestapo. All the worries about getting arrested, beaten or taken to a labor camp were far away.

That night, Christmas Eve, I gathered with hundreds of people in Times Square. All around me the energy was electric. The square was filled with bright lights, loud music, and spirited laughter. It seemed many people had too much to drink. I suppose it looked as though we were all sharing a good time. But I was rapidly becoming sad and lonely, especially as I remembered Christmases past with my family.

Growing up in Hamburg, Christmas was a much more intimate, familial affair. My parents set up the tree in the dining room and closed the doors until Christmas Eve. We would eat a light, delicious meal in the living room, served on Mother's Meissen china with its pretty patterns of blue onions and flowers. After dinner, the entire family would sing Christmas carols until my parents would finally open the sliding doors of the dining room, revealing the tree aglow with candles on the branches. There were four small tables around the tree: one for each of the children and one for our maid, Fräulein Liesel. Each table was covered with unwrapped presents. We would celebrate Christmas for two full days. On the second day, we would always visit relatives and receive more presents. Many of the Jewish families we knew celebrated Christmas in Germany.

Meissen china

As I walked away from Times Square back to my room, I thought about how far apart from one another my family had become. I pictured Mother, Oma, and Gladys celebrating together in the warmth of the apartment on Bendlerstrasse. I wondered if Werner was celebrating Christmas in Santiago. Was George celebrating with a family of strangers in England? I could not allow myself to think about my father's situation. I was now three thousand miles away, but despite the terrors of my Germany, I felt homesick.

I spent Christmas Day writing letters to Mother, Werner, and Aunt Martha. I was unable to write to George, not knowing where he was. I found it impossible to wait until Monday to begin searching for a job. Mother had given me a list of contacts in New York. I planned to visit each one, bringing them greetings from my parents, and asking for any job leads. As peculiar as it was, I ventured out on Christmas, traipsing all over the city to find three different acquaintances. They were all very welcoming but had no suggestions for employment, as their minds were focused on the holiday. One family invited me to stay for lunch, for which I was grateful.

Sunday evening, I met with Walter Singer, who had been an instructor at the *Gartenbauschule* and was now employed at a nursery on Staten Island. He invited me to stay for dinner. Mr. Singer was very happy to see me but explained he could not help with my job search. The Depression was still affecting the job market. New York was overcrowded with immigrants, and winter was the worst time to find a job in landscape architecture.

Some of the people on my contact list were other immigrants, who had been living in the United States for less than a year, or maybe a bit longer. They were still struggling to fit in. To my surprise they complained about the American culture and the food. They missed their homeland and the lifestyle they were accustomed to. Perhaps they had left Germany before the Nazis revealed the depths of their inhumanity. In reality, they were longing for a time and lifestyle that no longer existed back home in Germany. They did not seem to appreciate the freedom of their new, adopted country.

Before I left Germany, Gladys had given me advice about social behavior in America. It all came in very handy. For example, she said I should always let ladies exit the elevator first and remember to always say, "You're welcome."

One day, I was riding in the subway. It was very crowded and a man stepped on my foot. He politely apologized, and I replied, "You're welcome."

Then he lost his balance and stepped on my foot again. Once more, he apologized sincerely. So I said, "You're welcome" again. A lady sitting nearby smiled at me and explained my response was incorrect. Soon, we were all laughing. The gentleman excused himself once more and, coached by the lady, I said, "It is okay." Charmed, the man offered to take me out for lunch. We ate at another automat, and I thanked him before continuing my search for employment.

On December 30, I turned nineteen years old. I had been in America for one week, my money was dwindling, and I was far from finding a job. Convinced little opportunity existed for me in New York, I had no choice but to turn to the Salomons for advice. They invited me to come to Philadelphia and stay with them in Swarthmore.

Professor Salomon paid for the train ticket and met me in Philadelphia at the station.

The Salomons' house was right on campus, on a street lined with stately elms. George took me on a tour of the beautifully landscaped campus. It felt so good to be among gardens again. Swarthmore had expansive lawns and, best of all, Scott Arboretum: over three hundred acres of ornamental trees, shrubs, and flowers from all over the world, carefully chosen for the local climate and conditions so — according to its mission — the plants "could be used by people of average means living in the Philadelphia area."

There were collections of rhododendrons, azaleas, lilacs, hydrangeas, dogwoods, conifers, and many more. It was heavenly to walk the campus, even though most of the plants were cut back and dormant for the winter. The forsythia, however, were just about to break open. As George and I walked through the campus, he pointed out an area with large flowering trees. Each meadow had a romantic name and George explained in the summertime this was where the boys and girls would meet. He did not explain much, but it was obvious he had more experience with romance than I did.

Professor Salomon recommended me to an administrator and arranged an interview. Landscape architecture was an uncommon career at the time. When I told him I was a trained landscape architect, he did not seem to believe a young man of nineteen could have the education I claimed to have. The longer we talked, however, the more convinced he became I was telling the truth. We walked across the campus while he asked me questions about various plants. I answered all his questions and gave him additional information when I knew it.

The administrator offered me a position as a landscape architect at the college, and I accepted the job. However, it didn't actually solve my immediate situation. It was January. There was snow on the ground, and the job did not start until the first of April. Soon, I would no longer be able to support myself. I could never impose on the Salomons for so long. The job offer felt like a bittersweet victory, and I continued my search for other employment.

The following evening we had dinner guests at my request, Dr. and Mrs. Levy from Philadelphia. They were friends of Gladys', and she had written and told them about me. Professor Salomon had been kind enough to call and arrange the gathering.

Dr. Levy was a well-respected doctor, though he looked more like an eccentric scientist, with his slim build and wire-rim glasses. Mrs. Levy was shorter than her husband and rounder, with a warm and friendly demeanor. She was about the same age as my mother. I did as Gladys had encouraged me to do. I shared stories about what was happening in Germany and what Hitler was all about. The Levys seemed quite moved.

Before the meal was over, they invited me to come stay with them in Philadelphia, where I might have better luck finding work. I went with them after dinner, whole-heartedly thanking the Salomons for their hospitality.

During the two weeks I stayed with the Levys, they treated me like a son, providing me with a comfortable room, good food, and earnestly asking about my progress. Continuing my job search, I visited some of the local landscape architecture offices, but no one was hiring. Neither were the local nurseries, nor was Longwood Gardens, the beautiful estate of industrialist Pierre du Pont. I was very impressed walking around Longwood Gardens, which featured acres of lawns, shaped shrubs, reflection ponds, majestic trees, and a huge variety of flowers. Du Pont had built dazzling fountains, an elegant conservatory, and most recently, a vertically planted wall of roses. It also included a school where both students and the general public could receive instruction in the arts of horticulture and floriculture.

The Levys were invited to many high society affairs and asked me to accompany them. The parties, usually held in large homes, gave me more exposure to American food and culture. At one dinner I was served an avocado, a fruit I had never seen or tasted. It was delicious. It has been a favorite of mine ever since.

At the first party, Mrs. Levy introduced me to the host who asked for details on life in Germany. I responded by sharing a few of my personal experiences, trying my best to describe it all in English. Other guests were listening and also became interested in my stories. Everyone seemed fascinated and intrigued, but they didn't appear to be taking it all seriously. After this party, I became a popular guest, receiving several invitations to events. At one party, I was even scheduled to tell my stories as part of the evening's "entertainment."

I began to realize people enjoyed the drama and suspense of my storytelling but were simply unable to believe Hitler, the savior of Germany's economy, could commit such atrocities. It was frustrating until I thought of Gladys, reminding me to tell my stories to convince Americans of the impending threat of war.

Finally, one night at a fancy dinner party, I became so exasperated by my audience's disbelief that, in the middle of speaking, I asked the hostess if she would permit me to take off my shirt in order to prove the validity of my story. She couldn't say no; everyone was hanging off his or her seat waiting for me to finish. I removed my shirt, revealing the scars from the nails. Everyone fell silent. Then the guests really started to listen. Afterward, I received many questions. "How could Hitler possibly be arming Germany for war?" No one wanted to believe it could happen. Germany was so far away they couldn't comprehend Hitler's activities could ever interrupt their comfortable lives. Although it was fun to be invited to parties, I felt I was not accomplishing anything.

My father had advised me to stay on the East Coast to find a job. The West, in his mind, was a vast, wild, dangerous, and unpredictable place filled with cowboys, Indians, and train robbers. Father was a well-educated man and well-traveled in Europe, but his knowledge of the American West was based on the American Westerns we watched in the Hamburg movie theaters. While still in Germany I had written to a landscape architect named Ms. Aronstein who had graduated from the *Gartenbauschule* in Ahlem. She had become an American citizen and established her business in a city called San Mateo, a suburb of San Francisco. In her reply she described California as having a mild climate where one could work year round in the landscape business.

I wrote her another letter from Philadelphia. She responded, assuring me I would have no trouble finding work in the landscape industry, possibly even as a landscape architect in Northern California. I decided to take a chance and go to San Francisco, despite the risk of cowboys, Indians, and train robbers. The Levys did not want me to go, mostly because it was so far away. I felt I was already three thousand miles from my home. What was another three thousand if it meant I would find employment? Furthermore, if it didn't pan out, I would find a way to make enough money to return in April to the position at Swarthmore.

Mrs. Levy assisted with the purchase of a Greyhound bus ticket, which I couldn't have afforded on my own. She packed a bag of food and took me to the bus station in Philadelphia. She hugged me tightly, as if this would be our last embrace. It was a painful farewell, as close as I could get to saying goodbye to my mother again. I boarded the bus and embarked on a journey for yet another world.

CHAPTER 7
The Shelter of a Rhododendron

A mature *Rhododendron* (rhododendron) in Golden Gate Park (photo by etsai)

I sat in the front of the bus, absorbing the towns, cities, farms, and vast open spaces that filled the window as the bus rocked down the highway, the growl of its engine rising and falling as we slowed into each station. A couple days in, a tire suddenly blew, and the bus lurched enough to make the passengers gasp. The driver, Fred, had become my friend, and I helped him change the flat tire, sweating from the exertion even in the winter chill.

Fred was concerned about the icy roads and how the winter winds could whip up big piles of snow, like great sand dunes. He was afraid we would hit black ice, which we inevitably did in the Dakotas. The bus lost traction and began sliding one way and then the other while Fred tried to make small corrections with the useless steering wheel and pumps of the brake pedal. Finally, we ran into a snow bank on the side of the road. Had we been moving faster at the time we would have been much worse off. Fred and I got out of the bus and shoveled the snow bank away while the other passengers watched us from the windows.

Luckily, he always carried two shovels, and I was pleased that I had good gloves with me. They were my ski gloves; the same pair I'd worn on the Schneekoppe.

I also helped Fred store luggage in the compartment beneath the bus and then pull it all out when a passenger reached his or her destination. It seemed like the suitcase we were looking for was always in the back of the bunch.

We stopped at night to sleep. Fred and the other passengers rented rooms at motor lodges. I didn't realize this would happen and explained to Fred I had no money for a room. He allowed me to sleep on the bus. He even took me out to dinner a couple of times. Sitting on the red vinyl seats in diners, most of our conversations were about the places we passed. He told me the names of each state we crossed and the names of the towns we drove through and what was going on in them. He gave me a lecture on the Great Depression, how difficult it was for people to work. He told me about President Roosevelt and the Works Progress Administration he created to put the country back to work.

Fred loved my father's impression of the Wild West. We had a good laugh over it, imagining cowboys and Indians on ponies surrounding the Greyhound Bus. When we stopped one late afternoon in Cheyenne, Wyoming, Fred recommended I take a local bus for a side trip to see the real Indians of the West, living on a reservation. "Go see 'em for yourself," he said.

The Native Americans, subdued and stoic, wore feathered headdresses — probably for the tourists — and sold jewelry, baskets, and blankets. Not once, of course, did they threaten me with a tomahawk or arrow.

The next day, Fred had to leave to drive another route. I was sad to say goodbye, but he introduced me to the next driver, telling him of my situation. "You better take good care of Ernest here," he said, pronouncing my name in the American way that I would soon adopt.

I helped the new driver with the suitcases. He wasn't much interested in conversation, but he kept his word to Fred and let me sleep on the bus at night.

Seven days later, we arrived at the Greyhound station at Fifth and Mission in downtown San Francisco. When I got out of the bus, the loudspeaker was on, and I heard an impassioned voice speaking in German. It was Hitler. He spoke about the strength of the Nazi Party and the recovery of a nation on his sixth anniversary as the leader of Germany. It was January 30, 1939. There I was, more than six thousand miles from Berlin, listening to Hitler's menacing voice.

Had I listened more, I would have been even more wounded, hearing his unveiled threats against Europe's Jews.

> *"In the course of my life I have very often been a prophet, and have usually been ridiculed for it. During the time of my struggle for power it was in the first instance only the Jewish race that received my prophecies with laughter when I said that I would one day take over the leadership of the State, and with it that of the whole nation, and that I would then among other things settle the Jewish problem. Their laughter was uproarious, but I think that for some time now they have been laughing on the other side of their face. Today I will once more be a prophet: if the international Jewish financiers in and outside Europe should succeed in plunging the nations once more into a world war, then the result will not be the Bolshevizing of the Earth, and thus the victory of Jewry, but the annihilation of the Jewish race in Europe!"*

I found a pay phone, inserted a nickel and called Ms. Aronstein. A man answered the phone and informed me she was sick. I was very disappointed and told him I would call back the next day.

The man replied, "No, I'm sorry. Ms. Aronstein has had a nervous breakdown. She will most likely need at least three months to recover."

Hanging up the phone, I found a bench and sat down, feeling like I, too, would have a nervous breakdown or maybe a heart attack. What had I done? I had just crossed this huge, strange country with next to no money but with all my hopes based on this one contact. Now it was a dead end.

This was it, I thought, the end of the line. Then I remembered what Mother once told me, "When all goes wrong, step outside, and take a deep breath."

I put my suitcase into storage and stepped out into the fresh San Francisco morning air. I noticed that the entire block between Mission and Market had shops with flowers and other plants. There were small and large shops, each representing a nursery company. The thought occurred to me that perhaps they would have a job opening.

In Germany, a person would rarely approach a stranger and ask for a job. I was very reluctant to ask for help at this moment, despite my situation, yet I couldn't walk away from the familiarity of the flower market. I walked to the end of the block, turned around, and walked back, again, and again, enough to graze a trail in the cement. After an hour and a half, one of the flower shop owners stepped out from his stand and stopped me.

"Are you looking for someone?" he asked. I told him my predicament and my profession. The man introduced himself as Mr. Harry Perlstein, the owner of the Nursery Exchange in Half Moon Bay. (He went on to develop one of the largest greenhouse production nurseries in Northern California.) After listening to me for a short while, he offered me a cup of coffee and a blueberry muffin and then said, "Why don't you go talk to someone on the staff at the Strybing Arboretum. Perhaps they'll have a job for you." He gave me directions to Golden Gate Park. With a sliver of hope, I walked up and down — more up than down it seemed — the hilly streets of San Francisco, a few miles to the Arboretum.

I was always most comfortable around plants and trees. At the entrance of the Arboretum, which at that time was just across the street from the Japanese Tea Garden, I asked one of the gardeners where I would find Mr. Eric Walther, the director, the name Mr. Perlstein had given me. I was directed to a small wooden structure, which was Mr. Walther's office, although it looked more like a tool shed. Evidently, funds were very limited, and there was no money to build an office structure.

Mr. Walther listened to my story. He was the garden's first director and had served in this position since 1937 (he would remain at the helm until his retirement in 1957). He had a wonderful training in horticulture and botany, and he was most interested in my training. When I asked him about getting a job in the Arboretum he told me he would love to hire me, which gave me hope.

"But I'm sorry," he said, "I can only offer a position to you after you have been in the city of San Francisco for one year. That's when you will have established residency."

My heart sank again. He recommended I see a nurseryman named Victor Reiter, Jr. "His office and home are about twelve blocks from here at 1195 Stanyan Street."

I thanked him for the lead. Mr. Walther then asked if I'd like to tour the gardens. I learned he was obsessed with horticulture, loved cats, and had a very healthy ego — what I characterized then as a typical German. He was experimenting with a variety of plants from many parts of the world. He pointed out the rhododendron dell next to the California Academy of Sciences. "I'm sure they look familiar to you. Several came from Germany. Look, they're just starting to bloom."

I nodded. Indeed they were blooming, earlier here than in Germany, encouraged by the California climate. Mr. Walther promised he would call Victor Reiter to let him know I was coming. I thanked him again and went on my way.

Mr. Reiter graciously welcomed me and showed me around his home, his extensive garden, and his commercial nursery behind the home. Mr. Reiter's father had built the house on Stanyan Street. They had acquired three extra parcels of land from the Sutro family, which they had developed into a marvelous garden and nursery. It contained a rare red flowering New Zealand Christmas tree and an even rarer *Magnolia campbelli* (Campbell's magnolia tree). His specialty was hybridizing new plants, especially fuchsias. Victor was one of the original members of the California Horticultural Society, which began shortly after the Big Freeze of 1933, one of the coldest winters on record.

He told me more about the Society while feeding me coffee and cookies. On my empty stomach, a cookie never tasted so good.

Victor did not need help in the nursery and didn't know of any jobs locally. "I would suggest you try Los Angeles," he said. "Because of the movie industry, the Depression is lifting more rapidly in Southern California than it is in the north."

I didn't have the money for a bus to go south, and it was a much longer walk to Los Angeles than it was from the Flower Mart downtown to Golden Gate Park. It was good advice that I couldn't take, but Victor encouraged me to keep in touch and someday, perhaps, join the Horticultural Society.

By the time I said goodbye and found myself back on the sidewalk, it was evening. I didn't have enough money for a hotel. I could have stayed with Victor overnight, but I was too proud to admit that I had no place to go. I wanted to impress him so he would give me a job. As a cool fog fell over the city and the light began to fade, my situation seemed rather bleak.

I then remembered the rhododendrons in Golden Gate Park. I started walking back that way, picturing myself with George Salomon as we played fort beneath the bushy plants in the Salomons' garden outside of Hamburg. I found the rhododendron with the longest legs and the most space beneath its leaves and branches. Then I gathered pine needles and laid them on the ground inside to make a soft bed. I used Uncle Wilhelm's wonderful overcoat as a blanket. Exhausted, I slept very well in my rhododendron shelter.

The next morning I walked across the street to the Conservatory, a beautiful white-domed structure that had been imported from Europe and reconstructed in Golden Gate Park in the late 1870s. At the Conservatory's entrance I introduced myself to the lady manager. She let me use the bathroom facilities so I could clean up and shave. I carried my toiletries in the big pocket of my overcoat. Afterwards, she gave me a tour. The building was brought over in crates from Europe, most likely from England. The Conservatory's entrance was about two stories high, and it housed all kinds of tropical plants such as palms, banana trees, rubber trees, and a great variety of orchids. In one section, there was a lotus and lily pond. Some forty years later, my business partners and I would be asked to prepare designs for a complete renovation of these interior gardens.

The manager also allowed me to use the phone. I called Dr. Gassman, a friend of the Levys. He had heard from my kind hosts in Philadelphia and was expecting my call. He offered to pick me up from the bus station and insisted I stay with him for a few nights.

I walked the miles back to the Greyhound station, where I met Dr. Gassman. He and his wife lived in an apartment in the Marina District. During the drive to their house I admired the many wonderful Victorian houses in Pacific Heights, with their painted trim and ornate details. Driving down steep Fillmore Street, with a wide view of the San Francisco Bay in the distance, nearly scared me to death.

When we arrived at the Gassmans' house I took a shower and put on clean clothes. Dr. and Mrs. Gassman were most kind to me. For their hospitality, after my travels and in the midst of such uncertainty, I felt a deep and profound gratitude. Without them, I would have been homeless.

Not only did Dr. Gassman provide me with room and board, he arranged an interview for me with Mrs. Sigmund Stern (Rosalie Meyer Stern). Widowed in 1928, her husband had been president of Levi Strauss & Company. A Jewish community and civic leader, she wanted to leave something lasting in honor of her husband. In 1931, she donated to the city a magnificent, thirty-three acre wooded parcel along Sloat Boulevard, between 19th and 34th Avenues, to be used for free Sunday afternoon concerts and other recreation. It became known as Stern Grove, a Sunset District treasure to this day.

The interview took place at her lovely residence in Pacific Heights. Her butler had me wait at the door. Mrs. Stern appeared and invited me into her living room. She also showed me her small garden and explained that each spring she hires three Mexican workers to spade her ten-acre estate in Atherton, a country town south of San Francisco. She asked me, "Do you know how to spade?"

I couldn't help but smile as I told her I had quite a bit of experience with spading. She then said in a friendly but somewhat crude manor that because of my black hair and accent, I could pass as one of her Mexican workers, and thus hired me as a gardener. I was elated.

She offered me a job at ninety dollars a month, including the use of a small bedroom and bath over the garage, plus I was allowed to eat any fruit and vegetables produced on the grounds. My training in horticulture and landscape architecture never even came up.

On February 3, 1939, I bid the Gassmans farewell as Mrs. Stern's chauffeur took my suitcase to the car, and I climbed in for the ride to Atherton and my first job in America.

The estate on Atherton Avenue was in an exclusive area of large mansions and gardens close to Stanford University. The house was surrounded by several beautiful native *Quercus agrifolia* (California oaks), some with a spread of more than sixty feet. These trees provide shade during the summer, but do not allow any plants to grow beneath their branches. They don't tolerate any water in the summer. California oaks are native and thus well suited to the region's dry climate and short rainy season. If you develop the area underneath the canopy with new ground plantings, you run the risk of over saturating the soil with water, killing these big, beautiful trees.

Toward the rear of the estate was the garage — where I now lived — along with the greenhouses and the fruit and vegetable gardens. The room assigned to me was very small and the roof sloped steeply over the bed. After hitting my head several times, I learned not to sit up too quickly upon awakening. With my first check I bought a used hot plate, several small pots and a small frying pan so I could do some basic cooking. I wrote a letter to my mother asking her how to cook rice — something filling and inexpensive to keep me going. With my second paycheck, I bought a secondhand bicycle, which was very important because it meant I no longer had to walk back and forth to get dinner or groceries. It took me forty-five minutes to walk to a small café for dinner and the same to walk back. I was working manual labor all day so by the time I arrived back on the estate after dinner, I was hungry again. Just to tide me over, I would take a pocketful of those packaged saltines from the restaurant and snack on them while I walked home. The bicycle markedly improved my quality of life. I was no longer hungry all the time.

We spaded all over the estate. Flower borders needed to be prepared for spring and summer plantings. We spaded between shrubs and trees as the winter rains had germinated plentiful weeds. This was one way to get rid of them and make the place look cultivated. We spaded all day long. This is what we were hired for.

After several days of spading, the head gardener approached me.

"Ernest, you did not tell me the truth."

I did not know what he meant. Was I going to lose my job? What did I tell him? What did I say?

"You must know something about plants because you spade under the weeds but not under the plants, while our other workers just dig under everything."

Relieved, I explained I was trained in horticulture and had graduated as a landscape architect.

The gardener listened, his eyes lighting up and asked, "What do you know about *Tuberous begonias* (begonias)?"

I soon found myself in the greenhouse handling a begonia seeding operation. Shortly thereafter, the head gardener put me in charge of several greenhouses.

Several weeks later, the head gardener approached Mrs. Stern and told her that he and his wife had never had a vacation in the ten years he had worked for her. They agreed the couple could take a three-month vacation in Sweden, his homeland, where he had been a marine architect before moving to the United States. He recommended to Mrs. Stern I take his place while he was gone since I knew more about horticulture than he did.

Suddenly, I was going to be in charge of ten permanent workers and a ten-acre estate. I could hear the words of my teacher on my first day at the *Gartenbauschule* as he shook his finger at me: "Young man, those who graduate from this school will someday be *supervising* workers who are spading."

Before leaving, the head gardener introduced me to his counterpart at the Edward E. Heller Estate, which was next to the Stern Estate. The Heller Estate gardener, in turn, introduced me to other head gardeners in the area, who all knew each other and met together periodically. Most of them were either from Germany or England and were well trained. They invited me into their circle, offering me advice. We exchanged plants if we had more than we needed. They even invited me for dinner a few times. During a couple weekends, when the head gardener of the Heller Estate was gone, I would go and check in on things for him.

Despite my young age, the workers on the Stern Estate accepted me as head gardener when they realized I knew a lot more than anyone else did about plants. They were not trained gardeners, but I never let them feel they did not know much. They were used to people treating them as lesser. It was not in my nature to treat people this way, and after what I had experienced in Germany, I felt all the more strongly about treating everyone with equal respect.

One day, Mrs. Stern came to find me in the greenhouse.

"Ernest, do you know how to drive?" she asked. When I replied I did, she asked me to drive her into San Francisco. Her chauffeur was ill, and she had an appointment in the city. After this episode, I drove a number of times. I was not nervous except I did not know the streets of San Francisco very well, especially with so many one-way streets, but I learned quickly. Herr Glaubitz had taught me well in Aunt Martha's big Chrysler.

Mrs. Stern hosted many parties. One time, she asked me to help serve the dinner because she was short some maids. There I was, just as my mother predicted: working as a chauffeur, a butler, and a gardener.

Mrs. Stern asked me afterwards where I had learned to do such tasks. I didn't want to admit to her I had learned butlering at night school in Germany. I didn't want to do this kind of work on a regular basis. At the same time, I considered it part of my job to do it upon request. Instead, I told her my aunt, Martha, hosted dinner parties, and I had learned by observation.

It was great fun meeting Mrs. Stern's guests. She always introduced me as her gardener, and people enjoyed talking with me about their own gardens. I was also in charge of arranging floral displays in the big house. Mrs. Stern wrote the names of the flowers in beautiful calligraphy on cards placed in front of each centerpiece and the lovely containers flanking the doorways, so her guests could identify them. One day, while arranging the flowers in their vases, I grew nostalgic, remembering that as a boy I would help Mother arrange flowers in our Hamburg apartment. She took such great joy in it. It was hard to be patient as I slowly amassed the money to bring her to the United States. There was still a long way to go to have enough for her affidavit.

My mother's passport picture, 1941

On a day off I spent some precious savings on a Greyhound ticket from Menlo Park to San Francisco for a meeting of the California Horticultural Society. Victor Reiter had invited me as his guest; in fact, he paid for the first year of my membership. Since then, except for my years in the military, I have paid for the last seventy-four years.

When I arrived at the Commercial Club, where the Society met, a woman greeted me, recognizing my name from when Victor had mentioned it. She introduced herself as Ms. Cora Brandt, the Society's secretary, a volunteer position. I will never forget her kindness. She introduced me to other members and made me feel at home. She never made me feel less for being only nineteen years old. As I talked with the other members, they were amazed at my plant knowledge. Victor shook my hand and asked about my work on the Stern Estate before we took our seats for the monthly lecture.

Several of the head gardeners I had met in the area were also members. The head gardener from the Heller Estate was at the meeting and offered me a ride home. After that, I never had to worry about transportation to Society meetings.

After I had been working for Mrs. Stern for four months, her daughter, Mrs. Walter Haas, asked me to help her with a large party. Mrs. Haas lived on the property at the back of the estate. I planted annuals and perennials in her garden and created colorful, cascading flower baskets that I hung from the oak trees. On the day of the party, I served as valet, parking the guests' cars. Mrs. Haas had created nametags for everyone, including me. As a bearded gentleman rose slowly out of his car, leaning heavily on a well-worn cane, he looked curiously at my name.

"Are you related to the family who founded the Wertheim Department Stores in Germany?"

I told him about Uncle Wilhelm and Aunt Martha. He introduced himself as Alfred Hertz. He had been the music director of the San Francisco Symphony from 1915 until 1930. Since then, he had been involved in relief activities to assist musicians affected by the Depression. He was also a guest conductor, including for performances on The Standard Hour radio broadcast. He asked about my situation, and I told him I was the temporary head gardener for Mrs. Stern and explained about my training in Germany. Mr. Hertz seemed quite taken by the fact I was so young, yet so knowledgeable in my field, and fairly well spoken.

Later in the day, he asked Mrs. Haas if I could speak to the guests. However, I did not talk about Germany. In fact, I hardly spoke on the subject after Philadelphia because I was very discouraged at that point. Instead, I spoke about gardens, hiking, California flora, and my work, using my storytelling skills to engage them in the topic. My talk was well received. Mrs. Haas paid me for my work and gave me a bonus, which I happily stowed under my bed.

When the head gardener and his wife returned from their vacation, I had been working for Mrs. Stern for six months instead of the three for which she had originally hired me. I had grown quite comfortable in my routine so it was very disappointing when she called me in to see her one day to thank me for my service. She told me she had to let me go; "I do not need two head gardeners," she said. She was always very businesslike in her manner.

I was suddenly out of work.

Mrs. Stern arranged for her chauffeur to give me a ride back to San Francisco and allowed me to leave my things at her estate until I found a new job. I secured one that very afternoon at the Golden Gate Nursery, way down towards the end of Geary Street near the Cliff House. I rented a room right away in the Richmond District, not far from the nursery.

I was placed on a crew with two other men. The first day I worked really hard, and the other two men just sat around. It made me so angry. This happened the second day, too, and the third. When the boss showed up, they told him I was not pulling my weight, and he yelled at me. After one week, I quit. I simply did not show up one morning and never collected my pay.

I then worked on a crew for a landscape contracting and maintenance company in Palo Alto called Stebbins and Truax, named after two ladies who were graduates of a women's school for horticulture. I had met them at the California Horticultural Society. They did landscape maintenance work for some of the larger estates inside and outside of the city, one of them being the Mark Hopkins Estate in Menlo Park, the country home of the railroad tycoon. Mrs. Hopkins was a fine lady who was very interested in gardening.

Soon thereafter, I began a job on the Flood Estate in Atherton with Stebbins and Truax. The six hundred-acre Flood Estate was off of Middlefield Road and had once been home to a beautiful mansion known as Linden Towers. James Clair Flood had made his fortune mining silver, notably in Nevada's Comstock Lode, but he had met an untimely death while traveling in 1889.

While working on the estate, I met Thomas Church. He was already considered one of the leaders of landscape architecture on the West Coast. He was very pleased to find a member of the ground crew knew how to read and follow drawings. We maintained a lovely acquaintance in the years ahead.

I left my room in San Francisco's Richmond District and rented a room in Palo Alto from two girls who had a hair salon. They allowed me to use their kitchen to cook, which was a pretty good arrangement.

Soon the heavy, winter rains came. The wet ground became too difficult to work, and the company dismissed the whole crew. The next day, while buying a few groceries at Safeway, I told the cashier about my wet weather unemployment. He knew a doctor who, as a hobby, kept several greenhouses full of orchids in a town called Los Altos. The clerk took my number and promised to tell the doctor when he came in next. Sure enough, the doctor called me. I rode my bike about a half-hour to Los Altos and got the job. The doctor did not trust that I knew enough and told me I would get paid by the piece: one price for a five-inch pot, another for a six-inch pot, and so on. About thirty-five thousand orchids needed to be transplanted.

The first few days I did not make much money, but once I got the routine down, I was able to earn almost twenty dollars a day. That was a substantial amount of money. When I worked for Stebbins and Truax, I had made four dollars a day. I worked as many hours as I could, and the doctor was very satisfied. I took the Safeway clerk and his girlfriend out for dinner to say thank you.

Unfortunately, this job lasted only a few months before someone bought the doctor's entire orchid collection for what he alluded to be a great price. Once again, I was out of a job.

Without an immediate lead, I had no choice but to try and find temporary work through the California State Employment Office in Mayfield, just south of Palo Alto. This took a great deal of courage. For one, going to a governmental office in Germany as a Jewish person was no pleasure. You never knew if you would come out. Even though I was in America and knew it wouldn't be the same, I couldn't help but feel anxious. The dread and danger of such offices had become a part of me.

Secondly, in my circles in Germany, you were always recommended to the person who interviewed you. That was how you got a job. We didn't use employment agencies. The idea was quite foreign to me, so up until then, I had avoided going there.

The morning after putting in my application, I received a phone call from the agency to help a Mrs. Smith by mowing her lawn and cleaning up leaves. Mrs. Smith had a small house in Palo Alto. There was a lawn in front of the house divided by a straight concrete walkway. It led to her front door and a quaint porch that ran the width of the house, where she enjoyed sitting on a wicker chair and looking out over the garden. The place was well cared for. Palo Alto was just a small university town in 1939, a simple, nice place to live. I introduced myself at the door, and she pointed to a small shed beside the house where the mower and gardening tools were kept.

"Please put everything away when you are done and come to the back door."

A few hours later, with clippings in the trash and equipment back in the shed, I approached the rear door to collect my wages and noticed the fruit trees in her back garden needed some care. Casually, I mentioned they needed pruning. Until then Mrs. Smith had been friendly, but rather swiftly she became quite angry.

"What do you know about the pruning of fruit trees?" she hissed.

I explained about my training, and her countenance immediately shifted to delight. She hired me to prune the trees, explaining she was more used to getting people from the agency who worked to buy their next bottle of wine.

"I have never encountered anyone from the agency who has training in horticulture," Mrs. Smith said. She was so pleased she called the employment office to praise my work.

The next morning, I received another phone call from the employment office with another day job. This continued for a brief stretch. Each day I worked ten or more hours, and by the end of two weeks, I had a regular maintenance route providing me with work seven days a week. I used my bike for transportation, pulling a small cart behind it with my packed lunch and some used tools I had purchased. At first I did just cleanup work, mowing lawns, raking leaves, cleaning walks and patios, and doing some pruning. It was nothing very exciting; but it was work, and people appreciated that I knew what I was doing.

I followed what news I could. Czechoslovakia had long ceased to exist as a sovereign nation. In May 1939, Hitler and Mussolini had signed the Pact of Steel, becoming fascist allies. This did not bode well. On August 23, 1939, the Nazi-Soviet Pact surprised the world. It had just gone from bad to worse.

Then, on September 1, I heard on the radio that Hitler had invaded Poland. On September 3, when Hitler failed to respond to an ultimatum, British Prime Minister Chamberlain announced to his people, "This country is at war with Germany." The United Kingdom, France, New Zealand, and Australia all declared war against the Nazis. Could my mother somehow still get out of Germany? As challenging as it was, I had to remain hopeful. I continued working seven days a week, living frugally, and saving for Mother's voyage and any other costs that might arise in her immigration.

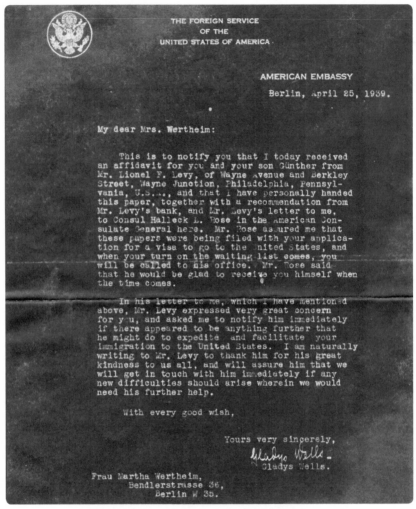

THE FOREIGN SERVICE
OF THE
UNITED STATES OF AMERICA

AMERICAN EMBASSY

Berlin, April 25, 1939.

My dear Mrs. Wertheim:

This is to notify you that I today received an affidavit for you and your son Günther from Mr. Lionel F. Levy, of Wayne Avenue and Berkley Street, Wayne Junction, Philadelphia, Pennsylvania, U.S.A., and that I have personally handed this paper, together with a recommendation from Mr. Levy's bank, and Mr. Levy's letter to me, to Consul Halleck L. Rose in the American Consulate General here. Mr. Rose assured me that these papers were being filed with your application for a visa to go to the United States, and when your turn on the waiting list comes, you will be called to his office. Mr. Rose said that he would be glad to receive you himself when the time comes.

In his letter to me, which I have mentioned above, Mr. Levy expressed very great concern for you, and asked me to notify him immediately if there appeared to be anything further that he might do to expedite and facilitate your immigration to the United States. I am naturally writing to Mr. Levy to thank him for his great kindness to us all, and will assure him that we will get in touch with him immediately if any new difficulties should arise wherein we would need his further help.

With every good wish,

Yours very sincerely,

Gladys Wells.

Frau Martha Wertheim,
Bendlerstrasse 36,
Berlin W 35.

Gladys Wells, still in Berlin, was trying to help my mother from within the American Embassy, and the Levys in Philadelphia sponsored my mother and brother, 1939

With the exception of my involvement in the California Horticultural Society, my social life was very limited. I highly valued the exchange of information at Society meetings with men and women working in gardens and nurseries all over Northern California, as well as with people who loved plants as much as I did. Some members were self-taught horticulture enthusiasts. A fellow named Bob Sachs worked for the post office and was a collector of *Primulas*, a genus of some five hundred species of ornamental flowers, including the primrose. Professor Mitchell from UC Berkeley was the first president of the Society and was not in the nursery business. Dr. Fred Coe, a dear friend of Victor Reiter, was a doctor in the U.S. Navy. The diverse membership included many gifted people.

Meetings always featured a good speaker in the first half and a discussion of plant materials brought by members in the second half. I served on the plant material selection committee. We would look at all the plants and decide which ones we wanted to discuss. We would call on the member who brought the plant to introduce it, followed by an open discussion. Years later, I would take charge of the committee, running it for a number of years, and contacting people before each meeting to ask them to bring interesting specimens.

I also took a course in plant propagation given by Percy "Jock" Brydon, director of the UC Berkeley Botanical Garden. The subject was Propagation of Woody Ornamentals. Topnotch people like Victor Reiter and Eric Walther, as well as other nursery owners and park directors were also in the class. With so much talent in the room, it was more of a round table discussion than a lecture. At first I took a Greyhound bus from Palo Alto to San Francisco and then took another bus to Berkeley. As time went on, I received a ride from Bill Schmidt, a nursery owner in Palo Alto.

When I wasn't working I would venture out to the World's Fair on Treasure Island, situated in the middle of San Francisco Bay. It was fun to ride the ferry from San Francisco. The fair was very impressive, with fascinating exhibits and exquisite architecture built just for the event. The fair's theme was "Pageant of the Pacific." It celebrated the opening of the two new bridges spanning the San Francisco Bay, the Golden Gate Bridge (1937) and the San Francisco-Oakland Bay Bridge (1936), and it served to showcase the goods of nations bordering the Pacific Ocean. Best of all, it featured many outstanding gardens with plants from all around the Pacific Rim. The fair introduced new species to California nurseries like *Trachelospermum jasminoides* (star jasmine) and a new hybrid of *Magnolia grandiflora* (southern magnolia or bull bay). My friends at the California Horticultural Society were very animated in discussions of the new flora.

By early 1940, a couple months after my twentieth birthday, I bought a car, a Dodge coupe, for three hundred dollars cash. It was a terrific experience to have my own automobile in America. It gave me new independence, allowing me to travel all over the Bay Area to do my work. It was a major success for me.

In early spring, I took an entire weekend off for the first time in the more than one year since I had started working regularly in America. A friend from the Society invited me to go skiing.

Before our departure date I bought my first pair of skis from a shop on Market Street in San Francisco. A very pretty and charming woman named Miss Hildebrandt worked there. Her father, Dr. Joel Hildebrandt, was an avid skier and managed the 1936 U.S. Olympic Ski Team. He was also a member of the Sierra Club (serving as president from 1937-1940), and a famous chemistry professor at UC Berkeley. Dr. Hildebrandt learned to ski in Europe and was an advocate for the sport, encouraging the Sierra Club to install one of the first rope tows in the Lake Tahoe area.

My friend and I drove northeast towards Lake Tahoe on Friday afternoon because we needed to arrive in daylight to find the Sierra Club cabin, which was located between Highway 40 and the Southern Pacific train sheds. We parked on the highway near the Sierra Club main lodge, the Clair Tappaan Lodge, and trekked the rest of the way. The cabin was a simple one-room shed with an outhouse about twenty feet away. There was no running water, but there was a wood stove and a good stack of firewood that served for both heating and cooking. There was also an icebox, which we filled with snow to keep our food fresh. Nearby was a small stream, not completely frozen, from which we hauled back buckets of water.

We stayed Friday and Saturday night. Each morning we walked down to the train shed, crossed the tracks, and walked to the Sugar Bowl ski resort. It was brand new, having just opened in December 1939. Sugar Bowl was the first ski resort in California to have a chairlift. However, I could not afford the lift, so I used the rope tow.

It was really the only good alpine skiing in the Northern Sierra Nevada mountains at the time. Highway 80 wouldn't be constructed until 1964, so Highway 40 was the hub for winter sports.

Also during the spring of 1940, I became reacquainted with Alfred Hertz and his wife, whom I had met at Mrs. Haas's party. They were with another couple and were getting ready for a hike up Mount Tamalpais in Marin County, north of San Francisco. "Would you care to join us?" Mr. Hertz asked.

It was a rare day off, and I gratefully accepted the offer. We took a bus to a German restaurant about half way up the mountain where we had refreshments and talked. It reminded me of the *hütte* at the peak of Schneekoppe. I had no idea such a place existed in America. Then, we all hiked up to the top of Mount Tamalpais. It was quite beautiful.

Before going our separate ways Mr. Hertz told me to call him. When I did, he and his wife hired me to design a garden at their home in Sea Cliff.

Right on the ocean in San Francisco, the site presented an interesting challenge. I had to find plants that could survive the wind and salt air. The Hertzes were a good contact for me since Mr. Hertz was so well known and had a wide circle of friends.

Finally by May 1940, I had raised enough money for Mother's affidavit and opened up a Wells Fargo bank account. This would provide an official record of the money. I wrote to my mother encouraging her to do all she could on her end with the paperwork, knowing how hard it had been for me and that it was becoming more difficult to leave Germany every day.

One day, early in the summer of 1940, I received a letter from Mother. My father had been released from a camp again and returned to Oma's house, but he was not well. Mother was taking care of him while also trying to earn a living. By then, Denmark, Norway, Holland, and Belgium had fallen to Hitler's relentless war machine. In France, the Nazis would occupy Paris by mid-June. There was no good news coming from Europe. Even more, the United States, fearing that enemy spies might enter America, had significantly reduced the number of visas to be issued in 1940; the majority of them were given to German Jews already outside of Germany. The U.S. had also added requirements, including proof of permission to leave Germany and proof the prospective immigrant had booked passage to the Western Hemisphere. It still was possible to get my mother to America, but it was getting more unlikely every day. It was hard not to feel helpless. All I could do was keep working and saving money.

That summer, two ladies hired me to design large perennial borders around their home on University Avenue in Palo Alto. It was more than one hundred feet long on both sides of the house, a huge amount of space to dress with plants. I knew my perennials well, so I was able to create a border that was in bloom year round. I certainly couldn't conduct an orchestra like Mr. Hertz, but I could conduct a perennial garden. I purchased the plants and installed them myself. It turned out so well, they told others about it, resulting in more design work.

In Berkeley, there were a number of German immigrants who came from Hamburg, and I was invited a number of times for Sunday afternoon *Kaffeeklatsch*. I met Mrs. F. Walton who was having her home — at 1521 La Loma Avenue in Berkeley — designed by Oskar Gerson, a refugee architect from Blankenese near Hamburg, where the Salomons had lived. Mrs. Walton needed a landscape architect to collaborate with her architect and design the house's garden. Working with Oskar was a delight, and I could barely contain my excitement. It was my first totally new project in the United States and the genuine beginning of my career in landscape architecture. Because of my commute, Mrs. Walton offered me a room to stay over as needed, which was very kind. We had dinner together, along with Mrs. Walton's daughter, who was a little older than I. We enjoyed each other's company and often took excursions to the World's Fair. There was no courting involved; we were more like brother and sister.

I gradually acquired other design-oriented jobs. I dropped most of my garden maintenance clients in favor of those who needed design work, for which my expertise was truly needed. This was much more enjoyable and profitable.

In addition to corresponding regularly with Mother and Aunt Martha, I also wrote to George Salomon and my old friend, Lore. She and her cousin and his family had successfully immigrated in 1939 to Louisville, Kentucky, via South America. I was always eager to receive her letters. All were signed, "With love, Lore." I was still quite naïve in the ways of women and love. I was under the impression that if you signed a letter "With love," it was literally what you meant. I was quite pleased this beautiful girl was in love with me. I was earning a steady income now, and I was tired of being alone. In December 1940, I decided to drive to Louisville and ask Lore to marry me.

The Louisville trip was going to be lengthy; but since there was no landscape work during the rainy season, it was easy to take time off. I wrote and told her I was coming for a visit, but didn't tell her why. If I was going to propose, I felt I had to plan to stay for a couple of months until we came back to California together.

On my way to Louisville, I stopped at Donner Lake Resort in the Sierras and skied for a few days. A couple named Herbert and Ollie Brook, who had come from Vienna, were operating the resort for the season. We sat talking in the lodge that first afternoon, and I told Ollie what I was about to do.

She was silent for a moment. "Have you actually said anything yet to Lore about marriage?"

"No," I said.

"I would suggest you write Lore a letter today and tell her of your intentions."

I mailed the letter the following morning.

In the meantime, the Brooks offered me a bed in the dormitory for thirty-five dollars a week and free meals if I would drive their station wagon to pick up guests at the Truckee train station. In addition, I drove skiers up to Donner Summit, so they could walk to Sugar Bowl. I also received free tickets for the Sugar Bowl lift. Occasionally, I would get a tip for taking care of a guest's luggage.

I extended my stay, managing to squeeze in a fair amount of skiing. I regularly walked up to the top of Mount Lincoln and skied down to Donner Lake.

After a bit more than a week, I received an answer from Lore. This was quite prompt.

"Dear Ernst, I am so sorry to disappoint you, but I am engaged to be married to my cousin. The wedding will likely take place this summer."

Lore continued, telling me how much my friendship meant to her and she hoped we would always stay in touch.

That was the end of my trip to Louisville.

Instead, I stayed at the Donner Lake Resort for two months. It was fantastic. I made some lifelong friends during this period. We skied together and celebrated the New Year together as well. Among them were a handful of young professionals from Los Angeles who, like me, had escaped from the Nazis. There were also several families from Vienna who knew each other and had come together to ski. Having emigrated earlier than I, most of them had brought their money out of Germany or Austria and had a much easier time than I did. Several of the professionals were architects. One was Paul Laszlo, a Hungarian-born contemporary architect and interior designer, who in 1936 left behind rising career in Stuttgart, Germany. He had set up a Beverly Hills office and was already very well known, popular with the wealthy, political and acting elite.

"Come to LA," said an American trained architect named Keith. There was plenty of work there in the sunshine he said; landscape architects were doing well in Southern California. I remembered receiving similar advice from Victor the day I had arrived in California. Keith gave me his office address and phone number. "Let me know when you get into Hollywood, and we'll have lunch together."

I had only one suitcase with me, plus my skis. That night in the dorms, I thought, well, the Palo Alto work is on hold during the wet season. I have my car. I can always drive back. I decided to head south.

The next day I made plans to caravan down with my new friends, Gottfried Reinhardt and his wife. Gottfried was a pleasant fellow, born in Berlin, with a thick mane of wavy, brown hair. He left Germany in 1932 and became a director and producer in Hollywood. His father, Max Reinhardt, followed him soon thereafter. Max also made his mark in Hollywood. Gottfried was working for Metro-Goldwyn-Mayer studios and had just produced his first film, *Comrade X*, starring Greta Garbo, Clark Gable, and Hedy Lamarr. He told terrific stories of the actors and their personalities.

Gottfried and his wife decided to return to Los Angeles by way of Route 395 and Conway Summit near Mono Lake. They had driven along the California coast most of the way up and wanted to see more of the state, plus they wanted to ski Conway Summit.

I drove my Dodge coup behind them until we got to Conway. Since we had two cars, we parked one at the base and drove the other car up to the top of the summit road, where we took a short rope tow and then climbed the rest of the way up. We skied down a marvelously long way in six inches of new powder.

The next day I found my way from Highways 395 and 14 to Sepulveda Boulevard (now Highway 405) and turned onto Highway 101 and into Hollywood. I called Keith from the road, and we scheduled to meet at his office at noon for lunch. I arrived right on time and entered a room with a very high ceiling, lots of light, and a number of simple drafting tables. Everything was very informal.

My friend was busy at his drafting table and jumped up to greet me with great delight, "I am so glad you came. Ernest, how was the skiing? Listen, I have a great job in Beverly Hills, but I cannot get a building permit without a landscape plan. Would you consider doing this for me? You can work in this office. I have a free table."

Of course I said yes.

Instead of going out for lunch, we got into Keith's car and drove out Sunset Boulevard to Beverly Hills. The job was on a pleasant street planted with Jacaranda trees that were just coming into bloom, with their lovely fern-like foliage and abundance of delicate, lavender flowers. I had never seen such a tree before. The house was about one hundred feet from the sidewalk. It was a rather good-sized home, with a Spanish-style tile roof and covered porches, but it did not dominate the property because the lot was large enough to feel like a park.

It was my job to locate the pool, the bathhouse, the paved area around the pool, and a sitting area with surrounding gardens. It was a large property with ample room for gardens in a wonderful neighborhood, and I was going to design it.

I was delighted. I had done nothing of this size since I had come to California. My friend offered me a lump sum for the work which appeared, to me at least, rather generous.

We never got around to having lunch.

My friend suggested I stay at the Roosevelt Hotel, which was close to his office and to Hollywood Boulevard. I worked all afternoon before heading to the hotel.

The room was a bit expensive, but I had nowhere else to stay, so I splurged. Lying in bed, sleep coming fast, I thought about my situation. I realized this new project would take some time to complete. The timing would be tricky, but I could get back to Palo Alto in time for the late spring season of 1941. I yawned and fell asleep, not knowing that my life had just completely changed course.

CHAPTER 8

Sometimes a Dandelion is not a Weed

Taraxacum officinale (common dandelion)
Photo by Stephen Rees © 123RF.com

My first morning in Southern California during March of 1941, I was up bright and early to start working on the design of the Beverly Hills garden. Back in Keith's office, I quickly realized the site plan I was provided did not have enough information. I needed to go back to the job site to gather information about existing conditions and take photographs.

Vine Street, Hollywood, looking north from Sunset Blvd, early morning, 1939

Afterwards, I decided to continue on to the Brentwood neighborhood, only a short jaunt by car. I had the address of a lady named Esther, a dear friend of Oma's, who had immigrated years earlier.

I arrived at a wonderful, ranch-style house with a pretty garden, just off of Sunset Boulevard. When Esther came to the door, I told her who I was. She was most delighted and asked me to stay for lunch. She asked about my grandmother and mother as well as my journey and work. After lunch, another gentleman rang her doorbell.

"Oh good, I wanted to introduce you," said Esther.

The man was her gardener, Rudi Brook. Rudi was also a German refugee. In Germany he had been a judge, but it was impossible for him to become an attorney in California without going back to school to learn the American legal system. Instead he went into the landscape maintenance business.

When Rudi heard I had just arrived in Los Angeles, he told me he had a room for rent. He lived in the Hollywood Hills, rather close to the office of my architect friend. I took the room sight unseen, pleased to know I would have a roof over my head at a reasonable price. The Roosevelt Hotel was far too expensive for me.

The following evening I followed Rudi's directions to his home. Rudi introduced me to his wife, Eva, and showed me my room. It was simple and small, nine feet by twelve feet, with a bed, a closet for my clothes, a couple of chairs, and a radio. I shared the bathroom with the family. There was a nice window, which looked out toward other well-kept houses in the neighborhood.

On the first Sunday after I arrived, Eva invited me to *Kaffeeklatsch*. She hosted one every Sunday afternoon for their large group of German friends with coffee and tea, pastries, black forest cake, and good conversation. Rudi had asked for my help planting a large tree for one of his clients, which was a rather labor-intensive operation that took longer than expected. By the time we returned, all the other guests had arrived. When Rudi and I showed up, we looked quite dirty and were in need of a shower; however, since Rudi was very popular with the group, we decided to skip our primping. Rudi introduced me to his business partner in his gardening enterprise, another Jewish refugee named Fred Odenheimer, a nice fellow. We made a little small talk, and then Fred introduced me to his sister, a pretty young brunette named Margrit. I was unaware that Eva had casually planned to set us up, as we were roughly the same age and younger than everyone else at the gathering.

I do not recall what she was wearing — most likely plain slacks — however I remember very clearly that she was soft spoken, quite shy, and had stunning blue eyes. Our conversation was fairly dull. We talked about the various cakes on the table: lemon meringue, chocolate cake with buttercream frosting, and coconut pound cake. At the time, no one discussed calories or nutrition. I felt awkward because of my disheveled appearance. In all honesty, I was much more interested in meeting the other guests. Most of them were European immigrants, who had worked to reestablish their careers in the United States. Many had come years earlier with some funds from their homeland, but they all had struggled to make a living. I was very interested to hear how they had done it, and I was also eager to ask them about acquiring visas and the logistics of bringing over family members.

Margrit

The next morning, unbeknownst to me, Eva called Margrit and told her I had raved about her after she left. This was not true because we had spent hardly any time talking to each other with so many other guests whom I was keen to meet. Eva told me Margrit had noticed me, but I thought I couldn't have made much of an impression, so disheveled from tree planting. I was not aware Mrs. Brook was a matchmaker.

Margrit decided to take another look. Eva suggested she come by to deliver the photographs she had taken of the Brooks' children. She lived only a short distance away. When she arrived we all looked at the wonderful pictures. She was a very talented, young photographer.

We were very proper with one another. I was getting ready to go to Beverly Hills and asked Margrit if she would be interested in accompanying me to see my garden design project. She agreed to come along.

On the way back we stopped for lunch. I asked about her family. The Odenheimers had come to the United States in a gradual wave. The first to arrive was Margrit's sister, Lotti. She was fortunate to be invited by an exchange student who had stayed with the Odenheimers at their home in Emmendingen, Germany. Lotti stayed in New York City for a while and then moved to Hollywood, where she taught piano and voice. Fred had gone to the Netherlands and learned his father's tobacco business. His associates in the U.S. sent him an affidavit allowing him to immigrate, at first settling in Connecticut. Margrit and her mother immigrated to Hollywood in 1937. Fred joined them in Southern California, and they built a house with money their father had left for them after his death. Margrit attended high school in Hollywood for her final two years. I learned her birthday was May 29, 1921. She was two-and-a-half years younger than me.

I also learned Margrit loved to ski. Emmendingen is situated southwest of the Black Forest mountain range in southwestern Germany, and the Odenheimer children grew up skiing in the foothills. Margrit was somewhat shy and didn't call much attention to herself in everyday circumstances, but on the ski hill, as I soon would discover, it was a different story. I told her about my recent skiing adventures at Sugar Bowl near Donner Summit and on Conway Summit. Her blue eyes sparkled.

"I will only marry a man who will take me skiing for the rest of my life," she said.

When the bill came, I looked in my wallet. I had forgotten to bring money. The only things in it were the two special two-dollar bills from Gladys I was saving for good luck. I had to ask Margrit to pay for lunch, promising to pay her back, which I did.

Margrit and I started dating. I do not think we fell in love right away, but our mutual love of skiing created interest in one another. From this grew a friendship.

Margrit

One day we went for a hike in the Hollywood Hills. We lost track of time. It was growing dark fast, so I suggested we return by heading straight downhill, ignoring the switchbacks of the path. Unfortunately, we went through some poison oak. Normally, I would have instructed Margrit to take her clothes off and wash herself as soon as she got home, but I simply couldn't bring myself to speak of such personal matters.

Poor Margrit woke up the next day with the worst case of poison oak I had ever seen. She had broken out all over her body and was really suffering. It put her in a sick bed under the doctor's care for two weeks. I thought this might be the end of our budding relationship.

I went to visit her and brought her the most beautiful flowers I could find: giant blue delphiniums — big and full with velvety stocks — from the Vetterle and Reinelt Nursery. They were special because Frank Reinelt had just hybridized them. She looked at them silently, with a slight frown, before thanking me politely.

"What's wrong?" I asked. "Don't you like them?"

Margrit admitted she liked smaller, simpler flowers best, "I like dandelions," she said. Despite having offended her with delphiniums, she must have liked me well enough because she asked me to come back and visit her again.

I could actually see Margrit's house from my bedroom window. As we got to know each other better, we sometimes communicated at night via a strong flashlight. I had not planned on staying in Los Angeles for long, but now, there was a very good reason to extend my stay. I wrote to Mother and told her about Margrit. Mother responded positively, which was typical of her warm nature.

We were still waiting for Mother's number to come up and every day there was more news of the war raging in Europe. In her last letter she mentioned Gladys, who was still renting a room from Oma even though there was no longer an American ambassador in Berlin. Ambassador Wilson had been recalled to the U.S. in November 1938 for urgent discussions following *Kristallnacht,* and he never went back to Germany. Since then, a U.S. Chargé d'Affaires had been assigned to look over the embassy. Gladys stayed until the Nazis took Oma's apartment and forced them out. To my best understanding, this happened in the second half of 1940 or the beginning of 1941, the details muddled by the chaos of the times. I also came to learn that Mother's letters did not always share exactly what her life was like, perhaps to protect me from the pain it would have caused.

I wrote Mother weekly but mail took a long time to get from Los Angeles to Berlin and back again. Letters were not thought to be censored, and Mother probably could have told me as much as she wanted. However, we were trained to be careful because one never really knew when the Nazis would read your mail. Even in the peaceful sunshine of Southern California, our immigrant community constantly thought about the despair and destruction taking place in Europe. At Rudi's home, there was much discussion about the situation. People would get mail from various countries describing the war and conditions in Europe, and new refugees kept showing up.

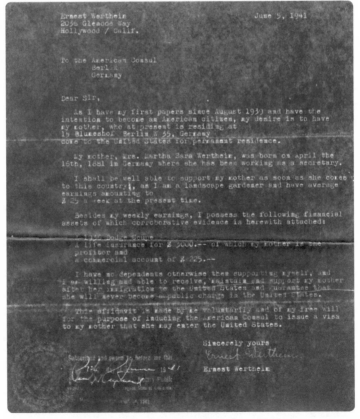

Letter to the American Consulate, 1941

I started looking for additional work designing gardens since I was going to stay in the Los Angeles area, but this was not easy. I did not know many people. I contacted my skiing friends from Donner Lake, Hans and Ini Strakosch. They were building a house in Pacific Palisades, not far from Santa Monica. Paul Laszlo, who I also met at Donner Lake, had designed their house. Hans and Ini hired me to design their garden, and I had the opportunity to work with Paul. It was a tremendous learning experience. The Strakosch garden was a bank and a hillside; the property had a level area with a beautiful view and another hillside beyond. Working with Paul, the project architect, I developed an informal planting plan, created shaded areas, and put in Arizona flagstone for the patio. The garden turned out very nicely. As a result I did several other projects in the neighborhood, including — years later and after the war — a garden for Thomas Mann, the famous author who had come to the United States in 1939 and to California in 1942.

I decided to form a small landscape-contracting firm so I could not only design gardens but also install them. I established a bank account at the Beverly Hills National Bank and Trust with only a hundred dollars. It wasn't much. Nonetheless, the president of the bank welcomed me and took great care to make me feel at home, even though I was just a very small customer. Probably because of this extra attention, I kept this account for many years even when I no longer lived there. The bank was finally taken over by Wells Fargo.

In order to have success with my new firm, I was missing one skill. In Los Angeles, gardens required irrigation. This was something I had not learned about in Germany with its abundance of rain. For a while, I sketched designs at night while working part-time during the day for an irrigation contractor so I could learn how to design irrigation systems. I learned how to put pipes together and how to space sprinklers according to their performance. I learned about the need for a backflow prevention valve and how to use a controller, which was a brand new invention. The most important lessons were to calculate the pipe sizes and how many sprinklers each valve could support. Today most people would hire an irrigation consultant, but at the time, I had to educate myself as I worked through the design.

I found more work as time went on. Besides jobs through my Donner Lake friends, I started developing friendships with a number of other people. I traveled to the better subdivisions around Los Angeles County, observing workers and contractors until I found Harold, who worked hard and knew what he was doing. I introduced myself. After we became further acquainted, I asked him if he wanted to be the foreman for the construction of gardens I would design. He agreed, and this arrangement worked out well during the second half of 1941. We kept ourselves very busy.

While doing these rounds, I also met Cliff May, a developer working just east of Pacific Palisades. He would become best known and remembered for developing the suburban, postwar, dream house, the California ranch house. He also went on to design the *Sunset Magazine* building in Menlo Park. He asked me to landscape his home garden. The front garden was very simple with a vast lawn and low plantings that stretched along the house, understated so they would not hide the architecture of the house itself. We used *Trachelospermum jasminoides* (star jasmine), both as a vine and as a groundcover, along with *Pelargonium peltatum* (ivy geraniums), which came in several colors and would bloom for months in the warm climate. Both *Lantana montevidensis* (trailing lantana or weeping lantana) and *Bougainvillea* (bougainvillea) also gave bloom for several months, and they, too, were incorporated into the plantings. We also used *Daphne odora marginata* (winter daphne), near the entrance for its fragrance, along with *Citrus x meyeri* (dwarf Meyer lemon), *Choisya ternata* (Mexican orange), and *Bouvardia* (bouvardia). After the end of the Second World War, Cliff May's garden would appear on the cover of *Life Magazine*.

Landscape firms in Southern California used *Hedera canariensis* (Canary Island ivy), as a quick groundcover because it required very little water and grew fast. As I gained experience, I learned my German clients disliked ivy because it was too closely associated with death and cemeteries. I thought of Opa's grave. I explored substitutes, such as *Hibiscus* (hibiscus) and *Nerium oleander* (oleander). Roses were very popular, and most ladies wanted the roses in their gardens to cut for the house. I placed roses against the house with a boxwood hedge as an edging. I preferred to use one or two varieties so the bed was very orderly.

In order to install gardens, I had to have plants. This required money to purchase the plants, which I didn't have much of, so I established credit with the local nurseries. One of these places was Evans and Reeves in Westwood, not far from the UCLA campus. Mr. Hugh Evans was a first class plantsman with great horticultural knowledge, and we really hit it off. His nursery worked frequently with Hollywood movie stars. This connection created multiple relationships lasting a lifetime. Hugh Evans had two sons closer to my age, Jack and Bill. Both men were well trained in plants and landscape design. Jack died at an early age, while Bill was hired by Walt Disney to transform eighty acres of Anaheim orange groves into a lush theme park filled with tropical plants. During his many years with Disney, Bill was also chief landscape architect of Disney World and EPCOT Center, as well as Disney Paris, Tokyo, and Hong Kong. Hugh Evans took me out to several of his projects, talking me through the designs and the plant material used. In turn, I would share with him my design experience. My friendship with Hugh developed during these projects. Before the war, I was not well acquainted with either Bill or Jack; this came later when I would become even more active in the California Horticultural Society.

Margrit worked for a photographer who provided contacts for me. Both of us had a little spending money, enabling us to have a pleasant social life. We often went to double features at the movies. We especially enjoyed going to a drive-in restaurant for milkshakes.

Photo of me by Margrit, 1941

In March 1941, Margrit and I went skiing together for the first time near June Lake in Mono County. I had heard the mountains were good for skiing in the eastern Sierra Nevada, not far from Yosemite, in what is now the Mammoth Mountain Ski Area. The ski area did not exist at the time so our plan was to climb the mountains, perhaps even to the top of 10,909-foot Carson Peak, and ski back down.

Since her mother would not allow us to stay overnight, I picked her up at one o'clock in the morning, and we drove all night. We had a glorious time, skiing all day long. Margrit was a terrific skier and enjoyed the exertion of the climbing as well. After our last run, we drove home again, eight hours with one stop for dinner.

As we neared Los Angeles, I became very sleepy and had to stop for a while. I certainly didn't want to endanger either of us. This meant we did not arrive back at Margrit's house until well after midnight, which was several hours later than I had promised. Mrs. Odenheimer waited up for us, and boy, did she give us a dressing down for being late. Mrs. Odenheimer may have had her doubts about me, but after that trip, Margrit was convinced I was a suitable boyfriend. We courted all through the spring and summer.

One day in August 1941, I called and told her to dress up. "I am taking you out to dinner, it's a celebration."

"A celebration of what?" she asked.

"I will tell you when we are there."

I picked her up, and we went to a Swedish restaurant where they served a smorgasbord, which was very helpful with a small food budget.

After we helped ourselves to dessert and were sitting back down at our table, with its flickering candle reflecting off the china plates that held our cake and pastries, I said, "You must have wondered what the special occasion is."

"Yes," she said.

I pulled out a black velvet box from my pocket and opened it to reveal a small ring. I couldn't afford a diamond so it was just a simple, shiny gold band. Margrit let me put it on her finger.

"I promise I will take you skiing for the rest of your life," I said, holding her ringed-hand across the table. "What do you say?"

Margrit smiled at me, her eyes sparkling, and nodded.

We were both very excited. Margrit, who didn't like glittery or elaborate things, appreciated the simplicity of her band, a dandelion in the jewelry world, I suppose.

Our engagement would have to remain a secret for the time being. Her mother did not think I was good enough for her daughter, maybe because my shoes needed new soles. I always helped clear and clean the dishes after a meal, which I think made somewhat of an impression on Mrs. Odenheimer; however, this was clearly not enough to qualify me as a good husband. I needed more time to prove myself as a provider.

I felt joy in my life, but it was often clouded over when I thought of Mother. She finally received a letter from the U.S. government granting her an immigration visa. My affidavit of support had gone through, but the American embassy in Berlin was closed. The British Royal Air Force had started attacks on Berlin in 1940. Sometime in 1941, the embassy was hit. Mother was told to pick up her visa for the United States in Switzerland or a similar country. This was impossible because she needed a visa to go to any of those countries, and none were available to her. She came up with the idea of applying for a visa to Italy since it was allied with Germany. I arranged for her to ship all her furniture to Genoa, where it was placed in temporary storage. I also booked passage on an Italian liner to the United States. This was one of her last options because in June, Hitler broke his pact with Stalin and invaded Russia and other republics in the Soviet Union; therefore, going east was not an option.

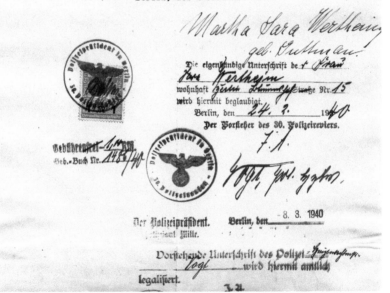

The list of my mother's belongings, 1940

The Italian visa led to a dead end, so we searched for another solution. Mother had heard from other refugees that you could go through Cuba to immigrate to the United States. I started investigating the process as soon as I received her letter suggesting the idea. At the time, the United States had a consulate in Cuba. From Havana, she could sail to America. The hard thing was finding an attorney in Cuba who was willing to handle this. There were many deals made under the table, which allowed me to purchase a visa for her to enter Cuba for three thousand dollars. I asked several friends for a loan and sent the money. I wrote to Mother with the news, and we waited.

Meanwhile Mother and I continued to write each other. She told me in one letter that starting September 1, 1941, all Jewish people had to wear a yellow Star of David on their clothing with the word *Jude* inscribed in the middle.

In another particular letter that arrived via a friend of my mother's, Mrs. Falkenberg, Mother told me she and my father had gotten a divorce. She wrote, "It needed to be done. Don't blame your father." She said the Nazis insisted she and my father be divorced in order for her to leave Germany by herself. After his arrest on *Kristallnacht* in November of 1938, my father had been sent back to Berlin some months later and forced to work in slave labor as a street sweeper. As best as I could decipher, he might have been in and out of prison work camps a couple of times since then. The divorce had become official on August 6, 1940, but Mother had waited quite some time to tell me. She waited some time to tell me many things it seemed.

Since I was so close to Mother, the news of the divorce affected me deeply. In some ways I felt Mother had been deserted. On the other hand, she had taken care of herself and her family for so long without my father's presence or assistance. I decided to treat it as just another thing that happened and to believe Mother's reasoning.

On Sunday, December 7, 1941, Margrit and I drove to Mount Baldy, east of Los Angeles in the national forest, for a day of skiing. Since there were no ski lifts, we climbed to the top where we had a leisurely lunch before we skied down.

It was about four thirty in the afternoon when we returned to my car, the sun low near the horizon. We were about an hour away from home, and I was determined to get Margrit back on time. Once on the highway, she switched on the radio. She liked to listen to classical music in the car. Instead, we heard nothing but news broadcasts. The Japanese had bombed Pearl Harbor on the island of Oahu in Hawaii.

The announcement made me sick to my stomach. If the United States was at war with Japan, it was also at war with Germany because in September 1940, Germany, Italy, and Japan had signed the Tripartite Pact. In the coming weeks, they would be referred to as the Axis alliance.

Mother's Cuban visa had not arrived. Now, I no longer had any way to help her. Margrit, seeming to read my mind, gently squeezed my shoulder.

We caught up on all the news as we drove. The first reports to the public were broadcast while we were climbing the mountain. San Francisco declared a state of emergency. The radio instructed people to turn off lights. The government was afraid of an attack from the Pacific.

That evening in Hollywood and all along the Pacific Coast, we pinned up dark paper and heavy drapes, whatever we could find, for a mandatory black out. Unless we had justified business, all citizens were instructed to stay in their houses with lights off or blacked out windows until thirty minutes after daylight the next day. Many people in Los Angeles and San Francisco listened for the sound of airplanes. Luckily, they did not come.

The following day, President Roosevelt made his famous pronouncement. "Yesterday, December 7, 1941, a date which will live in infamy, the United States of America was suddenly and deliberately attacked by naval and air forces of the Empire of Japan."

Though the numbers didn't come right away, a day or two after the bombing we learned eight battleships in Pearl Harbor were damaged, with five sunk. Three destroyers and six other vessels were lost along with almost two hundred aircraft. The casualty list totaled 2,335 servicemen and sixty-eight civilians killed, with 1,178 Americans wounded.

On December 11, Germany and Italy declared war on the United States. The European and Western Pacific wars merged to become a global conflict with the Axis powers of Japan, Germany, and Italy against America, Britain, France, and their allies. America closed its borders to the Japanese and Germans.

I had three goals when I immigrated to America — to make a living, to become a citizen, and to bring Mother to my newly adopted country. The latter was now impossible for me to accomplish. I had paid for the shipping of her belongings, her passage on the liner, and her affidavit and visas. All the money and property were now lost.

Worse though, much worse, was that after December 7, 1941, there was no more direct communication between Germany and the United States. I no longer received letters from Mother. We were completely separated, now and forever.

Some of these things I want to forget — all of my experiences in Germany, my inability to get Mother out in time, losing so many friends and family, and a disappearance of a way of life. Between March and December of 1941, I had seen a doctor who told me I should forget the troubles in Germany, and much of the time, I have been able to do so.

The fact I was in love with Margrit also changed things. When you're attracted to another person, the excitement occupies your mind. For me, falling in love was burdened with confusion and heartache. Margrit and I would go out to a movie or buy a milkshake at the drive-in — romantic things — and I would think, should I really be doing this? Shouldn't this money go into the bank for Mother? My love for Mother was very strong, but not the same feeling I had for my girlfriend. In retrospect, I believe I did not devote enough attention to preparing things for Mother. I was, perhaps, sidetracked by my work and on developing my relationship with Margrit. There are too many unknowns, too many external forces to account for when trying to understand if things would have been different had my efforts been more singularly focused.

These days, I rarely speak in German. When Margrit's mother was getting older and seemed to be slowing down, she would surprise us by reciting poems in flawless German. Sometimes when I can't think of a word in English, it comes back crystal clear in German. It's all down there, hidden, and it surfaces at funny times and with mixed emotions.

Just a few days after Pearl Harbor, I received my draft notice. I was to report for duty in the United States Army on February 3, 1942. Like everyone else I had been required to register for the draft on my twenty-first birthday in 1940, even though I was not yet a citizen. I had procured a draft deferment because of the responsibility for my mother. With this responsibility forcibly gone, my deferment had been cancelled.

Immediately after the bombing of Pearl Harbor, President Roosevelt issued Presidential Proclamations 2525, 2526, and 2527 to authorize the United States to detain potentially dangerous enemy aliens. This branded German, Italian, and Japanese nationals as "enemy aliens," authorizing internment as well as travel and property ownership restrictions. The Department of Justice (DOJ) formed its Alien Enemy Control Unit. Tens of thousands of German, Italian, and Japanese aliens were ultimately arrested. It was a period of great uncertainty.

On January 14, 1942, President Roosevelt issued Presidential Proclamation 2537, requiring aliens from the enemy countries — Italy, Germany, and Japan — to register with the DOJ. Such persons were then issued a Certificate of Identification for Aliens of Enemy Nationality. As a follow-up to the Alien Registration Act of 1940, Proclamation 2537 facilitated the beginning of full-scale internment of Japanese Americans the following month. About one hundred and ten thousand Japanese-Americans would be placed into camps.

The tragedy of the Japanese-American internment camps is widely known, although still underrepresented in U.S. history. It was terrible. Less well known is that the U.S. government ended up interning over eleven thousand persons of German ancestry, as well as many Italians, too. For those not interned at a camp, enemy aliens could not enter federally designated restricted areas. As a result, thousands of people, now classified as enemy aliens, living in areas adjacent to shipyards, docks, power plants, and defense factories had to find new homes. I never thought I would see this in America. Getting my enemy alien registration card felt eerily similar to the "J" on my German passport.

Although not interned or displaced, Margrit's family had to turn in their cameras and other similar items to the government. We were told any change of address, employment or name must be reported to the FBI.

We were still very fortunate, more so than those sent to internment camps, who experienced such harsh discrimination and exclusion. I could still continue to run my business with my current customers, and Margrit and I could still go skiing.

About the middle of January, with her mother's permission, Margrit and I drove up to Soda Springs for three days of skiing near Donner Summit. By then, I think Mrs. Odenheimer knew she could trust me to be respectful of her daughter. Maybe her decision had to do with knowing this would be our last ski trip together before I would become a soldier.

We earned free skiing in Soda Springs, close to Sugar Bowl, by helping Ollie and Herb Brook address and stuff envelopes with an announcement letting their customers know they would be running the Soda Springs Hotel during the winter of 1941-42, undeterred by the war. Margrit stayed in the women's dormitory, and I stayed in the men's dormitory. We were very proper. This was her first visit to the mountains on Highway 40 near Donner Summit, and she loved it. The snowfall was abundant that winter, and the skiing was great. We were able to laugh and ski and forget about my imminent departure.

The day we were to leave, and after we had already checked out, we decided to play the slot machines in the lobby, just for fun. I placed a nickel into one of the machines and won the jackpot. We went back to the front desk and registered for another two nights.

Back in Los Angeles, I had three gardens under construction. Luckily, I had an excellent foreman in Harold. I decided to turn over the business to him, letting him have all the profits from these jobs. I felt it was more important to satisfy my clients than take profit for myself. I visited all the nurseries to which I owed money and explained I had been drafted, but I would pay them back a small amount at a time.

I said goodbye to my friends in Los Angeles. I left my car with Margrit, as well as my other belongings.

On February 3, 1942, we hugged goodbye. It was not easy. Margrit was my first real girlfriend and now my wife-to-be; yet we did not know what would happen in the future. I didn't want to let her go once she was in my arms. For a young man, I had already endured so many painful and uncertain farewells.

Then, it was my turn to board the bus to the recruitment center in downtown Los Angeles, where I would become a United States enemy alien soldier.

CHAPTER 9
The Prettiest Lawn In Fort Sill

Lawn
Photo by Michael Ploujnikov

My first day in the United States Army was very strange. I was told, in a rather public format, to strip down for a medical examination. Toilets and showers were all open as well. Even the dormitories at the *Gartenbauschule* had been private compared to this. We listened to an orientation — much as one might expect from a scene in a movie — and were assigned footlockers, the only place in the entire camp that resembled anything like privacy.

"If anything is stolen from your footlocker, you will be court-marshaled," said the sergeant, to emphasize that if a soldier left his footlocker open he created the temptation for theft and had to take the responsibility.

The officers interviewed each of us to see where we might best serve. There was much discussion among the new recruits about what we wanted our assignment to be. I knew I did not want to be in the cavalry. I wanted nothing to do with horses or mules; I did not like my experience at Ahlem when we had to guide horses through the rows of trees. Horses and I did not get along very well. There was also the memory of the human waste we brought out into the fields by horse and wagon — that awful smell and the fear of excrement pouring out on you when opening the spout of the tank. My desire was to get into the ski or parachute troops.

By afternoon, once declared healthy, we were sworn in. This ceremony was rather impressive. It created great pride in having been accepted into the U.S. Army, entrusted to bring peace to the nation.

At about 1330, we had our first meal. We were all starving by this time, especially after waiting in line for so long. The food was bland, salty, and mushy. But we were young and needed sustenance, so we wolfed it down anyway.

I was assigned to field artillery, and the very next day, Uncle Sam shipped me out on a troop train to Fort Sill, Oklahoma, for three months of basic training. My life was suddenly so different from the one I had known in the winter sunshine of Los Angeles while building a thriving business and falling in love. I had no choice but to be on that jostling train, in a new, stiff uniform. In such a foreign situation, I did what I've always done, engage the people around me and make the best of it.

To accommodate the many waves of draftees coming through Fort Sill, new wooden barracks had been quickly built. The long, simple, prefab buildings were thirty-five by one hundred feet and about forty feet apart. There were beds against the walls on both sides and a long aisle through the center that allowed officers to inspect their enlisted men's uniforms, postures, and trunks. Each sergeant had a private bedroom at the entrance, which we had no choice but to pass when entering or leaving the barracks. One of the first things they trained us to do was to salute and say, "Yes Sir!"

At dusk we were summoned out onto the parade ground and watched the flag be lowered for the night. Gathering everyone to witness this ceremony was intended to build pride, camaraderie, and a sense of purpose. Yet as I saluted the red, white, and blue flag coming down the pole, I felt yearning and conflict. I was German, but I wanted so desperately to be recognized as American, to feel American. How American could I be after three years in this country? Looking around at my fellow trainees, I thought, *Am I one of them or am I the enemy? Am I both? How will they see me?* I certainly couldn't hide my accent or my name.

Luckily, we were kept so busy in those first few weeks my accent didn't seem to matter to anyone. We were all under incredible pressure to learn and perform the simplest tasks with precision. For example, when making our beds, it had to be just so. If someone did not do it right, he had to do thirty push-ups in front of all the other men. There was an officer who would inspect our daily tasks, including the cleaning of our rifles, which — like everything else — needed to be perfect. I had an advantage over most of the other fellows because the Nazis taught me how to clean and carry a rifle during my last year in *Oberrealschule*. Of course, I didn't tell anyone in basic where I had learned this skill. The Nazis also taught me how to shoot a rifle, but not accurately. This detail I learned at Fort Sill.

Every day we awoke at 0530, dressed quickly, and reported to the parade grounds for exercise. We then showered, made our beds, and went to breakfast. During the first few days we learned to march and our trainers worked to get everybody into shape as quickly as possible. We ran an obstacle course, practiced loading and shooting our guns, learned to climb over walls, and to carry heavy loads on our backs. During the first week or two, we lost some people because they were just not able to take the rigors of training, either physically or mentally.

After our group "looked more like soldiers," the officers introduced us to the big artillery guns, and we learned how to operate them: loading, shooting, cleaning, and transporting.

Like most of Oklahoma, the parade ground was a dusty, windy, flat expanse of land. As we marched and jogged in formation, we kicked up terrible clouds of dirt that had everyone choking and coughing. Fort Sill authorities decided to plant grass to keep the dust down. Though my company captain read on my record I was a landscape architect, he had no idea what that was and simply assigned me to a wheelbarrow detail. Our first job was to create a level area and import planting soil to bring everything to a grade that would drain. It became obvious no one in our crew knew how to do this job. I explained to the captain I was trained in this field and he said, "Okay, you're in charge."

After the grading was finished, we had to prepare a good seed bed. The soil we imported for the lawn was quite sandy with little humus. I suggested to the captain we add manure, which I knew was sitting piled up outside the stables. I recommended we request a load of it from the cavalry, turn it several times, after which it would become valuable compost material. Once our request was granted, we worked it into our seedbed. I also oversaw the spreading of Milorganite fertilizer over the seedbed, which was then raked into the top inch of soil.

Next came the seeding. I did most of it, hand-seeding the area and then carefully raking the seeds into the top half-inch of soil. It is an art to do this evenly and at the optimum depth. You have to hold the rake up slightly so you don't use the total weight of the rake to scratch the soil.

After the seeding, it was important to keep the area well watered without disturbing the seedbed. Because of the sun and the wind, the top two inches or so dried out very quickly. I was elected to do most of the watering, but the colonel in charge of maintenance questioned my approach. I explained when the seeds start to germinate, they need ample water. If the seedlings dry out even once, there is no chance for recovery. Choosing one section, I applied water only once a day to illustrate how fewer seedlings would grow.

This demonstration did the trick, and the news spread rapidly. The colonel put out a directive of how to prepare the seedbed and water the seeds, and he asked me to give a demonstration for each company. I think if there had been an officer training school for landscape maintenance, I would have been accepted with open arms! I might even have been selected for the teaching staff.

Since it was early spring, the seeds germinated in just over a week. Our company won the award for the best lawn. Of course, landscape architecture is a more complicated field than just planting grass, but we did have the prettiest lawn in Fort Sill.

After that, I didn't have to worry about being rejected by my peers because of my German heritage. Americans, it seemed, greatly value big fields of grass.

During the three months of marching, conditioning, firearm training, lawn planting, wheelbarrow pushing, and "Yes Sir"-ing Margrit and I wrote to each other every week. We were eager to be together, but we had to wait and see what future the military had in store for me. Most soldiers were sent on to other camps to become part of different divisions or to specialize in a particular skill. Each division had its own training camp, and new divisions were being formed all the time as the army built up its troops.

America hadn't started ground attacks yet, so we weren't yet sent to the front lines. Most of the early strikes following the attack on Pearl Harbor involved naval ships and aircraft carriers already in active service.

In April 1942, I was transferred to a unit called Flash and Sound. We received special training in locating an enemy gun position by either sound or sight. The irony that I dodged military service in Nazi Germany with a falsified report of bad hearing was not lost on me. My hearing was excellent as were my powers of observation, and I excelled in this training. It also helped I knew how to operate transit survey equipment from my training as a landscape architect. While in this unit, I was selected for Officer's Candidate School. The other candidates and I got to know each other right away. We were all strangers when we started training, but in the close quarters of the barracks — with officer training awaiting us — we made new friends.

The morning we packed up, I was called aside by the colonel in charge.

"Private Wertheim, I am very sorry. Because you are not a U.S. citizen, you cannot become an officer."

I faced him, trying not to let my disappointment show. I had applied for citizenship papers soon after I arrived in California, but there was a five-year waiting period to qualify. I watched all my new friends get on the bus before turning on my heels and returning to the barracks, heartbroken. Here I was in my new country, willing to serve as a soldier, and suddenly I was not good enough. It felt like Germany all over again. Later, when the company captain learned of this, he offered me the position of company clerk. I think he liked me because I helped him get a promotion with the best lawn on the base.

This wasn't so bad. There was a certain amount of security in the post — it meant I would be in Fort Sill for a while.

I called Margrit that night to tell her the news and we talked over our situation. My clerk job was supposed to keep me at Fort Sill for several months, or even longer. On the other hand, my army salary was only twenty-one dollars a month, out of which I had to send ten dollars to the nurseries and some more to pay back the loans for the Cuban visa, most of which came from friends and other private sources. If married, I was allowed to live off-base, but I could provide little for my new wife and our room and board. Margrit would have to get a job to support herself, and at anytime, I might be reassigned and shipped out. It was all so temporary.

Nonetheless, we were young and in love. Our desire to be together overrode all the obstacles and unknowns. We decided she would come to Lawton, Oklahoma, and we would get married. We were both very excited.

I started my desk job right away and was suddenly a part of the training company staff, a brand new environment and job. The work was simple, but it was difficult serving as a private when most of my coworkers were sergeants. After all, I had become accustomed to being a leader in my landscape career. The sergeants continually greeted new recruits, repeating the same gruff script I had heard upon my arrival. I processed the new troop's paperwork, soon learning to type rapidly with two fingers (still my current method).

Margrit broke the news to her mother that we were engaged. She bought a Greyhound bus ticket from Los Angeles to Lawton in mid-June, giving her time to wrap up her work and get her things together.

I wrote a letter to my Uncle Ernst Hellinger to say hello and ask him what advice he could give me about getting married — what things I needed to know? Uncle Ernst was an uncle twice removed, but had been a dear friend of my mother's throughout my childhood. I think he might have been sweet on her. He was now a mathematics professor at Northwestern University. Because he was Jewish, he had been removed from his position at the University of Frankfurt in 1938 and sent to Dachau Concentration Camp. After six weeks was released on the condition that he emigrate immediately. He had come to the United States in late February 1939, after friends found him the position at Northwestern.

His reply letter was most congratulatory, but he could not advise me, he said. He had been a bachelor all his life. However, he did send one hundred dollars as a wedding gift, a large amount of money. We decided to use part of it as the deposit to rent a room in Lawton and part of it for Greyhound tickets and two nights at a hotel in Oklahoma City for our "honeymoon."

In late March of 1942, Congress had passed a law that allowed anyone serving in the army to become a citizen as long as he or she did not have a criminal record. The Second War Powers Act of 1942 exempted non-citizen service members from most naturalization requirements if "serving honorably in the U.S. Armed Forces." My swearing-in date was scheduled for the week prior to Margrit's arrival. I called her to proudly report she would be marrying an American citizen. This was a big deal for many reasons. It meant I could go to officer's training after all, but most importantly, we would not be enemy aliens anymore. The news of Japanese-Americans being sent to internment camps like Manzanar was on the front page of the newspaper by then. In the fear and uncertainty of wartime, who knew what would happen to Germans who were not citizens. Our status as Americans would assure Margrit's safety.

Citizenship required me to pass a test about general United States history and government. I had only a month to study and barely any spare time. I usually got off work at 1800 unless the captain had something else in mind, and then I stayed later. I often had to work on weekends as well.

There were no books at the Fort from which to study, so as soon as I had a free hour, I took the bus into Lawton to the public library. The librarian, a kind elderly lady, advised me on which books I should read, but she was reluctant to check out books to me. She didn't trust soldiers because they often didn't bring them back. She explained the men would receive orders, be shipped out the next day, and abandon the books at the Fort or take the books with them. I assured her I would return the book because I was a clerk on the base. She checked out one book to me. When I returned it a few days later, she knew she could trust me and checked out the rest without any further hesitation.

What I learned in the books about United States history shocked me. I had no idea about the Civil War. I didn't know slavery had ever existed in America. I only knew about cowboys and Indians and that everyone in the U.S. became a millionaire. In San Francisco and Los Angeles, I didn't see segregation. It may have existed, and I'm sure it did, but it was nothing compared to the Jim Crow ways of the deep South. Honestly, I wasn't exposed to many black people in California. In Germany, we rarely saw a dark-skinned person in our comings and goings. When we did, we assumed they were from India. What had been done to African Americans during the time of slavery and since was something I had never heard about and couldn't quickly understand. I didn't think such a thing could happen in this country.

In Oklahoma, it was an entirely different story than in California. I suppose it was similar to the southern states. I saw black people in town but they often kept their heads down or eyes averted as they passed. I became aware of signs in front of restaurants that read: "White Only." On the bus from the army base to Lawton, the black people had to sit in the back of the bus. I thought I had left such discrimination behind in Germany. It was a sad reality to learn about my beloved America.

On June 7, 1942, I joined a good-sized group of soldiers in the recreation hall for our citizenship test and ceremony. An Army judge told us to raise our right hands and repeat after him. I swore the Oath of Allegiance, and quite suddenly, I was declared a U.S. citizen. It was a very exciting moment.

There was no celebration afterward. A few of us shook hands before returning to our duties, but inside I celebrated for days. I had new roots. Margrit was going to marry a U.S. citizen.

A few days later, Margrit arrived in Lawton. It was a Thursday evening when I greeted the girl I loved at the bus station. She looked beautiful despite the long journey.

That first night she stayed in a hotel in Lawton, and I returned to the base. I would keep my bunk, which I would use when I had to stay overnight at the base for one reason or another. I certainly wouldn't be there for the next couple nights. My request had been granted for a three-day leave to get married, find a place to live, and be with my bride in Oklahoma City.

The next morning we looked for a room and found a simple, inexpensive one in a private home. It had a shared bathroom and not much privacy, but we could afford it. From there we walked to the Comanche County Courthouse. Bert Fielden, one of my friends from the base, who was also German, came with us to be our witness.

The courthouse was an old building and a sign pointed up a long, very steep staircase. Both of us wondered, "Did we really have to climb up there?" We hoped it wasn't a metaphor for our future together. At the top, there was one small office that belonged to the judge. He instructed us to come in.

Standing inside the office was a Native American man in full traditional dress, wearing clothes made of animal hides with beads sewn in and fringed at the ends. He also wore a large, colorful feather headpiece. His long, dark braids framed his tanned and angled face. He was quite a sight, especially for Margrit.

The judge asked to see our marriage certificate, which we had already filled out except for the signatures of our witness and the Justice of the Peace.

The judge told us we needed two witnesses. This came as a surprise and for a moment we wondered what to do. Then we both looked at the Indian and back at each other. He agreed to be our second witness.

We were quite a sight for a wedding party. Me in my regular enlisted man's uniform; Bert in his uniform; the Native American in his head dress; the judge in his robes; and Margrit, without a bouquet or a formal white wedding gown, looking absolutely beautiful in a simple summer dress. The judge led us through a standard civil ceremony. Bert signed our wedding certificate and the Native American signed an X for his name.

There was no pomp, no frills, no photographer, no wedding party, but it didn't matter. I leaned in and kissed my wife, and I looked into her eyes, feeling nothing but sheer joy. She smiled lovingly back at me. We thanked Bert, said our goodbyes, and rushed to the Greyhound station to catch the bus to Oklahoma City. It was June 13, 1942.

My beautiful bride

At the open door to our hotel room in Oklahoma City, I picked Margrit up in my arms and carried her over the threshold, both of us smiling and laughing with unsuppressed joy. We hung not one, but two "Do Not Disturb" signs on the door.

I repeated my initial vow to Margrit that I would take her skiing every season "for as long as we both shall live." I would only break this pact for two seasons when General MacArthur would not give me leave. We didn't know it then, but skiing together would stretch beyond our ninetieth birthdays. Even babies would be planned around the ski season. I renewed this marriage agreement every year until our fiftieth wedding anniversary at which time Margrit wrote a lovely poem stating she would not ask for a renewal until another fifty years had passed.

On Saturday morning, Margrit and I reluctantly left the sanctuary of our hotel room to go to lunch with some relatives of hers who lived in Oklahoma City. For the wedding luncheon, we ate hot dogs in their garden, which Margrit would never forget. We had no wedding cake or wedding party, but we had each other, which was exciting enough. Every dollar saved was important.

It was wonderful to have time to ourselves, even if it only lasted two-and-a-half days. Back in Lawton we settled into our new routine as a military husband and wife. I took the bus to the base three times a week, working twenty-four hour shifts and working on weekends when required. My army salary increased from twenty-one to twenty-eight dollars a month, because I was married. Margrit found a job at a local photo studio and often worked long hours. It was a simple army life, but it was wonderful because we were together.

When winter came I received a furlough. Margrit and I took a troop train to Los Angeles to visit her mother and to go skiing. Doing things with Margrit was always wonderful. She accepted so many inconveniences and embraced the adventure. We sat together on the floor of the troop train all the way from Lawton to Albuquerque where we had a layover. We were young and discomforts didn't matter as long as we achieved our main goal.

When we arrived at her mother's house in Hollywood, it was quiet. Margrit's brother, Fred, and a number of our friends had left to serve in the military. Fred and a few others were in the 10th Mountain Division that trained in Colorado. Since all of them were skiers, this appointment didn't seem so bad.

After a couple days, we took the train north to Norden on Highway 40 just before Donner Pass. We did not have enough gasoline coupons to use my car, which was stored in Margrit's mother's garage, so we took the train to Sacramento and transferred to a train headed to Reno.

It felt great to be at the top of Sugar Bowl Resort again, powdery snow flying by as we leaned and turned and sped down the mountain. The Brooks at Soda Springs were happy to see us. Our friends Hans and Ini Strakosch, whose garden I had designed the previous year, skied with us as well. We remained lifelong friends with the Brooks and Strakosches after this experience.

We spent three terrific days skiing at Sugar Bowl and were scheduled to stay several days longer, but on that third day, government officials arrived at the hotel to shut it down. Because the resort was close to the Southern Pacific tracks — now used for transporting troops and war supplies — the officials told the Brooks they had to close for security reasons. The sudden change was hard on all of us, but the country was at war and no one argued with such restrictions.

Sugar Bowl, circa 1941

We all boarded the train together heading toward Bakersfield. There, the others caught a bus bound for Hollywood, but Margrit and I boarded an eastbound train and took the southern route via Texas to Lawton.

One April morning in 1943, I arrived at my desk to find transfer papers. I was to go to Fort Washington, Maryland, for Officer's Candidate School and training in intelligence. I was going to be an officer after all! This was great, except that my train was leaving Fort Sill in less than four hours. I called Margrit at the photo studio and told her I'd sort things out when I got to Maryland and then send for her.

But Margrit had plans of her own. When I arrived at the Fort Sill train depot, there she was. In just those few hours she had quit her job, packed all our things, paid the balance of our room, closed our bank account, and met me at the station. How she managed all this, I will never know. It was a terrific achievement.

"You didn't think you were going to leave me behind, did you?" she said.

It was a long trip, but we had tickets to eat in the dining car, where we met other couples. When we arrived in Washington, D.C., we went to the housing bureau and received a list of available rentals. A taxi driver drove us around and around, but we did not find anything we liked. The rooms were either in parts of town with sour-faced landlords or were rather dark and dingy. It was very important to me to find safe and pleasant housing for my young bride. I was discouraged. We were tired from our journey, the cost of the taxi was going up by the minute, and I needed to report to Fort Washington soon, which was outside of the city.

The taxi driver, a middle aged man, was very friendly and sympathetic. It seemed that he came to like us during our unsuccessful search because he offered us a possible solution.

"My wife and I have a basement room for rent in our house," he said, "Would you like to see it?"

He drove us to his home, a small, very clean house with a tiny garden in a well-kept, lower middle-class neighborhood. He introduced us to his wife, who was very pleasant and gracious as she showed us the room. It was half a floor below the grade with a separate entrance and a bath. It was perfectly adequate. We had only a small room in Lawton, so this actually offered more privacy. The price was right, too, and we said yes. I was especially pleased because Margrit would not be completely alone as I sensed this couple would look out for her. The husband even offered Margrit a ride into town in his taxi when she needed to go, allowing that it worked with his schedule. I kissed my beautiful wife goodbye, and our new landlord drove me to the bus station, where I caught a military bus to the base.

The expectations were high in officer candidate training, which appealed to me. Physically, it included very tough daily exercise: an obstacle course that went up and down the hilly countryside; long distance hikes; lots of calisthenics; and drill after drill. Fortunately I was in good condition and was able catch up with those who had begun their training a few weeks earlier. Academically, we worked day and night. We learned about military law and the rules of the Geneva Convention in the treatment of prisoners. We read maps, learned strategies and tactics, and improved our communication and leadership skills.

Our trainers emphasized the importance of understanding our role as leaders and decision-makers, while at the same time being respectful of officers of higher rank. It was assumed everybody knew how to shoot a rifle and use standard weapons.

I knew the importance of this training and wanted to succeed, so I worked very hard. Not all candidates made it to the end. Some were dropped, while others tried to get away with things, but cheating or behavioral indiscretions rarely went unnoticed. I was never very good at tests and was not specifically trained in American examinations, but I knew how to study. Most of the candidates were either university graduates or sports figures. We had one person who was an opera singer and another who was the son of a famous department store owner. We also had candidates who, like me, spoke more than one language.

This should not imply that the smartest men all became officers. I knew a number of enlisted men who had the ability or educational qualifications to become officers but did not wish to be leaders. I yearned for the responsibility and leadership. My experience in Germany had forced me to mature at an early age, and in California, I was running my own business.

Part of our training involved giving commands to large groups of men. I did not have a very strong voice, and my experience in speaking to a large audience had ended in grade school when I failed to remember the poem I was supposed to recite. But an officer needed to make himself heard, so on the weekends Margrit helped me. We found a large field where I practiced giving commands to her. She would stand far away, and if she could not hear my voice, she would raise her right arm. If she heard me loud and clear, she raised her left arm. We would do this for a couple hours at a time, and it helped tremendously. Like many things in life, this practice had its time and place. I do not recommend yelling at one's spouse as a normal routine.

All the officer candidates could go to town every other weekend. The army provided big cattle-car type buses that drove us into town and back to the fort again on Sunday evening. Margrit found a good job working for Kodak. This allowed us enough of a budget to eat out most Saturday nights, usually at our favorite French restaurant. Sometimes we joined other married officer candidates and their wives for dinner. On Sundays, we took walks around the neighborhood where there were lovely, tall trees providing shade in the hot and humid city. We thoroughly enjoyed our weekends off. On some weekends the officer candidates were required to go on field trips or we stayed in camp. On the camp weekends, visitors were allowed to come to the fort for a few hours and eat with us in the dining hall. Margrit came out a few times when she didn't have to work. The wives of the troops had a chance to meet each other here so friendships developed. The wives often did things together in town.

On July 13, 1943, I completed the ninety-day course and became a second lieutenant, another "ninety-day wonder," a World War II officer who had neither participated in college ROTC nor graduated from a military academy. (Today, young men and women still may become military officers through officer candidate schools.)

As a second lieutenant in the U.S. Army

After graduation I had a two-week leave before having to report to Camp Patrick Henry outside of Newport News, Virginia. Margrit and I decided to visit Uncle Alfred and Aunt Hilde Traube, who had made it out of Germany at the end of 1939. They lived in the Forest Hills neighborhood of Queens, across the river from Manhattan. It was a lovely reunion, but tinged — whether I liked it or not — with painful memories. For the first time in almost five years, I was with family again but not with Mother. Hilde was, after all, my mother's younger sister. She had been there throughout my childhood, pre-Hitler, and during my adolescence, when life had changed for all of us in Nazi Germany.

Just as I was forced to do, my aunt and uncle had to abandon all their assets in Germany to get out and save themselves. It was not an easy life for them in America. Aunt Hilde earned money as a masseuse, and she traveled around Long Island with her massage table to customers' homes. Uncle Alfred, who had been a well-known and respected attorney in Germany, was a clerk in an upscale Manhattan hotel. He had noticeably aged from his experience in the prison work camp. Having gone in to rescue my father at *Sachsenhausen*, I understood at least a bit of the horror he must have known.

They were gracious hosts welcoming us into their house. However, I couldn't wait to take my bride sightseeing in Manhattan, so one day we ventured into the city. I knew exactly where I wanted to start our tour, at the top of the Empire State building, just as I had with George Salomon. Standing at the top I glanced at Margrit, the wind blowing her hair away from her face as she took in the skyscrapers, Central Park, and the bustling boulevards. Margrit then informed me she didn't like being on top of the building, so we quickly made our way around the observation deck and back down. As we walked to Rockefeller Plaza and all around the city, I pointed out famous buildings, and Margrit snapped photographs with her Leica camera.

My uncle and aunt suggested we go to the Five Finger Lakes in upstate New York because it was quite beautiful. We rented an inexpensive, rustic cabin beside one of the lakes, which included the use of a boat. We rowed out onto the lake, spending hours exploring the shoreline and picking wild strawberries. In the evenings we held each other and talked and laughed. It was peaceful and very romantic, a wonderful few days together that we wished would never end. As we reluctantly left, we declared it our real honeymoon, far superior to a hot dog lunch in Oklahoma City.

I reported for duty at Camp Patrick Henry, and we found a small room to rent in Newport News while I applied for officer's quarters. It was the end of July and quite hot. Camp Patrick Henry was really just a staging place for officers and enlisted men who were waiting for assignments either overseas or elsewhere in the United States. At first it seemed our stay there would be very temporary, but I was given my first intelligence job based at the camp. I was to go aboard a Liberty ship in

Chesapeake Bay to gain intelligence while reviewing how American soldiers treated the POWs held on board.

I was partnered with an FBI agent, and we both wore the insignia of the Inspector General's Office. A couple of enlisted Navy men motored us out in a small boat to the ship in the bay. As we neared the lightly laden Liberty ship, it loomed high overhead. The only way up was to climb a long rope ladder. I was not a good swimmer and was a bit fearful, but I grabbed the rope ladder and climbed without hesitation. As an officer, you never wilt. When I reached the top and looked over the edge of the ship's railing, I saw a crowd of men on the deck, all of them in German army uniforms. My heart seemed to seize for a moment given my past experience, and my immediate instinct was to head back down the ladder. Instead, I took a deep breath and hopped over the railing onto the deck, waiting for the FBI agent to join me.

We reported to the ship's captain, as instructed, telling him and anyone else who asked that our mission was to make certain the prisoners were being treated in accordance with the Geneva Convention. Of course, that was not our aim at all. While engaging the prisoners in casual discussion about how they were being treated, we were to observe the quality of their uniforms and shoes to determine whether Allied bombings were having any significant effect on factory output. We knew we must be careful of watchful Nazis amongst the group so as not to cause trouble for the more friendly soldiers who spoke with us.

I began talking to the German soldiers using *Platt Deutsch* (Low German dialect), which I had learned at *Oberrealschule*. No one taught German in the United States knew this form of the language, but every schoolchild in the general area of Hamburg, educated during Hitler's reign, would have been required to speak it.

One young soldier told me he was a farmer from Hamburg. I asked him where he did his farming, knowing very well there were no farms within the city limits. He was surprised when I began naming farming areas outside the city and nodded when I mentioned the name of his hometown. It was in the Alten Land area across the Elbe River from

Hamburg. I told him what I knew of the farms there and the crops they grew, explaining that I used to go there as a boy. This loosened up the prisoner, and we began to talk about his farm. We discovered my father and I had met the young man's grandfather when, after a day hike, we had stopped at a *Biergarten* (pub) run by the soldier's family. The young man obviously missed his home and lit up as I described the outdoor area of the small restaurant, which I remembered well. It had an arbor covered with wisteria, under which my father drank beer and I drank *Apfelsaft* (apple juice).

The German soldier, now at ease, was willing to continue our discussion. The other soldiers, particularly any Nazi spies, were not interested in our conversation about his grandfather's farm, so they walked away from us. He told me he was relieved he would not be mistreated, as the Nazis had told him he most surely would be if captured.

I mentioned I sometimes enjoyed watching the large passenger liners come down the Elbe River, like the Europa and the Bremen.

"I did too," said the young man, "but no liners come down the river anymore. The Hamburg harbor is now home to submarines."

This was incredibly valuable information. Hiding my excitement, I told the soldier I couldn't believe it. What could they possibly have done with all the beautiful old elm trees all along the river? I shared that I was a landscape architect, and I was interested in hearing more about it. The soldier explained the elm trees had been dug up several years earlier, and the contractors had used cranes to place the trees into very large boxes so they could move them around. Where they once had stood rooted to the ground, the Germans had built a submarine terminal submerged under a large concrete platform. After completion of the platform, the elm trees, in their large containers, were repositioned at their original locations, as camouflage, so aerial photographs would reveal nothing. I told him I hoped he would see his grandfather again soon and assured him he would not be mistreated. Caught up in his own relief and nostalgia, and believing I was only there to check on his treatment, he did not seem to realize what he had just revealed to me.

After returning to shore, I reported my findings to my commanding officer. He arranged for me to be driven immediately to the Pentagon near Washington, D.C. and called to say I was coming with important information. By the time I arrived and was escorted into the secure building, a group of senior officials had gathered to hear my report, including someone from the Army Air Force intelligence department.

After my presentation, they sent requests to England for more recent aerial photos of the area. In the meantime, they asked me to identify the location on a map. When the pictures arrived a few days later, the submarine base and its camouflage were easily noticeable. Within days, the base was successfully bombed.

Meanwhile, Margrit had quickly found a job in photography. We were soon assigned an apartment through officer housing, our first real home together. We had almost no money so our bed was a mattress on the floor and our tables, chairs, and shelves were orange crates stacked creatively, but we loved having our own place. I cooked us simple meals over which we talked about Margrit's work, our lives, and what was in the news, everything except my missions, which were classified. We didn't have much, but it didn't matter in the least. We were happy and felt we had nothing to complain about. This routine lasted for only three weeks.

During one of my visits to the Pentagon in the summer of 1943, a high-ranking officer asked me if I would volunteer to enter Germany to report on the destruction of bridges and other important structures along the south side of the Elbe River. While I recognized the risks of a top secret mission, I accepted the assignment because I felt I could provide special knowledge that few others could — I knew the terrain and countryside and I could speak Low German, the dialect spoken in this region. The officer in charge assembled a group of officers and enlisted men, each with a different expertise needed to complete this mission.

Our training involved both academic study and field training. We covered the geography of the area and what was expected of us, but our camaraderie was equally significant since we would need each other to succeed. Assigned to an undercover and highly secretive mission, we could only talk to each other about it. It was difficult to keep all this from my wife, but secrecy was extremely important.

In September 1943, I received orders to leave for Camp Stoneman in Pittsburg, California, a small city east of San Francisco. I was surprised. I didn't know why the Army would have me embark for Europe from the West Coast. Intelligence team members never traveled together and often arrived at their destination at different times and in different ways. Still, it seemed strange, but as a soldier, I learned not to question orders.

We were sad to leave our cozy apartment after such a short time. We packed our few belongings and boarded a passenger train, yet again. We decided to stop in Chicago to visit my uncle, Ernst Hellinger, who had been so generous with our wedding gift.

He showed us around Northwestern University and the town of Evanston. He made us comfortable for the night in his apartment. We learned he struggled with finances despite his position at Northwestern. We also discussed the fate of various family members, which greatly saddened me. This would be the last time we would see Uncle Ernst.

During our visit, he told us about his sister, Hanna, who had assisted with my affidavit. She had done well becoming a sociology professor at Purdue University and marrying fellow professor, Karl Meissner, a prominent physicist who also had escaped Germany. They lived in Lafayette, Indiana. I would visit her in later years, specifically to thank her for sponsoring my immigration.

Between Chicago and San Francisco we had a private room on the train. This was a fantastic luxury. We also enjoyed eating in the dining car, courtesy of Uncle Sam.

We knew that from Camp Stoneman, I would soon be leaving again. I worried about leaving Margrit on her own before she had found housing or a job. She assured me she would be fine, and really what choice did we have? When we reached Oakland, California, I had to say goodbye to my bride. This was extremely difficult because we did not know if we would ever see each other again.

I was at Camp Stoneman for less than a day before I was ordered onto a troop train from Oakland to Fort Lewis, Washington. The trip lasted for a full day and part of the night. No one knew what would happen next. We were like many parcels being shipped to destinations unknown. Fort Lewis was a large camp amongst fir trees making it look as though it had been placed in a forest. What a great contrast there was between the barren landscape of Oklahoma and this lush site in the Pacific Northwest. Around the main building was a landscape of rhododendrons, azaleas, and pink dogwoods.

By now I knew the routine all too well. I reported to the commanding officer, was escorted to the barracks, and went to the dining hall, where I met my peers. Shortly thereafter, I made my way to bed. Three days later we were bused to Portland, Oregon, where I boarded a Liberty ship and headed out to sea. I didn't know where the ship was going but guessed we would go through the Panama Canal and on to Europe.

I was assigned to the officers' quarters. But after depositing my gear in the trunk by my cot, I spent most of the long voyage leaning over the port side of the ship vomiting or huddled on a cushioned chair on the deck, gulping in fresh air to keep from being sick again. It was a much different ride on this type of vessel than the passenger ship that brought me to New York. We sailed south beyond Central America, and I thought perhaps I would be dropped off in Chile. However, the ship turned west, crossing the landless South Pacific. Our ship did not take a straight path, zigzagging constantly as the crew kept watch for enemy submarines. Periodically, we practiced getting out the lifeboats, just in case the ship was damaged. We ended up seeing no other vessels the whole voyage. It was just us out there on the endless blue.

When we at last reached land some thirty days later, eleven officers and I were put ashore near Townsville, Queensland, in Australia. Why was I in Australia?

No one met us. We began walking in the hot, humid landscape until we came to a small, dusty café at the edge of town. We were all very thirsty but had no Australian money. We convinced the weathered owner to take our American money and ordered milk. We knew better than to trust water in a foreign country. He would only serve us one glass from which we each took a few sips before reluctantly passing it along. We asked around and managed to obtain the phone number of the army camp and then asked to use the phone. Soon, a private from the base picked us up in a troop truck.

We were assigned quarters in what appeared to be a temporary camp, and we waited for further orders from Army headquarters in Brisbane.

In our free time, while awaiting our various assignments, we often went into Townsville on a streetcar, taking in a movie at the Winter Garden Theatre, exploring the town, or having a meal together. I noticed the men got drunk faster on Australian beer. I tended to steer clear of alcohol in those days.

Finally, I received orders from General Douglas MacArthur's headquarters in Brisbane. I was to go immediately to Port Moresby in Papua New Guinea, which was about three hundred miles from Australia near the southeastern end of the large island of New Guinea. I was to establish a new base censor office there.

It was October 1943 — some month-and-a-half after saying goodbye to Margrit in Oakland — when I boarded a troop airplane for Port Moresby. It was my first time flying, which was quite exciting. Our plane was a C-47 Skytrain, the Army's two-propeller workhorse for moving troops and supplies. We sat on metal benches on the sides with our backs to the windows, so I wasn't able to see much except when I occasionally twisted around to get a glimpse of the sky or the land below. Our gear was strapped down to the floor in the middle of the plane.

We landed on a paved airstrip in a clearing surrounded by tropical forest. Disembarking was like stepping into a warm shower, the humidity pasting my clothes to my skin. A few of the men tittered, and I looked around to see why. I was shocked to see native Papuan women walking along the airstrip wearing no clothing above the waist.

Everyone soon grew used to this custom. The Papuan men wore only loincloths, and both men and women kept their curly hair in large round Afros.

An old photo of natives in Papua New Guinea at the Village of Kamali

I was given a small unit to train, which eventually grew to forty-five people most of whom spoke more than one language. Our unit was the base censor, and it was our job to check mail and make sure the contents did not reveal military plans, secrets or strategies — anything that might potentially hurt the war effort if it fell into the wrong hands. This meant we were responsible for reviewing all the mail from the officers in our region. We also spot checked the enlisted solders' mail, which their commanding officers were supposed to censor. We were located in a standard office building in town, but we slept in the small military camp outside of town, sharing four-person tents and a typical camp-style kitchen.

As the office grew in numbers a captain became the head of the unit. This captain, an American who had been a businessman in Australia, had no idea what censorship was really all about. Our captain did not like foreigners, which made leading our unit a challenge. We had a number of men who were refugees from various European countries, although many of us had become U.S. citizens. He would send only American-born officers to teach various company officers about censorship. His excuse was our accents. This caused me further anxiety about speaking in front of an audience.

Except for the natives and the surrounding jungle, Port Moresby reminded me of some of the small towns in New England I had seen, with colonial-style buildings and lush, green surroundings. It was a small, coastal town full of Australian businessmen. As the capital and largest city in Papua New Guinea, it was a high profile target for Japan in its goal of disrupting the Allies' access to Asia thus making it of particular interest to General MacArthur. Even though there were many camps distributed within a five-mile radius from the center of town, we did not mix with other soldiers because we were all focused on our own jobs. Aside from the American soldiers stationed in the camps, there were some Papuan youth hired by the Army. They were educated in English and trained to drive vehicles.

On my first evening at my new post, I walked to the officer's club, a straw hut built on stilts that protruded over the water. I asked an officer seated at a table if I could join him, and we started talking. He was a captain, a fighter pilot. When I asked him how long he had been at Port Moresby, he replied, "The question is how much longer I'll be here?"

He told me the pilots had a fairly good idea of when they would die simply by counting the airplanes remaining on the landing strip each day. He explained they were not receiving any replacement planes or pilots. "My squadron has only seven planes left, so I estimate I have a maximum of three weeks to live."

I listened in shock. Still, the captain's main concern was not to fall into enemy hands. The next time we met, three days later, he gave me a letter for his parents and girlfriend and asked me to mail it if he was shot down. A week later, another pilot found me at my tent. My friend, the captain, had been shot down as he predicted. I mailed his letter without censorship. I had known the man for less than two weeks, but I have never forgotten him.

At first I was not alarmed to arrive in Papua New Guinea instead of Europe as anticipated. I would go along with whatever the military had in mind for me. Yet as the days went by, and I received no new orders to put me on a transport towards Europe, I began to look into my situation and soon discovered my arrival in Australia was the result of an Army snafu.

It was lucky I had friends at headquarters in Brisbane in General MacArthur's office, otherwise I might never have known what happened. Evidently, when my European mission leader discovered I had been sent to Australia without his knowledge, he wrote out orders for me to return to Washington, D.C., from which I would then continue on to London. The orders were accompanied with a letter to General MacArthur asking him, if I was available, to comply with the attached orders. MacArthur, however, decided he did not want to lose my expertise in intelligence and replied I was not available.

I had mixed feelings. I was worried about the rest of my intelligence team, who depended on my firsthand knowledge of the German terrain and Low German dialect. I felt like a traitor to these men. On the other hand, if the General thought I was needed in the Pacific theatre, it was my duty to follow his command. This was not the only Army snafu I witnessed, but that didn't make it any easier to abandon my team and its mission in Europe. Once again, it was time for me to make the best out of an unexpected turn of events.

As the weeks went by, I began to explore the surrounding flora during my down time. There were wonderful large-leafed palms and ferns as well as shrubs that were either full of small, delicate blossoms or exploding with bright, waxy flowers the size of a hat. I collected samples and drew pictures in a journal of what I discovered.

After about a month in Papua, I was very pleased to receive a letter from Margrit. She had found a room to rent in Berkeley and a job with a photographer in San Francisco. Though I missed her terribly, I was very proud of her and comforted by her ability to take care of herself. I wrote back and asked her to send me some seeds so I could start a vegetable garden; the seeds arrived a few weeks later. During my free time, I prepared beds and planted them, nurturing the young plants as they arose from the soil: lettuce, tomatoes, cucumbers, carrots, and radishes. Things grew very quickly in the tropical conditions. It rained almost every afternoon, the greenhouse conditions cooled only occasionally by a sea breeze.

By this time the rest of the men, who watched me investigate the plant life and work in my garden, had bestowed upon me a nickname, "Lieutenant Flowers." Things move very quickly in wartime though and people are moved quickly too. I never did get to see my garden grow ripe and ready to eat.

After a while, I was taken out of the censorship group and joined various investigations. Frequently, I searched for planes that had been shot down in order to find the crew and direct ships to rescue them. I also went on several bombing runs over Rabaul, on the island of New Britain. While the crew flew, navigated, and bombed the targets, my job was one of keen observation, with and without binoculars, carefully recording all I saw. I would report on the number, type, and positions of the Japanese ships; the condition of the airport; and the number of planes on the ground. I came to know many pilots and airmen on the base, even though they were always coming and going.

One time I went on a supply trip to Darwin, Australia. There was a real camaraderie between the captain and this crew, and they considered me one of their own while I was on board. I hoped to have a good meal in Darwin and, more importantly, to pick up some food supplies for my unit back in Papua New Guinea.

We took off in a C-54, a four-propeller plane, and were over the Coral Sea when one engine failed. I looked at the others with concern but the captain said he was sure we could make it to Darwin on three engines. Then a second engine quit.

There was just time for the captain to give calm directions for a water landing, and we all put on life jackets as the plane sped closer and closer to the sea. The radio operator sent an SOS with our position to the Australians. All I could think of was Margrit in San Francisco and how she would respond to the news I drowned in the Pacific Ocean.

"Hold on for dear life, we are about to land!" yelled the captain. We splashed hard into the water. A moment later, several well-trained members of the crew quickly launched two life boats into which we all piled, tying them together before rowing away from the plane. We watched it slowly fill with water and then sink, disappearing below the surface of the sea until it was as if no plane had ever been there.

We had no weapons of any kind, no radio. We were truly sitting ducks should an enemy plane pass overhead. We had nothing to do but sit, row, and worry. The captain asked me to entertain the crew by telling about my experiences in Nazi Germany. I launched into the stories of my life, my father's kidnappings, and the darkening days under Hitler's reign. They especially liked hearing about my missions on the ski slopes of Schneekoppe. I went on to describe *Sachsenhausen* and *Kristallnacht*. They had very little knowledge of what happened under Hitler, and this provided a diversion for the crew while we rowed toward Australia. It also kept me from worrying. We were picked up four hours later by two PT boats and eventually returned to Port Moresby. I was glad to be back, even without supplies and a good meal in Darwin. So many years later, I can still see the crash clearly, feel the rubber of the raft, and smell the salty sea. I don't think you forget the near misses. Somehow, you learn to cope with such things.

Soon after, I received urgent orders to lead an expedition to find a C-47 plane that had disappeared and presumably crashed in the sea near the island. The crash was kept secret because aboard the plane were twenty-seven intelligence officers, the last time so many would fly together.

I was assigned a B-25 crew, but searching from the sky, we could see no sign of the plane in the surrounding water. No other planes or PT boats could find it either. I suggested to the commanding general that perhaps the plane had gone down in an area we referred to as "the saddle," a hanging valley in the Owen Stanley Mountain Range. The mountains rose in the center of Papua New Guinea like a giant spine towering over the dense, warm jungles below. These mountaintops, rising to over 13,000-feet, were often covered with snow in winter. The saddle between the ridges was frequently fogged in during the early afternoon, and the bomber and fighter pilots always wanted to return through the saddle to Moresby before the fog settled thick in the canyon bed.

During the search flight in this area, I noted a substantial snow blanket on the higher parts of the mountains near the saddle and realized the snow might be concealing the wreckage. I requested permission to organize a search party.

My team was all native Papuans, who served as guides, laborers, and carriers. Guides cleared the way with machetes so we could climb through the hot, thick jungle. It took several days, and it was a very tough trek, even for people who were in good shape.

As an added challenge, communication with the natives was not always easy and several had brought their families along. We established camp in the late afternoon each day. I was not allowed to be a part of the main camp with the women and children. The Papuan men were very polite to me. They provided me with a tent and a hammock in an area outside their circle and brought me food the women had prepared.

We made our final camp in the high hills of the jungle and I instructed my team to get out their cold weather gear for our search up on the ridge. As we climbed higher the wind grew icy cold until we suddenly found ourselves in snow. The native people were not used to the cold. The "warm clothing" they brought consisted of light army jackets and thin blankets they wore like shawls; there weren't enough to go around. My team and I followed the ridgeline above the saddle, searching until we spotted the tip of a wing. The plane lay mostly buried and sickeningly severed in the snow. We carried small spades, usually used for digging foxholes, and employed them to remove the snow from around the plane so we could gain access.

There were no survivors. I was used to seeing dead bodies by then, but it was still not a job I would easily volunteer for twice. A couple of my crew were not used to seeing the dead, which added difficulty to the painstaking job of dragging corpses out of the plane. In some cases the bodies were not in one piece. As for me, I reminded myself I was the officer in charge. I had to get this done. Having to manage my Papuan team helped me keep my emotions at bay, suppressing my own response to the horror.

Finding the plane was very important. On board were intelligence records, and it was good to know none of them would fall into enemy hands. I recovered some classified material and burned the rest, using the papers to start fires in an attempt to keep my people warm. We also took off some of the dead officers' uniforms to put on my team. We emptied the plane's cabin of anything of value and dug shallow graves for the bodies. I could keep the natives only a short time in the freezing temperature before sending them back down to our base camp over a thousand feet lower on the mountain.

By the end, I was running short of team members able to work with me, since I kept sending them back to stay warm. My foreman then asked for some of the women to come up. They worked very hard, too.

I was inside the plane when the foreman burst in and very anxiously told me one of the young women was turning blue. I followed him out and saw a native girl violently shivering, overcome by the cold. I took off my jacket, wrapped it around her, and rubbed and massaged her arms, legs, and back to keep the blood circulating. I then hoisted her into my arms and over my shoulder and took off walking as fast as I could down the steep mountainside to camp. It was a fortunate thing she was slender and not too heavy. When we reached the camp, I enlisted other women to keep massaging her and to keep the girl close to the campfire.

Within hours, she recovered. With this I earned the respect of the native tribe, and later that evening I found my tent inside their camp circle, a welcomed part of their family.

Trekking back down the mountain, a bit more easily now since the Papuans had cleared a path on the way up, I could hear in my rucksack the jangling of the dog tags we had taken off all the dead. It was sad to lose so many valuable officers, so many men; but it was war. It was good we could tell the families they were not just missing in action; it was good that we could send their dog tags home. War forces you to compartmentalize your emotions and experiences, tucking them away, not knowing how they will be processed later.

Back at the post, the commanding general, Lieutenant General George C. Kenney, thanked the natives for their hard work by supplying them with provisions they needed in their village. Because money meant nothing to them, we arranged for some of the young men to attend the educational facilities nearby and provided them with medicine. I received a standing invitation to visit their village.

Our knowledge of the C-47 plane was kept very secret. Apart from the Papuans, a couple commanding officers and myself, no one knew of our mission at the time. General MacArthur would soon be informed, but I wouldn't find this out until much later. He would tell me himself.

Because I was moving around so much, my mail usually came in small clusters, so I would receive several letters from Margrit all at once. I would open them chronologically, based on the postmark date, savoring each one, and usually opening only two a day to help stretch out my bounty. At night, she was taking courses in Japanese, thinking this might allow her to join me. The Army needed translators so much they were even hiring civilians — both men and women — to help in the war effort.

"We can be together," she wrote. All this was done for love, and I was so grateful for it. Looking back, I believe this time of independence was important for Margrit. Until the war, most women in the U.S. didn't live such an autonomous lifestyle — fending for themselves, learning how capable they were in what had been a "man's world."

I also received a letter from a friend in my old censor unit in Port Moresby, teasing me about the lush, flavorful tomatoes they harvested from my garden. "Dear Lieutenant Flowers," it began, and ended with a taunting description of a very delicious salad of green lettuce and tomatoes.

Then I received a letter I did not expect.

It was from Mrs. Falkenberg, the friend of Mother's. She had somehow escaped from the *Theresienstadt* concentration camp to Switzerland. She wrote to tell me about the fate of Oma and Mother, who were both interned in the camp with her. The jungle around me disappeared as I read the letter. It was written in German; as a result, it had probably remained in the censor office for a while before being sent on to me.

My grandmother died first. Afterwards, Mother seemed to stop caring what happened to her, quickly growing weaker. But even in this condition, wrote Mrs. Falkenberg, Mother still showed great kindness to everyone around her. Mrs. Falkenberg described one incident in which a young woman was having labor contractions, and Mother helped by donating her watch so the woman's contractions could be timed.

"Your mother died not long after that."

My body felt very heavy. I could see her in our Hamburg apartment, humming under her breath as she arranged tulips in a vase; I could hear her voice as we discussed *The Magic Mountain* by Thomas Mann; I could feel her embrace at the Hamburg train station as we said our last goodbye.

An obituary announcing the deaths of Oma and Mother,
which Aunt Hilde likely had published in New York

With the success of my recent assignments, I changed my second lieutenant's gold bar for the silver bar of a first lieutenant. Mother would never see this. She would never meet my wife. She would never see Manhattan from the Empire State Building or squint in California sunshine. There was so much I wished I could have told her, shown her, and done for her.

It was almost a relief when I realized the time. I hastily put the letter in my back pocket and reported to the commander to find out about my next mission.

I was shipped out to Finschhafen on the eastern coast of New Guinea, facing New Britain. It was even warmer and more humid than at Port Moresby, merely gently raining when it wasn't pouring during monsoon season. My job was to train officers how to censor the letters of their troops. Normally, this was done with a small group of officers sitting around a table. But one day, soon after I arrived, a colonel asked me to come to his headquarters. He drove me in his jeep to a natural amphitheater outside of the army camp, where he assembled an entire regiment to hear what I had to say about censorship. I had never done this before. Looking out over the large group all looking back at me, I was overcome with nerves and wondered if I would become paralyzed and unable to remember what I was supposed to say, just as I had as a schoolboy. I suddenly imagined the arena was in ancient Rome, and I was a prisoner, awaiting Caeser's decision with a signal of his hand as to whether I would live or die. Dying would mean a gate would open and out would charge a hungry, angry lion. I remembered Margrit helping me train my voice in the field, and I thought of my responsibility as an officer.

I started by telling the men a soldier should never write home about the officers taking out the nurses and the Red Cross women. The men laughed, and their laughter gave me the confidence to continue on with more serious information about censorship. After this positive experience, I slowly gained confidence about presenting lectures and addressing an audience, large or small. I am thankful to the Army for helping me overcome my fear of public speaking. It has been useful to me during my entire career.

In late December 1943, I was assigned to the 1st Marine Division. Their mission was to invade and take over the Japanese airfield at Cape Glouster on the island of New Britain to the northeast of New Guinea. My job was to take notes about the operation and the extent of Japanese resistance. This landing would isolate and make less effective the major Japanese base at Rabaul, on the northeast side of the island. Taking Cape Gloucester would also provide safe passage for the Allies through the straits separating New Britain from New Guinea.

As the soldiers were making preparations for the next morning's landing, Tokyo Rose came on the radio. Tokyo Rose was the name given to the English-speaking women, spreading Japanese propaganda over the radio to disrupt the morale of Allied soldiers. In her high-pitched voice, she announced exactly where the marines were headed for their landing. The men were so anxious they recklessly drank jungle juice — a combination of strong alcohol and coconut milk — and climbed palm trees. They were so drunk they kept falling off. I called the MPs to calm them, making certain no one was arrested, because they were all needed the next morning. It was Christmas Day, though I didn't realize it at the time.

In the dawn light, the men were very quiet as they boarded an LST (Landing Ship, Tank) filled with trucks, jeeps, and supplies. In my possession was a large manila envelope, sent to me a few days before by courier from MacArthur's headquarters, with instructions to hand it to the captain of the ship as soon as we left the shores of New Guinea. None of the Marine officers knew about this.

Inside were orders instructing the captain to change course and use a different landing place than the one Tokyo Rose had announced. Relaying this information was part of my duty as an intelligence officer, and it was highly important it was distributed to a minimum number of people.

At Cape Gloucester, following a naval and air attack, we waded ashore and entered New Britain facing empty beaches and swampy terrain. The Marines met only a few rear-echelon Japanese troops in the thick jungle beyond the beach. I took careful notes about all that went on as the troops created a safe base.

We had a relatively dry period when I was there. The sand on the beach was black, and from my hammock I had a beautiful view of a very small island out on the horizon, silhouetted every night by a glowing orange sunset. Strangely — given the circumstances — it was a very romantic scene. I left several days later on a PT boat.

In contrast, the Marines who stayed had a hard time of it. The monsoon rains came in right after I left, and the men were constantly soaked, developing fungal and other skin diseases. Nevertheless, the objectives of the landing were met.

Aboard the PT boat, I received a new mission. I was to accompany Marines to extract a Swedish missionary, who was working with natives in some villages around Rabaul. It was arranged that we would meet a contact on an isolated beach far from town. The missionary didn't speak English, and none of the soldiers spoke Swedish, but the missionary and I both spoke German. We landed and walked the rest of the way so as not to call attention to the PT boat. When the missionary and I met, we began speaking right away. He told me about a nearby Japanese garrison. Once we were back on the PT boat, I began to gather valuable information about the location of Japanese troops and their movements in the Rabaul area, learning the Japanese had stronger air defenses than we had previously thought.

We took the missionary to the Marine's camp where I arranged for both of us to be taken immediately to Finschhafen so intelligence personnel could help me get my report to General MacArthur in Brisbane. It was our hope to get the missionary back to Sweden, but I never found out if that happened.

Ultimately, the intelligence gathered may have reinforced the plan to bypass and contain the Japanese base at Rabaul rather than try to capture it. I went on several intelligence missions of this nature, in and out of combat zones, as we pushed forward into Japanese controlled territory.

My next major mission, around October 1944, was to the main Philippine island of Luzon, which was occupied by the Japanese. I was to contact three separate groups of guerrillas there to learn where to drop food and supplies and to gather intelligence information about the strength and placement of the Japanese forces in the area.

I went through an indoctrination that included the necessary information and survival training. Afterwards, I flew to the Navy base at Seeadler Harbor on Manus Island in the Admiralty Islands, where I boarded a submarine. This was a real experience. I had never been in a submarine and did not realize how cramped the quarters would be. I shared a cabin with one of the Navy officers, and the officer and crew were most kind to me. They gave me a tour of the entire vessel. The sub traveled partly on the surface and partly underwater on the way to Luzon, constantly monitoring for communications from enemy ships or planes. Radio contact with the Filipino guerrilla group had been established but not directly from the submarine, so we could only go on relayed coordinates. It took several days to reach our destination.

When we neared the drop-off beach, I dressed in civilian clothes similar to those of the guerrillas, and the crew outfitted me with food and supplies for the jungle warriors, including rifles and radios. The captain told me the day and hour he would send a rubber raft ashore to pick me up. "The raft will wait no longer than three minutes after the rendezvous time," he said.

My immediate reaction was to ask the captain for another watch for backup. The captain, smiling slightly, took off his own waterproof watch and handed it to me. He also provided me with two flashlights and extra batteries, since that was how I would signal the raft from shore once I was in position and ready for pick up.

Sailors from the submarine rowed me to a beautiful, small beach. It was just outside of Subic Bay, about sixty miles northwest of Manila Bay on the western coast of Luzon. The crew quickly unloaded several boxes of rifles, which they buried in the sand while I kept an eye out for enemy soldiers. When they were all done, the sailors shook my hand and wished me good luck. In reality they should have saluted, but this was a much warmer way of saying goodbye. Then they silently rowed back to the submarine, which soon submerged out of sight.

I suddenly realized I was completely alone in enemy territory. A forest edged the beach, and I walked along it looking for a tree with a white blaze, a stroke of paint that marked the trail I needed to take into the jungle. I did not recognize the tree species, but they reminded me of birches. I felt like rejoicing when I found the mark.

Returning to the beach, I loaded my equipment and supplies on my back, including the radio parts, leaving the rifles buried in their hiding place. I entered the forest, my own gun ready, following the blazes leading me up a steep hill. My load was cumbersome and heavy. At the top of a plateau, I found the remains of a campfire and waited there as instructed until I heard the cry of a bird, the signal for my meeting with two of the guerillas. It was a big relief when two men appeared. I led them back down to the beach, and we carried all the materials to a hidden campsite where we covered them with dirt and brush.

It took nearly one-and-a-half days to get to the guerrilla camp. We slept out in the open for two nights, fed by local farm people, one of us always keeping watch. Although my guide did speak English, the local people spoke only their native language. It was a strange feeling not being able to understand what they were talking about.

When we arrived at the first guerrilla camp, the group insisted on having a festive party to celebrate the arrival of an American officer — one who oddly enough had a German accent. I was the first American officer they had seen since December 1941 or early 1942, after the Japanese invasion and MacArthur's withdrawal from the Philippine Archipelago. I did not have time for a party. I had to complete my mission and get back for my rendezvous on time. The guerrillas were an interesting bunch, a mix of American private businessmen, native Filipinos, local soldiers, and two American soldiers, who had set up camp in the mountains and went on missions to destroy Japanese posts and attack patrol operations. Two of the American civilians could also speak the local language. They helped me communicate to the guerrillas the urgency of my mission and agreed to accompany me for the rest of my trip. They also knew the island and the location of the next guerrilla camp. Before leaving their camp, I helped put their wireless radio together. We would have radio contact with them from then on.

Now a trio, we visited the two other guerrilla camps, where I helped build their radios and selected places for supply drops that would escape the notice of the Japanese. I made lists of supplies needed by the guerrillas and lists of Filipinos who had cooperated with the Japanese and needed to be apprehended. I also wrote down names of people who were willing and able to work on the construction of a proposed airstrip. This was extremely important information. Keeping myself alive to get it back to headquarters was the next step.

The two guerrillas continued as my guides through the forest, over farmland, and between rice paddies, as we made our way back to the beach site. I said goodbye, and they took off through the trees.

I was elated that evening, at the designated time, to see a light flash out in the bay. I clicked my flashlight in reply, and the sailors came to get me with the raft, equally happy to see me and hear I had been successful. I offered the captain back his watch, but he said to keep it as a souvenir. For several years afterwards, I would wear two watches.

As soon as I returned to New Guinea, I made my report and was asked to fly with the B-24 bomber crew out of Hollandia to help identify the drop sites from the air. Hollandia's location and bay made it a major supply port, which had contributed to the successful takeover of the island of Biak in August 1944, a critical turning point in the Pacific campaign that we hoped, in turn, would lead to successful invasions of the Japanese positions in the Philippines.

The plane was very full, and it was a long flight through the dark of night. We wondered if we would have enough fuel to get back. Flares by the guerrillas let us know they were in position for the drop, and it was gratifying to watch the supplies drift down by parachute toward the waiting men.

I did one more task, although not formally a part of the mission. I wrote to the parents of the American soldiers I had met to let them know their sons were alive and well. It was very rewarding when I received tearful letters of gratitude in return.

Shortly thereafter, I received my next mission. Reading my orders, I envisioned Margrit receiving a strange letter announcing my death. Even with everything I had done and experienced in the military thus far, I worried about this next assignment. I was to go befriend some headhunters.

CHAPTER 10
Lieutenant Flowers

Rhododendron 'Cristo Rey'-Vireya ('Cristo Rey' rhododendron)

Arrow was a Papuan man who had been hired by the U.S. Army as a civilian guide. He had helped me during the trek up the Owen Stanley Mountains to find the downed plane and its intelligence officers. Not all the tribes spoke the same language, and yet, we somehow managed to communicate using his language combined with body language. On this next mission, I hoped he would be able to communicate with the headhunters, who we wanted to assist us in our operations on New Guinea. We knew the Japanese soldiers who had occupied Hollandia had escaped into the mountains. My job was to solicit a particular tribe to be our watchdog and tell us where the Japanese were located, so we could send soldiers to their camp either to kill them or drive them deeper into the mountains.

On the appointed day, Arrow reported to me in Army fatigues, rather than the loincloth he wore in his village, and we set out in my jeep with a command car bearing a machine gun. We were in no man's land and could run into Japanese patrols at any time. When we could no longer drive through the jungle terrain, we set out with our packs and machetes through the thick trees and undergrowth towards where we thought we would find the headhunters' village.

We had been walking inland for about a half-hour when I stopped briefly to examine what looked like a rhododendron, a variety I had never seen before. The leaves and pretty yellow flowers were much smaller than those of a typical rhododendron. Arrow was used to my interest in plant life by then and nodded and smiled as I enthusiastically pointed it out before moving on.

Several native men stood guard at a dense group of trees near the village entrance. The people here were taller than the natives on the southern part of the island, made even taller still by a large crop of untrimmed hair. They looked at us suspiciously, bows and arrows in their hands and knives in animal hide sheaves at the waists of their skirts. This clothing was also different from all the other natives I had met, who wore only loincloths.

Arrow spoke to them, telling them who we were and our wish to speak to the chief of the village. They pointed at my rifle and machete, and Arrow translated they would take us into the village, but our weapons must stay here. Unarmed, we entered the village, guards on either side of us and one behind us. For the first few hours, we were under guard at all times.

The A-frame houses in the village were similar to the ones I had seen in other parts of New Guinea. The basic structure and floors were made of logs from local trees, tied together with rope created from reed-like leaves. The walls were also tightly woven from reeds, and the roofs were high-pitched and thatched. All the houses were stilted to accommodate rainforest floods. The women wore skirts with nothing on top, and the children, mostly naked, stared at us as we entered. Attached to the sides of the houses like artwork were skulls I soon learned belonged to warring tribes and Japanese soldiers.

Headhunter village in New Guinea, circa 1945

Once we were allowed to meet the chief everything became very cordial. He insisted we drink a welcome toast of liquor made by his tribesmen. Since I had stopped drinking alcohol, Arrow had to explain to him that I did not drink because my religion did not allow it. Instead, I hoisted water from my canteen that I had poured into one of their beautiful, ceramic cups. The chief was very interested in cultivating vegetables, and with Arrow translating, I had the chance to talk about plants and mentioned the rhododendron I had seen. He knew it well and said to be careful as the leaves were poisonous.

This plant, previously undiscovered by the Western world, would become known as the *Rhododendron vireya* (vireyas). After the war, the plants would be brought to the United States, and growers, including horticulturalists at the Strybing Arboretum in Golden Gate Park, would hybridize them to create many new colors. It is now a popular plant in climates with no freezing temperatures. They do very well in San Francisco and have the advantage of blooming several times a year.

We explained why we had come, and the headhunter chief was happy to provide detailed information about the locations of the Japanese encampments. The tribe detested the Japanese soldiers, who treated the natives very poorly and used them as slave labor. It was no wonder the tribesmen had made their heads into trophies.

A couple of the tribesmen pointed in the direction they had last seen Japanese troops. The tribe told us the Japanese preferred tunnels and caves to open camps. From just the first day of conversation, we learned a lot.

The chief agreed to help us uncover the exact whereabouts of the Japanese encampments. His tribe had no firearms, and he proposed that in exchange for his help we would give them arms. I agreed to do so after I returned to Hollandia.

We spent three days and four nights with the tribe. They took us out on searches, providing valuable intelligence about the number of Japanese soldiers in the area, where they were camped, and the conditions of their camps. It was important to keep track of them, because small Japanese patrols could do substantial damage. A few times we encountered enemy fire, and we managed to kill several enemy soldiers. We were able to acquire their rifles, but the chief preferred U.S. rifles because American ammunition was more readily available through our alliance. Now, all these years later, it is unsettling to think about killing without remorse. Back then, I had learned not to let feelings interfere with my job of eliminating the enemy.

When we accomplished our mission, we took three of the tribesmen back to Hollandia and issued them six rifles and ammunition. This was a great gift for them.

Guided by aerial photographs of the region, we spent a couple weeks visiting several other native villages in the mountains, often with challenging diplomatic sessions. Like the headhunters, most villages had guards we encountered first. We were not always allowed to meet the chief and had to work with the second or third man in command.

Shortly after New Year's Day 1945, I left Hollandia for the last time. I was assigned to join the 40th Division, which was formerly the California, Nevada, and Utah National Guards. They had recently arrived in the region after a series of more defensive and training oriented operations, and therefore, had not seen major combat action. I boarded a Liberty ship that would be part of the landing at Lingayen Gulf, on the northwest shores of Luzon, the largest island in the Philippines and home to the city of Manila.

On January 6, in advance of the landing, the U.S. Navy and Royal Australian Navy began heavy bombardments along the shores of the Lingayen Gulf. Japanese forces had controlled this area since the end of December 1941, when they had overrun Filipino and American positions. Those troops had joined the withdrawal of forces to the Bataan Peninsula, where MacArthur had hoped reinforcements would bolster his strength so he could hold the Philippines. But help never arrived. Instead, in early January 1942, the Japanese began a siege, the Battle of Bataan, on MacArthur's forces and three months later the majority would be forced to surrender, starving and too weak to fight. This led to the infamous Bataan Death March in April 1942, during which some seventy-five thousand Filipino and American soldiers, already weak, emaciated, and fighting off diseases, were forced to march almost a week with barely any food or water. Along the way, many were bayoneted or shot if they fell or stopped to try and get a sip from a muddy roadside puddle. Upward of ten thousand died during the march. For those who survived what awaited them was a horrific prisoner of war camp that would ultimately claim the lives of many thousands more.

But now, three years later, an armada had been assembled to retake Luzon, beginning with the Invasion of Lingayen Gulf. Destroyers, battle ships, cruisers, carriers, and Liberty ships like ours were all part of a huge convoy. Eight hundred different ships and over two hundred thousand men participated in the operation.

I was in charge of an intelligence group consisting of about fifteen men. As we set sail, there were many ships in the seas around us. It was exciting, the sheer number of men and vessels. As we entered the Sulu Sea near the islands of Mindanao and Negros, Japanese fighter planes and *kamikazes* (manned suicide aircraft) suddenly appeared like a small cloud in the sky. As they rapidly drew nearer, their target became clear. They were coming toward the aircraft carrier in our convoy, a few hundred feet away from our ship. Anti-aircraft guns from the surrounding gunner ships made a thunderous noise as they shot into the sky to protect the carrier. There was nothing we could do as passengers on a Liberty ship, possessing no weapons that could target the planes. I rushed with the rest to the port side of the ship to watch. We all started yelling like fans in the bleachers. "Get those bastards!" the men cried. The captain had to make some of the soldiers move to the starboard side, because with all of us on one side, our ship was off balance.

It was a real show, strangely exhilarating and frightening, but it was also like Russian roulette. No one knew which ships would go down. We all wore our life jackets, helpless except for knowing how to launch the lifeboats should *kamikazes*, bombs, torpedoes, or stray bullets find us. Suddenly, we felt very vulnerable.

A gunner on a nearby cruiser shot one of the Japanese planes, and everyone cheered. Another smoked and dove, and one more. The three Zeros went down in the water right next to the aircraft carrier. The others turned and flew away. The Japanese had not inflicted serious damage to the carrier, but the attack certainly had come close. It all happened so quickly that the carrier's planes did not even have a chance to take off. For many soldiers this was their first introduction to warfare, and after the adrenaline of the fight wore off, the rest of the trip was rather tense, both for seasoned and fresh troops alike.

It was January 9, just before sunrise, when we could see land silhouetted in the distance, along with flashes of light, as a great number of our naval ships bombarded the beaches. Before we knew it, in the midst of the noise and chaos, we were told it was time to man the landing crafts. I lead my men as we climbed down rope ladders over the side of the ship. Although the men had been trained to climb up and down such ladders, they were not trained to do so wearing all their equipment. We carried full packs, basic survival gear, and rifles. There were some anxious moments as the men maneuvered their way down. One soldier fell into the water but we quickly pulled him over the metal sides of our boat.

Once all my crew was aboard and the landing craft was filled to its capacity of thirty-six armed men, the Navy boatman moved us away at high speed, taking care not to suddenly pitch the fully loaded craft as he steered us to shore. Simultaneously, many boats from others ships were similarly guided as the Navy kept bombarding the beaches. In fact, we passed a number of gunships as we raced to our landing site. Most everybody in my boat was quiet. None of us knew what we would encounter when we hit the beach.

U.S. landing barges heading for Luzon, 1945

In the area where we landed, the boat could not get right up to the shore. I was the first to jump out of our landing craft, splashing into the water, signaling my men to do the same. Being the shortest, I was waist-deep and had to hold my rifle up above my head as I waded to the beach. I was not a combat soldier, but my instructions were to always carry a gun to protect myself. Too often I had needed to use it.

The Navy was still bombarding the forward area and the noise was unbelievable. As we arrived at the shore, our boys halted their fire. There was almost no opposition from the Japanese, who had apparently fled to the interior. We were very fortunate.

Unexpectedly, everything became strangely calm. I had barely set foot on dry sand when I turned back and saw in the distance a disturbance in the water, something speeding along like a giant shark toward our Liberty ship. Then came the explosion, flames leaping from the bow. A *kaiten* (a manned suicide torpedo) had hit our ship. On the beach, we watched like a bunch of statues as the vessel began to sink along with our supplies, ammunition, personal belongings, and hundreds of men and commanding officers, some of them personal friends.

The boatmen turned their empty crafts back into the waves, trying their best to rescue soldiers in the water. The fire on the ship was sending an ugly, gray cloud of smoke into the sky. Other ships sent boats to assist in the rescue. I roused my team out of their shock and confusion, as we turned our backs to the sea and the things we held dear, including our friends and fellow soldiers. We had orders to move towards a building a ways up the beach, so we advanced with our rifles at the ready.

My main job was to take over the enemy's radio station, their headquarters, and any printing press or similar resource. The next most important task was to establish contact with the guerrillas and work on building an airstrip.

I had the maps that were given to me during my prior visit by way of the submarine. The building up the beach had been a school before the Japanese soldiers claimed it. We searched in and around the abandoned classroom before setting up shop inside. I had my men put together our radio while others kept watch. Other troops arrived, passing right by us on the way to their own destinations while we stayed to secure the area near the beach and establish a base. I had been involved in several invasions, but this was more confusing than most. It was a massive operation with many different types of troops, each having a specific job to do.

With the radio set-up, I sent out messages to the local guerillas. They knew when they heard from me it was time to inform and gather local Filipinos — who were looking for work — and transport them back to our location by truck or foot. I had a list of names we had put together from the last time I was on the island. Most of the local population had already left the coastal area because our planes had dropped leaflets telling them to leave before the naval bombardment. This was also why the Japanese garrison had left for the interior. They knew they were outnumbered.

Next, I set up a makeshift office in which I would interview the locals. They needed to be screened and cleared for work. I also needed to employ those who spoke various local languages and dialects to help us communicate.

Once set-up, I assessed what supplies we had. All men had three days worth of K-rations: thick, fortified cheese crackers high in calories and one canteen of water. We had no tents or anything to sleep in and only the clothes on our backs.

Before evening set in, we used the small emergency spades in our packs and our hands to dig foxholes for protection from Japanese aircraft. We were afraid planes might bomb the easily seen schoolhouse, so we decided to sleep in foxholes a ways away. When I dug my foxhole, I came across an irrigation pipe. We had no idea there would be an irrigation system here. I reburied it and started digging a new hole nearby. Seeing me start on another foxhole sent the men laughing. "Of all the people to find an irrigation pipe, it would be you, Lieutenant Flowers." It was nice to inadvertently create some humor, so useful at that moment. No one knew what the next day would bring or, for that matter, the evening.

I assigned rotating guard duty through the night, three-hour shifts of four men at the perimeter of our camp. In the cover of darkness and the eerie silence after the morning's tumult, I could hear sobs and sniffles coming from more than a few foxholes. We had lost comrades, leaders, and friends. We had lost letters and pictures of loved ones left behind with the rest of our personal items on the ship. This would be the only time to grieve, the hours until it was your turn to go on watch. In combat, we never had a full night's sleep.

There are so many untold stories from the soldiers of war; stories we do not wish to relive in the telling. The hardest moments were when our peers were wounded, and we had no way to help them. There were never enough hands to transport all the injured to a field hospital. Too many times we watched them die right then and there. When we did not have time to dig a grave, we would honor our fallen with an offering of available flowers, many from plants unknown to even my trained eyes. We cut branches just below the dazzling tropical blossoms and stuck the base into the flesh of a halved coconut. This would make them last longer. A coconut is a wonderfully versatile fruit with many uses, but it cannot bring a man back to life.

Too frequently we had to choose to protect the able-bodied fighting force and let the wounded languish behind. This was never easy. We always hoped the medics would catch up with them, but we had minimal communication capabilities and rarely had the opportunity to radio the position of the wounded to someone who might be able to help.

Many times we sent two or three people back to carry someone who had been left behind. These soldiers risked their lives, far too often finding the wounded soldier had died. It was tough taking food from the packs of dead soldiers to distribute amongst the living. It had to be done for our own survival, yet we all felt guilty eating that next meal. We also had to collect the dog tags and, as conditions permitted, report the soldier had died so family could be notified. When it was one of my own men, I would write a letter to his family. Because there was no mail service for weeks at a time, I had to carry the unsent letters and dog tags, reminders of death, as we moved from camp to camp.

Our first full day ashore, the guerrillas and locals arrived at the schoolhouse to sign up for work. For the next two days it was my job to clear the workers and arrange their transportation to the landing strip site. Money was of no interest to the Filipinos since they already had plenty of useless Japanese currency. They agreed to work for food provided by the U.S. Army.

As the Filipinos lined up to work, I checked their names against the list of those who had cooperated with the Japanese. I was careful not to hire any of them. There were many who had cooperated, and they needed to be apprehended, primarily because we did not want them giving the Japanese information about our troop movements.

In the afternoon I took a break and walked out of the building to stretch my aching body. I saw our personnel loading the locals into trucks like sheep or cattle, barking at them, pushing them, and crowding them into the back of the vehicles. I approached the colonel in charge of transportation and told him I would not clear any more workers until his troops treated the Filipinos as if they were American workers or soldiers. I was furious.

He changed the manner of this interaction immediately. This, unfortunately, was one of many unjust treatments I witnessed during the war. The Filipinos looked different; therefore, it was assumed by too many they could be treated like dirt. It became habitual for the U.S. troops to mistreat the natives we were liberating, and to this day I have not forgotten this attitude. I was pleased the colonel, at least, saw what was happening and changed the tenor of his men.

The Mangaldan airstrip started out as a rice paddy about fifteen miles east of Lingayen. The land needed to be leveled for drainage by knocking down the plants without tearing out the roots to finally make a flat surface about twelve inches above the water level. Then, it was partially laid over with heavy steel matting (Marsden Matting). Rains would eventually raise the level of the muck, but the Marine colonel in charge, Colonel Jerome, had served in the Philippines before and was betting the upcoming three dry months was all he needed at Mangaldan.

The Army engineers and civilian workforce worked hard and fast and the first planes, MAG-24 and MAG-32 (Marine Aircraft Group), took off from Dagupan and landed on the strip on January 25, 1945. Combat operations began two days later.

Long before that, after I had cleared enough men to work on the airstrip, I went back to my regular duties, catching up with the 40th Division, which had advanced a good distance inland.

For the most part, it was my decision to join the division. For the landing, my basic orders came from MacArthur's headquarters, but I had a fair amount of freedom in the field with many of my decisions based on battle conditions. I always worked closely with other division intelligence officers, but I had many different "bosses" in the military, leading to some measure of autonomy. When I was on the search for the airplane in the Owen Stanley Mountains, I worked with the Army Air Force high brass only. When I was on the submarine, my contact was with Navy and Army headquarters. When I went to New Britain, it was with both the Marines and under MacArthur's orders. My original assignment in the Pacific theater was as a base censor, but then I was selected for special, secret missions having nothing to do with censorship.

Because I served so many different bosses, I was never promoted to captain. Many times the base censor's office didn't even know where I was. The intelligence officer of the 40th Division knew most of the time what I was doing, but he didn't hand out the promotions. None of this mattered much at the time though. We were all just doing our jobs, and I was determined to do mine to the best of my ability.

The 40th was to meet up with the 37th Division in a pincer maneuver at Camiling, over thirty miles inland to the south-southeast. This meant the two divisions would move in on the Japanese troops in a choreographed attack from both flanks. During the movement, my intelligence team had to apprehend government officials who had collaborated with the Japanese or harmed civilians. We learned of them from local police and guerrillas, both of whom helped us detain these officials.

This work depended heavily on guides and translators. At first, a few who I had met previously came along. They were most helpful but did not like to travel too far from their own base of operations. Due to local language variations we often needed new translators anyway as we moved through the island.

We knew barely anything about the local culture, which changed from one place to the next. Each area spoke a different dialect or language, and it was very difficult to know if the natives were telling the truth. Twice I went with a Filipino guide to supposedly meet with collaborators only to be led toward a Japanese patrol. On both occasions I discovered this danger just in time and was able to avoid the patrol or go around them, which was difficult to do. We were lucky we did not get killed. Japanese soldiers did not wish to surrender, because such an action dishonored them and their families.

We encouraged the locals to set up new regional governments, outside the influence of the Japanese or Japanese sympathizers. We had to encourage local radio stations to broadcast true information, no more Tokyo Rose. Food distribution was also critically important. Allied victories in the Pacific had made it harder for the Japanese to get their ships through to Manila, so they started confiscating food from the Filipinos. Our main purpose was to keep anyone from doing anything that would harm our progress; however, these situations were rarely simple. In retrospect, we could have done a much better job if we had more trained men, and of course, all our work was done in the heat of combat. We often had to leave before a job was done in order to stay with the advancing troops.

At night, we occasionally slept in tents, but more often we slept directly on the exposed ground. A couple of times, local Filipinos invited us to sleep in their homes on spare mattresses. A few times the locals kindly offered to kill and serve to us chickens and other animals. I always politely declined and suggested instead they keep their chickens, which laid eggs and provided food for many more people.

The 40th encountered several severely damaged bridges. The Army engineers had to repair them before we could cross with all our heavy equipment, and this caused a substantial delay in our flanking maneuver.

In the meantime, the 37th ran into far less opposition and made it to the meeting place outside Camiling. Communication between the two divisions was abruptly cut off. It became my job to establish contact with the intelligence officer of the 37th and inform him of our situation and when he could expect our troops. The only way to do so was to tell him in person.

No translator was available, so I packed up and set off immediately, wearing a farmer's outfit. My helmet and jacket were concealed in my rucksack. I would have to walk alone and at a good pace, most of the way through enemy territory.

At first, I walked through an area we controlled. Our engineers were working on a damaged bridge and some of our patrols had fanned out but only for so many miles.

Once I got past them, I stayed off the main road because the Japanese controlled the area. I walked through agricultural fields planted with grains and vegetables, and, of course, I walked through rice paddies. Most of the land was dotted with small farmhouses. Around the farmhouses, I saw chickens, pigs, and other farm animals, but hardly any cows. I avoided going through villages, although I did ride on one farm wagon pulled by horses.

Wherever there were trees or hedges I would take detours in case anyone was observing me. I was aware of some Japanese troop movements, and those I avoided since they were on roadways. I had to cross over streams several times, wading through the water because I thought it wise to avoid bridges. Where it was too deep or difficult to cross and I had to use the bridge, I observed the area for a long time to make sure there were no enemy troops nearby.

When night fell, it was difficult to walk in the dark. I had a flashlight but felt the light would draw attention, so I didn't want to use it. Choosing a dry spot in a field of tall native shrubs, I propped my bag up as a pillow and curled up to sleep with my rifle in the crook of my arm. Being used to foxholes, a protected area with shrubs around it served as a fine bed. I suppose I could have stayed the night on a farm, but I did not know if the natives were on our side or working with the Japanese. It was best not to take any chances.

A day and a half later, I reached the 37th. I quickly changed into my Amy uniform and searched for the intelligence officer. Announcing myself to the guard patrol, I was led through a courtyard and into a building, where I found my counterpart and exchanged information.

The task done, there was nothing to do but return to the 40th and report back to General Brush's headquarters. Whatever happened next was up to the generals in charge of each division. I walked through the entrance court when a loud voice called out, "Is there anyone here from the 40th Division?"

I approached the speaker, a full colonel, identified myself, and asked him what I could do for him. The colonel waved his arm toward a jeep and told me to speak to the person sitting in the front seat next to the driver. Walking toward the jeep, I noticed five stars on the license plate. As I got closer, I recognized the man sitting there. It was General Douglas MacArthur.

Saluting, I gave my name and rank, but I am certain I did not state my name very clearly. I was taken aback to see the general in a combat zone let alone to be speaking to him. To my great surprise, the general shook my hand.

"I'm glad to meet you, Lieutenant Wertheim."

He spread out a map on his knees and asked me to show him where the 40th Division was being held up and why. It turns out someone took a photograph of me with the general, but I was too busy illustrating information on the map and answering his questions to notice.

BULLETIN

VICTORY EDITION

Going over a map with General MacArthur

Then the general asked me to guide him to the 40th Division. This was a nice way of telling me what I was about to do. It seemed unwise to chance the life of the commanding general of the Southwest Pacific theater through no-man's land where we were sure to run into Japanese patrols. I expressed this to the general, but MacArthur insisted on going. I suggested the 37th Division could give us a couple of scout cars with machine guns, but the general would not hear of it.

"Climb in," he said, and we took off in his jeep, just the general, his driver, the general's aide, the colonel, and me. I felt an incredible responsibility on my shoulders.

The first half hour was smooth sailing. Then we ran into a Japanese patrol. The driver steered the jeep to the side of the road, and we quickly jumped out into a ditch, using the jeep as a shield.

"Can I borrow your rifle?" General MacArthur asked me. I handed it to him, feeling naked and vulnerable without my rifle and a strange sense of guilt that I should be trying to protect the general. Instead I watched as he shot three of the threatening Japanese soldiers. The rest fled. He handed me back my rifle. "I know it is military practice to clean a rifle after using it, but I will rely on you to do this for me."

While we continued our journey toward the 40th, MacArthur asked me about troop morale. It was not in my nature to skirt the truth (nor is it now). Besides, it was my job to pass on information with absolute accuracy. I had found that doing so almost always helped, so I did not hesitate in my reply.

"Well sir, you are not very popular with the men." Then added, "Often we do not have the right supplies. There have been times when we have run out of ammunition and food. Another complaint is it takes too long to transport wounded soldiers to the hospital."

"How about *your* morale, Lieutenant?" he replied.

I did hesitate before answering this time, taking a breath, "Well sir, you are not my favorite general, either."

MacArthur encouraged me to elaborate. I explained I had trained with a group of officers and soldiers to go into northern Germany, in advance of the landing in France, now known as D-Day, the June 6, 1944 invasion on the beaches of Normandy. I was the only person in the group well acquainted with the region west of the Elbe River, and therefore, an important part of the team, independent of the fact I spoke German fluently with the correct dialect for this area. I complained about the snafu that brought me to the South Pacific and about the general not releasing me when he was asked to send me back to Washington, D.C. I explained I felt I had deserted my team.

At that point MacArthur turned his body to face me where I sat in the back of the jeep. He told me his command was the stepchild of the war department. Most of the war supplies were headed to Europe, commanded by Generals Eisenhower, Clark, and Patton, and to battles in the Pacific commanded by Admiral Nimitz. He, in turn, had to fight for whatever he could get. He was short on airplanes to replace those that had been lost, and he didn't have enough men.

"By chance, I received word that a new officer who had been trained in intelligence work was in my command. Why do you think you were sent to New Britain to get the missionary out of Rabaul? Why do you think you were sent on the submarine to visit the guerrillas in Luzon, and why were you involved in the search for the intelligence plane? I needed you." I couldn't believe he could just rattle off my missions like that. Then he asked me, "If you were in my shoes and you had found an officer on your staff with your training, would you have sent him to Europe?"

"No sir," I answered immediately. MacArthur laughed. "Well, this means you also would have been a bastard."

He said he was glad to meet me in person. He expressed his sympathy for the loss of my mother and grandmother in the concentration camp. I couldn't believe he knew. I was really touched he had bothered to discover and remember my mother and grandmother's deaths. Likely, my mail was being read, and he found out from one of my intelligence friends at headquarters.

On the way back to the 40th Division, we came to the still unfinished bridge the Army engineers were building. General MacArthur asked me to go across and check with the officer in charge to see if we could cross the partially built bridge with the jeep.

I approached the colonel, whom I actually knew quite well, and asked him if General MacArthur could cross the bridge in his jeep. The colonel was very annoyed, insisting he was way too busy to joke around. "We were just attacked by a Japanese patrol, and we're behind schedule."

I simply handed him my binoculars and told him to look across the river at the jeep's license plate and passenger. The colonel glanced at me with irritation and grabbed the binoculars. When he returned them to me, he looked at me quizzically, his eyes big. He immediately became cooperative. He told me the beams were just far enough apart to take the jeep across, but someone would have to guide the driver. I told MacArthur's driver to follow me as I walked backward on the ten-inch wide beams, guiding him slowly over the bridge.

Those watching must have been holding their breath. As soon as we were back on the road, the colonel congratulated me on guiding the jeep successfully, then remembered himself, and saluted the general. MacArthur got out of the jeep and returned the colonel's salute by shaking his hand. He asked the colonel not to radio ahead he had been here, in case the enemy intercepted the message.

The general dropped me at Division headquarters, then bid me a warm goodbye. I saluted him. He returned my salute and immediately drove off.

Perhaps it was some of the engineers who leaked it, but during the next couple of days the men repeated the rumor they heard: "Did you know General MacArthur was here?" No one expected him to be on the front lines, let alone drop off one very privileged lieutenant. General Brush, the commanding general for the 40th Division, was especially annoyed MacArthur had not stopped to say hello.

Months later, the photograph of me with the general was printed in an Army publication. I went to headquarters and talked to the general's assistant, the colonel I'd met before, and asked if I could get a copy of the photograph. The colonel told me to come back in two days. When I did, the colonel said General MacArthur wanted to see me. I entered the general's office with a salute. In reply, the general rose from his seat and shook my hand, asking if I would like to have the photograph signed. I told him, of course, I would love to have his signature. During this visit we discussed various subjects. General MacArthur was a pleasant gentleman and very easy to talk to. I felt more at ease talking to him than to my own commanding officer. I was deeply impressed by this meeting and our prior encounter. I consider these moments my most prized experiences overseas.

During the rest of the way south to Clark Field and Manila, the 40th Division liberated several communities. Although the bulk of the Japanese Army had retreated to Manila, there were still a number of patrols along the way surprising us with gunfire. We experienced the most resistance in the bigger towns where the Japanese forces clung to their positions. We sorted through civilians for enemy collaborators, always considering the townspeople innocent until proven guilty as we listened carefully to testimony and gathered information. Some people considered dangerous to our troops or the civilian population were placed under house arrest pending official hearings about their guilt or innocence, while others were put in prison. In time, all the information was turned over to administrative agencies. This process involved endless handwritten reports, since we did not often have access to typewriters.

By January 28, 1945, the 40th Division had partially captured the complex of airfields known as Clark Field near Angeles City, over forty miles north of Manila. Established by the U.S. military in 1903, the Japanese had overrun the base and controlled it since January 1942, after dealing a critical blow to our air capabilities on December 8, 1941. Our forces needed to put Clark Field into operation immediately; however, the damage to the facilities was extensive, and the Japanese would not let the base go easily. Even after the air field was secured at the end of January, Japanese troops remained in the Zambales Mountains, which rose abruptly in a crescent against the far end of the base. The Japanese had blasted out caves to conceal large field artillery guns they fired on our troops to prevent them from working on the runways.

My intelligence unit established its quarters in a house on the base. One day we were relaxing for a rare moment when an artillery shell came whistling through an open window, passing through the living room and out another open window on the opposite side, exploding a nearby tree into kindling. We knew we had been very lucky, but we mourned the loss of the much-needed shade the tree provided.

Our planes tried bombing the Japanese hideouts, but they were unsuccessful. The caves also concealed anti-aircraft guns the Japanese used all too often with good results. The only thing to do was flush them out of the caves, one by one. It was dangerous and difficult as our infantry attacked the caves at night with flamethrowers, and climbed in afterwards to overpower the enemy in hand-to-hand combat. They found a large supply of canned food stashed in the caves. The Japanese had provisions to last for weeks; they were prepared for a long fight. However, it was our infantry soldiers who finally won the upper hand and fully secured Clark Field by neutralizing these enemy positions.

After about a week at Clark, I started to feel terrible pain and the heat of a rising temperature. I had Dengue fever, a tropical virus transmitted by mosquitos. They transported me to a tent hospital on the air base, where I lay for over a week sweating and trying to manage excruciating joint and muscle pains. Another name for the disease is "breakbone fever," and it is sometimes fatal. I had so little energy I had to crawl to the outhouse and could barely pull myself up on the toilet. I felt great shame and embarrassment about this illness, in contrast to the other men in the ward who had been injured in battle. When I got a bit better, I assisted the nurses in taking care of the wounded. It felt good to be useful again.

After I fully recovered and was back to work, a message came in from a platoon stopped by armed Philippine soldiers as they tried to cross a nearby bridge. The sergeant in charge withdrew his platoon and reported the problem to division headquarters. It now became my job to investigate.

I drove with the sergeant to the bridge. I introduced myself to the soldiers and asked who they were. They were a Hukbalahap guerrilla unit, or Huks, mostly peasants fighting against wealthy farmers. U.S. troops could not enter their area, they told me.

I had not heard of this group, and I requested a meeting with their leaders, which was arranged the following day. From the bridge, a couple of the guards led me to a farming village where I entered a small house that clearly served as both living quarters and conference room. I met two Filipino men and an American woman who translated for them. She explained they were communists, fighting for the rights of peasants. They had fought the Japanese but were also killing sugar plantation owners and other wealthy Filipinos. I had become very aware of the severe poverty throughout the Philippines, a country with no significant middle class. There were people who were quite wealthy, but the vast majority had almost nothing. Still, this did not rationalize their perspective in my mind. They insisted Allied troops would not be allowed in their territory, which included the farmland between Clark Field and Subic Bay. Yet they wanted the help of the United States and recognition of their plight as peasants in a country under siege. Despite their zeal, they were friendly and very polite but resolute in their cause.

They had a farmers' market with a rich abundance of food. I offered to buy some with my U.S. dollars, but they wanted only Japanese currency. I tried to explain Japanese money was worthless, but they insisted. When another officer and I came back the next day, we brought boxes of Japanese currency and loaded up our jeep with wonderful food we had not seen for months — eggs, chickens, and fresh fruit and vegetables. Returning to our unit with these prizes, we were the richest men in the world — we became everyone's friend.

The Huks — their actions, attitudes, and communist bent — worried me, and I felt it was important to promptly report this situation to General Krueger at the Army headquarters back at the Lingayen Gulf. Upon returning from the second meeting with the Huks, I hopped in my jeep and drove towards the Gulf. It was at least a four-hour drive to Lingayen. We were finally in control of the area, though there were still small groups of Japanese troops giving us problems. It was an important issue, so I had to risk it. I arrived at Sixth Army headquarters in the middle of the night, dead tired. I reported I had to give the general some important information. His aide woke him up, and I explained to a sleepy, soon-to-be four-star general what my visit was all about. No one in the Army, it seemed, had heard of the Huks before.

I told him what the Huks had said and why I had the impression they moved around, careful not to make their headquarters in one place. I explained they had their own small army of soldiers and presented a danger to our troops. For these reasons, we needed to be very aware of their positions and the size of their forces. We could not afford to have our flank exposed to them. This was certainly something Army headquarters had to know about.

General Krueger's secretary took down my verbal report and sent the completed report to General MacArthur in Hollandia and from there to Washington, D.C. It was apparent Washington had its hands full with other matters, primarily in Europe. Later, the Huks were found to be active on other islands, especially Panay, but the United States did little about it. It is my belief if the United States had done more about the Huks, the communists might never have gained the strength they did in the region after the end of the war.

Besides the farmers' market bonanza, one more good thing came out of this episode. I brought with me two big sacks of mail from the 40th Division, and the general made sure the mail was put on the plane carrying my report back to Hollandia. I also carried mail back to the division. This made me even more popular with the men, because we had not received mail for several weeks. When we were on the move, it often took a while for it to catch up with us.

I had several letters from Margrit. Her letters always gave me a temporary reprieve from my surroundings, even if it was just for those few glorious minutes of immersion. I always took her picture from my wallet and propped it up in front of me as I read her words.

We wrote weekly, but Margrit often wrote more frequently. She had more to tell than I did because so much of my work was confidential. Margrit wrote about her job, her friends, and about love and missing me. She described the lessons she was taking in Japanese. At times, we were able to read the same books, sharing our opinions and experiences through our exchange of letters. In one letter Margrit told me she had received a dozen red roses. Before leaving to go overseas, I prepaid to have them delivered to her on our anniversary.

I kept in touch with the Huk leaders and told them General Krueger had not received any instructions from Washington. Their killing of wealthy landholders continued. One morning, General Krueger arrived at the front lines and asked me what I thought should be done. My suggestion was to have a small unit raid the Huks' headquarters and detain all the leaders, putting them under house arrest, so the group would weaken without sufficient leadership. Under the general's instructions, a small unit of elite soldiers assembled, and we proceeded to the Huks' hideout. Although we attempted to keep this plan a secret, somehow they got wind of it and left just minutes before we arrived. The coffee in the cups was still hot.

They did, however, leave behind some important documents. One such document was a list of people to be killed. My name was the third on the list with the comment, "He let us down." I had not come up with a good solution to their problem. No one paid proper attention to the group's political movement, and after the war, it would get entirely out of hand with a strengthened communist party and an insurrection that would burn until 1954.

Despite my name being on their hit list, I sent a letter to the Huks at an address I had discovered amidst the documents from our otherwise unsuccessful raid. I tried to explain our government in Washington was busy fighting a war in Europe and simply did not attach a priority to the Huks' cause. This was a private letter, and I know it reached them.

Our troops moved toward Manila, trying to clear the region of the enemy. I told General Brush about a civilian internment camp in Manila at Santo Tomas University and recommended we concentrate on the liberation of those people. Brush suggested I join the 37th Division to participate. There was a great fear the Japanese would kill the prison camp inmates when they learned American forces were closing in on Manila.

Generals MacArthur and Mudge, in the "Flying Column" decree, authorized specialized elements of the 1st Cavalry to make a lightning thrust into the capital. Just after midnight on February 1, the 1st Cavalry began a race to Manila from the south, a dash through enemy lines while taking force only as necessary so as not to delay the rescue operation. In three days they would cover one hundred miles through enemy territory. As the U.S. Army pushed into Manila from the north, the scouts of the 37th Division and I were among the first to arrive at the Santo Tomas internment camp. It was a chaotic time with the military pressing into Manila, the Japanese continuing to fight rather than surrender, and the liberation of the internment camp. On arrival at Santo Tomas, my focus was to assess the situation and determine our course of action.

The prisoners — men, women, and children — were in terrible shape. The Japanese had been holding Americans and other Allied civilians at the university since 1942, after Allied forces had abandoned Manila. With steadily worsening conditions over the last three years, we would learn that about ten percent of the prisoners had already died, leaving approximately three thousand seven hundred survivors. The adults were gaunt from starvation, and many of the children were orphaned. It became immediately obvious they needed water, food, and medical treatment, none of which we had with us when we first reached the camp. I radioed for medical help and asked for food and water drops; however, with the push to Manila, communication was difficult. It was terribly painful to witness such anguish and feel so powerless.

The survivors looked to us as heroes, but we could not act as heroes. At the very basic level, we did not have the supplies or the know-how to care for everyone properly; we needed doctors and nurses. And as soldiers, we certainly were not prepared for nor had the training to deal with the psychological trauma of being held in the internment camp. We did our very best to provide immediate help, but it was simply not enough.

While trying to secure Santo Tomas University as well as liberate and assist the prisoners, we had to contend with Japanese still within the university. Not all of them had fled when we arrived, and they used the large campus to disrupt our efforts. They knew where to hide and attack our troops, who struggled to communicate with one another. I lost two members from my team. The Japanese also took some of the prisoners hostage. Meanwhile, I had to contend with the needs of the liberated prisoners, while also learning about their health, their nationality, and where they hoped to go once it was safe for them to leave. This was one of the most challenging situations I faced, made all the worse by not feeling adequately prepared or resourced to handle the situation.

The Army had a tough time securing Manila, with the ugly battle continuing a full month into March 1945. We were poorly prepared to handle a big city and the problems we encountered there. Our troops had been trained in jungle warfare, not block by block street fighting.

We were not aware the enemy was going to make a stand and burn part of the city. It was like nothing we had seen before, a terrible bloodbath. The Battle of Manila would claim over a thousand of our soldiers and perhaps twenty times that number of Japanese. Caught between these military forces, roughly one hundred thousand Filipino civilians would die at the hands of Japanese massacres and Allied artillery, bombs, and bullets. Later historians would compare the month long battle to Stalingrad, witnessing World War II's worst urban warfare.

In early March, I received orders to pull out with the 40th Division. We set sail from the Lingayen Gulf on March 15, 1945, and landed on Panay Island three days later. Fortunately, the Japanese had already retreated inland, and we met no resistance. It helped the Filipino guerrillas there were quite active. The civilians greeted us with revelry. We moved toward the capital of Ilio-Ilio City. There, we had decent quarters and even some good food as my unit did its usual round of interviewing and investigation. U.S. intelligence had determined the man who was serving as governor of Panay during the Japanese occupation was guilty of cooperating with the enemy, and he was placed under house arrest. My unit spent many hours interrogating him to learn the names of collaborators.

In addition, we learned a number of Americans were leaders in the guerrilla forces. They were very happy to see us and wondered how they could get home. Some of them still had their dog tags with their serial numbers to provide evidence they had survived by taking refuge in the jungle when Japan had rolled over these islands more than three years earlier. This issue had not been considered let alone addressed, and I reported it to General Brush to try to find a solution for these men.

After securing Panay, the division made landings on Negros Island. When my unit sailed to Negros on March 29, all the officers, myself included, drew straws — actually matchsticks — to decide who would be in charge of unloading all the supplies and equipment from our LST, even though none of us were trained in the science of unloading a ship. I chose the short stick, and it became my responsibility.

We landed in the late afternoon. Each company assigned ten men to help; however, since they were from various units, it was very difficult to command them. They wanted to be with their own units, with the men who had become their friends, and to do their assigned jobs. This unloading assignment kept them from doing their work.

Still, it was imperative that I motivate them to finish unloading before daylight when the landing crafts would become sitting ducks for Japanese Zeros. Heavy boxes for the signal corps made up much of the cargo. Pontoons were put in place between the LSTs and the shore. Trucks would back up from the beach, their tires carefully aligned on the pontoons, and the soldiers would load the trucks.

I divided the men into two teams. One team worked for an hour while the other team rested. This rest was necessary, because the labor was backbreaking, and the men had not eaten since lunch. At midnight, I asked the ship's captain for food and drink for my men, explaining that the soldiers had not eaten for twelve hours. The captain told me his orders were to deliver the ship to Negros; he was not required to feed Army soldiers.

I was very angry. I asked him, "Do you want your ship sunk, or do you want to leave here before daylight?" I stood my ground and finally convinced him the extra energy and morale would allow the men to work harder, possibly saving the ship. The captain softened up, and we were fed in shifts.

After eating, I took off my jacket with my silver lieutenant's bar and worked side-by-side with the men, taking no rest myself. My crew became unified, and our LST was unloaded before anyone else's. Our ship was the first to leave.

In the morning light, Japanese Zeros sank five of the ships remaining on the beach and damaged several others.

The next day General Brush, commanding officer for the 40th Division, called me to his office. He accused me of conduct unbecoming an officer for removing my jacket and working with the crew. The general said the action was not "officer-like" and I would likely be court-martialed.

"We lost five ships in the operation, but not mine," I said to the general. "I wanted to encourage my men." After a loaded pause, I continued. "But sir, before you court-martial me, I think you should check with General MacArthur."

The rumor of a court-martial went all over camp, from company to company. Then, suddenly, I never heard of it again. I think if Lieutenant Flowers had been court-martialed, General Brush would have gotten an ear full.

After the cargo was unloaded, I went to make contact with my own unit. We drove toward the capital city to take the Japanese naval headquarters building, an office building on the main square. With breakfast dishes containing half-eaten meals on the table, it was clear the Japanese fled shortly before our arrival. One of my men could read Japanese and identified a number of important papers that hadn't been burned. I stuffed many of them into a large rucksack, but there were still more that I couldn't carry out in one trip. I left a few guards to secure the place, while the rest of the unit headed for the radio station. We were only a couple hundred feet away when an explosion went off behind us. The Japanese had set time bombs that blew up the building, killing the men I had just put on duty there. We were stunned but had to move on to our next task at the radio station. Later, back at base, we reviewed the papers we had taken from the naval headquarters and discovered crucial information about the location of the Japanese fleet. Given our task at the radio station, we didn't have time to mourn the loss of our friends and comrades, the dear price paid for this information. It was just the way it was.

I boarded one of the naval ships still in the harbor and asked the captain to code my information and send it directly to General MacArthur. You never know what impact your work may have, but this data likely influenced one of the big naval battles that followed.

In the island's capital, Bacolod City, Negros, I knew there was a Japanese consulate, but I could not discover where. Then I learned of the consul's private residence. We inspected the house without knowing he had been running the consulate from this residence. There were a lot of lovely things in the house, but diplomatic items are handled quite differently than military ones, so I locked the place up and stationed two guards. When General Brush heard I had secured the site, he wanted to have the keys to inspect the house. I had heard some high-ranking officers confiscated items for themselves in these situations. The things in the house did not belong to them or me. I did not hand over the keys, telling him I would do so only on orders from General MacArthur. I obtained no such order. Already being out of favor with General Brush, this decision did not win me any more popularity in his office.

Through questioning some guerrillas, I learned of a Japanese lumber mill on the southern end of Negros. Lumber and milling machinery were like gold to the Army, because lumber had to be brought all the way from the United States which is a costly and time-consuming export. To try to secure the mill, I requested three armored jeeps and twelve infantrymen to accompany my small unit, but General Brush only gave me one scout car with a mounted machine gun. I had my own jeep, but no additional personnel. He was reluctant to deplete his forces because he was having problems with Japanese troops dug in on the mountain near the capital. I had my interpreter find four guerrilla-scouts willing to accompany us, all of them equipped with rifles. I had three of my team and the four guerillas for a total of eight of us to take over the entire mill, but off we went anyway. We travelled through unsecured territory where encountering the enemy was a real possibility, but I felt strongly the mission was worth it.

We made it through without an attack and stopped our vehicles just short of our destination. One of the guerrillas told me the mill area had a tremendous echo. As we approached the site on foot, climbing up a mountainside, we agreed we would not speak at all but write notes to each other. We watched every step we took so as not to step on a branch or crunch leaves under foot. We wanted to do nothing that might alert the Japanese of our presence.

We moved slowly, detouring to avoid stepping on anything that would create a noise. When we neared the ridge of the mountain, I motioned all to stay in a prone position, and we crept on our hands and knees up the last fifty feet or so.

Down below was an amazing sight, a large valley surrounded entirely by mountains creating a natural amphitheater. The mill was a sprawling complex. There were several mill buildings, two-story framed houses, and large piles of stacked lumber. The people down below, in miniature from our vista, were unloading logs from train cars.

I instructed my scouts to place themselves about a hundred feet apart along the perimeter. At a given time I would fire my rifle, and they should follow with shots, each of us firing about ten seconds apart. They crept away, and I waited to allow them enough time to get into position. Then, I fired. They did the same for six rounds.

I expected we would make a loud noise, but the volume and repetition exceeded my expectations. Our rifles created a terrific boom that kept echoing and sounding like the bombardment at Lingayen Gulf. It was a concert of gunfire. The Japanese workers below scrambled quickly out of buildings, piled onto the train in a panic, and left for the interior.

My men and I hiked down the hill. The tea was still warm when we reached the mill. We made notes about the amount of lumber and checked over the machinery.

I knew I had to get more troops to protect this valuable asset. I made my way back to my jeep, radioed on a secure frequency to MacArthur's headquarters, and reported our capture of the mill. The general's aid asked me if I thought a fighter plane could land on the road near my position. The road was paved but only twenty-feet wide at the most. The colonel said he thought that would do.

At a pre-arranged time, a special two-seater fighter plane flew overhead, looking for my jeep. I lit three flares to let the pilot know where he could land on the roadway. There was no guarantee it was long enough or wide enough; nonetheless, he landed safely. As soon as he came to a stop, I boarded the plane, and before I was even able to get my seatbelt in place, the proficient pilot turned the plane around and prepared for an immediate take off. As we quickly gathered speed, we held our breath because we were not certain if the road was straight enough. A moment later, we were up in the air, heading toward Clark Field. It was a beautiful sight to see the country from the air. I took in the expansive landscape as we made our way. When we landed at Clark Field, MacArthur's limousine driver was waiting for me. He drove me to the new headquarters in Manila, where the colonel led me to a large conference room.

Sitting around a table were General MacArthur; General Kenney, commander of Allied Air Forces in the Southwest Pacific Area (SWPA); General Krueger, commander of the Sixth Army; two other Army generals; and two Navy admirals. General MacArthur stood up from his chair and returned my salute. He shook my hand, welcomed me to the headquarters, and introduced me to the others at the conference table. We sat down, and I presented my report about the takeover of the lumber mill. There were a number of questions, and I pointed out the location of the mill on a map. Then I listened as the General MacArthur asked the other officers for their opinions on parachute troops landing at the site before giving instructions for the mission.

After two hours of deliberation, the General turned to me and asked when I had last eaten. It was about midnight, and thinking for a moment, I told him I had eaten K-rations at 0600. The General turned to the others, "Gentlemen, we will take a recess while I feed this officer."

The General took me to a small dining room and arranged for the meal by having the cook awakened. While we waited, MacArthur asked about General Brush and the threatened court-martial. I told him the whole story, while he sat with me as I ate. I had hardly finished when an officer came in and requested my presence to brief the parachute troops about the location of the lumber mill. I thanked the general and bid him farewell, once again.

That evening was most memorable. It was humbling and fascinating to see the leaders of the Army, Navy, and Allied Air Forces work together to address a problem and then all agree on a solution. General MacArthur's consideration also meant a great deal. The experience raised my spirits tremendously. I felt great pride in my small contribution.

In midsummer 1945, some guerrillas told me about an inhabited island between Panay and Negros in the Visayan Sea. The seas there were dotted with small lush islands. I decided to investigate. Along with another officer, an experienced sailor, we took a motorized sailboat out to the island.

We pulled up to a private dock with a fishing boat and two handsome sailboats, upon one a stately older gentleman was making repairs. From the end of the dock, there was a paved road surrounded by agricultural fields. It was a serene and peaceful setting, with no indication a brutal war was raging all around it. We had landed in some magical, isolated paradise. We walked up to the older gentleman and introduced ourselves as U.S. Army officers. He greeted us warmly and invited us into his home. He guided us down the path, past the fields, and through a beautiful, well-kept garden. There were familiar annuals, and I was most impressed by the orchids growing outside. In front of the house there was an eight-foot high hibiscus hedge in full bloom. He explained he was from a Spanish family who had owned the island for many generations. The Japanese had not touched it, probably deeming it too small to be of any interest, so the islanders were living on their miniature Eden without any intrusion from the war around them.

Inside the house, the gentleman introduced us to his wife and two beautiful daughters. The other officer and I smiled at one another. They made us at home, fed us delicious fresh food, and we stayed for three glorious days and two nights. It was a tropical island fantasy. We laughed in private about the temptation to just disappear and stay there forever, but, of course, we acted properly. After walking every inch of the lovely island, we returned to base, well fed and rested, and I filed my report.

At the beginning of August 1945, while in Manila, I was granted a forty-five day leave, my second leave since embarking overseas. I had been on the islands, mostly in combat, away from the mainland and my beautiful Margrit for nearly two full years. In a couple weeks, I was scheduled to fly back on a C-54 to San Francisco. I planned to spend every day with my bride and then return to Manila, where the Army was preparing for the invasion of Japan. On August 6 and 9, U.S. planes dropped the atomic bombs Little Boy and Fat Man on Hiroshima and Nagasaki, respectively. Japan surrendered on August 15, 1945.

This changed everything. Peace was around the corner and suddenly many soldiers were going back to the mainland. More transportation was needed, so I agreed to go back by ship instead. I boarded the Matson liner SS Monterey in late August. The Monterey had been a passenger liner before being commissioned for war use. In December 1941, she was one of the first ships to arrive with fresh troops in Hawaii, carrying over three thousand soldiers, and returned to the mainland with eight hundred of Pearl Harbor's wounded. The officers shared cabins that, despite its years of service, were plush and luxurious compared to what we were used to on the standard Liberty ship. The junior officers ate in an open cafeteria; however, senior officers were welcome to eat in the officers' dining room. While the food was not what you get on today's cruise ships, the food was much better than it had been in the field. We stopped in Pearl Harbor to refuel and take on food but were not allowed to go ashore. Just the same, we were in heaven.

It was a much more pleasant trip than my outward bound journey from Portland to Townsville, Australia. Then we slept on narrow bunks, stacked three or four high, and I was sick for a good part of the voyage. On board the Monterey, I slept comfortably, and there was even a library, where one could read leisurely.

On my return voyage, we heard the news of the formal signing of the surrender papers on September 2, 1945, aboard the USS Missouri, henceforth celebrated in the United States as V-J (Victory over Japan) Day.

I was very happy the war was over, but I was haunted knowing how many civilians our country had killed in the bombing of Hiroshima and Nagasaki. It was a grave decision about which I had mixed feelings. I knew many lives would have been lost in an invasion of Japan. I wondered how the Japanese population would take the defeat, a seemingly unthinkable dishonor in their culture.

Now, removed from my day-to-day survival and responsibilities, I suddenly had time to think about everything. How could the Japanese recover? How would Manila recover? What about Europe? What would happen to the victims in the concentration camps? Who would pay for all the destruction?

I also pondered my own fate. Until the atomic bombs, I was under the impression that I would return to Manila and continue my service after my forty-five day leave. With the war officially over, was this still the case? I didn't know where I was going next. The future was a complete mystery.

As our ship cruised into San Francisco Bay, under the Golden Gate Bridge, passing Alcatraz Island, and slowing into the dock at Fort Mason, I was overcome with an excitement that even exceeded the emotions I had felt when I spotted Lady Liberty for the first time. Nearly seven years later, I was now coming home rather than hoping to find a new country to call home. Almost all aboard sent a letter in advance to let family know of our ship's arrival.

We disembarked into a crowd of people — mostly wives, parents, sisters, brothers, and friends. Most ashore were looking anxiously for loved ones, for the husbands, fathers, sons, and brothers they hadn't seen in so long. They were looking for the lucky ones, the ones who had survived.

Amongst the horde, I somehow spotted Margrit. I pushed my way through tearful reunions and people patting me on the shoulder in welcome. In a moment, I was holding my wife tightly in my arms. It had been two years since I had embraced her, and I will never forget the wonderful feeling of that moment — the warmth of her body, her tenderness, her softness, and the feeling of love. Miraculously, I returned in one piece, and here was Margrit, her body pressed to mine.

A minute later, I heard a command to board the military transport buses immediately. We were heading to Camp Beale in Marysville, California, where I would be assigned a temporary duty. I looked intensely into Margrit's eyes, not wanting to look away.

"I will see you there," Margrit said.

My fellow soldiers and I spent the night at Camp Beale, but it is all a blur now. I do not even remember what we had for dinner. The next morning, a corporal, who was handling the papers for the returning troops, interviewed me. He asked me if I wanted to have my forty-five day paid leave. This was a strange question. I thought this was why I was returning to the United States; to take a paid vacation with my bride. I told him yes.

He then handed me a piece of paper stating I would serve for the duration of the war, which had just ended, plus an additional six months. I had signed these conditions when I was originally drafted, so I was very confused. I asked the corporal why I had to sign this again. He explained many troops returning from Europe had taken the paid leave only to then claim they had enough points to be discharged as soon as they were to return to work. The government caught on to this scheme and decided if soldiers wanted the paid leave, they also had to stay in the service for an additional six months. The corporal told me I was also eligible for a discharge now. I had to make a choice between getting paid or being discharged immediately without a dime in my pocket.

This was a major change in plans. I felt I had done my duty. I had many more points than I needed, so I told the corporal I would take a discharge instead of the forty-five days of leave. I made this decision in less than a minute.

Suddenly, I was free. Before I had time to truly comprehend the circumstances, I walked briskly out of the building, with my discharge papers in hand, to where Margrit was waiting for me by our car. After a long embrace, I told her I was a civilian again. We looked at each other, excited but perplexed. We both wondered aloud what would come next; we had been expecting a forty-five day paid honeymoon.

I suggested we drive back to San Francisco and stop at the Nut Tree restaurant for lunch, where we could discuss the future. At the time, the Nut Tree was a simple, small restaurant frequented by skiers having dinner on their way back to the Bay Area after a weekend on the slopes near Lake Tahoe.

We sat in a booth and began to deconstruct our situation. For almost four years, the government had taken care of me, and now, without warning, I was a civilian. I started as a private and an enemy alien and was retiring as a first lieutenant and a U.S. citizen. I was a landscape architect by training; however, with a four-year gap since I worked in the field, I had no clients, no projects and no income. How was I to re-enter the field? Where were my old contacts, and would they be open to hearing from me? Four years seemed like an eternity.

I longed to be carefree with Margrit in my arms, but as we ate lunch together and discussed the future, I was overcome with uneasiness. Now, I was a married man, and I had to take care of my wife.

Margrit smiled and told me she loved me. She had a job and a roof over her head — our heads — and things would work out one way or another. I looked into her crystal, blue eyes, her comforting smile, and responded, "Yes, somehow we will make it together."

CHAPTER 11

My Path Through the Landscape

Needles of the *Metasequoia glyptostroboides* (dawn redwood) in fall
Photo by Konrad Weiss © 123RF.com

That was as far as we got with plans for our future. Despite my anxiety, I delighted in watching Margrit light up as she enthusiastically told me about her job and new friends. As a result, we ventured no further than planning the rest of the day and discussing Margrit's idea for the upcoming ski season. Our old friends from Soda Springs, the

Brooks, were going to be operating Strawberry Lodge on Highway 50. We could work for our lodging and lift tickets. At some point we would have to drive to Los Angeles and visit her mother in Hollywood, because our skis were still in storage as were my drafting tools. Margrit couldn't wait to ski again and neither could I. However, I wondered if we had enough gas coupons to drive that far or if we should take the coastal train and save the ration coupons for my work?

Margrit explained that in addition to her work for the photographer in San Francisco, she had helped Herb and Ollie Brook when they operated Hotel Agua Caliente, just outside Sonoma. Margrit worked at the front desk, and when they were short a waitress, she helped out in the restaurant waiting on guests. She laughed when she told me how she mixed up the breakfast orders and how she got away with it using some charm and a big smile.

As I listened to my lovely wife describe her life in my absence, I saw how very independent she had become. For the last two years, Margrit had been on her own for the first time in her life. How well she had adapted!

Our conversation was light and giddy, like two young people on a first date. I shared with her my experiences on the SS Monterey. We avoided discussing any major decisions.

What a complexity of thoughts and emotions I juggled. It was our first meal together in what felt like a new life, yet, I was eating familiar food in a familiar restaurant. There was the world in my head of battlefields and survival, and the world in front of me that contained only Margrit. And then there was the world around us, the unconcerned buzz of other diners in conversation, the clinking of forks on plates and the smell of toasted bread, bacon, and warm apple pie.

Margrit drove us back to San Francisco in my car, which she had only used occasionally because of the gas rationing. She always liked to drive, and given that I had grown accustomed to driving on the left side of the road during the war, it was best she was the one behind the wheel.

It felt like a dream, winding along on the sunny highway beside this beautiful, loving woman, my wife, with classical music serenading us. There were no enemies to watch out for as we passed a western landscape unblemished by war's destruction.

At the beginning of my time abroad she lived in El Cerrito, just north of Berkeley, and took the train over the lower deck of the Bay Bridge to her job in San Francisco. For the past few months Margrit had been sharing a house with the Brooks in San Francisco. It was on Camino del Mar, between Ocean Beach and China Beach, at the edge of the upscale Sea Cliff neighborhood. When she opened the front door, Herbert and Ollie were there to greet me; it was wonderful to see my old friends. Margrit showed me around the neat, compact, three-bedroom house. As I put my bag down in our bedroom I found myself torn between wanting to visit with my friends and to just shut the door and hold my wife in my arms forever.

That evening, when we gathered in the dining room for dinner, the conversation focused on rationing and the bombings in Japan. No one pressed me for details of my time in the Southwest Pacific, for which I was grateful. I think they understood I had seen many horrible things and might not want to talk about them on my first day back, or anytime for that matter. Like Margrit, they did ask me about my trip back home on the SS Monterey. I told them how all the men aboard the Monterey were very disappointed when we stopped at Pearl Harbor and were not allowed to go ashore.

Our friends shared how they landed the opportunity to start the ski resort for Strawberry Lodge in Kyburz, California, about twenty minutes from South Lake Tahoe. Herbert and Ollie were eager to get back to the mountains. I was very happy for them, but I couldn't help but think their departure would mean Margrit and I would soon have to pay the full rent on the house.

My greatest concern, even on that first day, was I needed to start earning money as soon as possible. My Army pay would run out in two months. Margrit had her job working for a photography studio but did not earn enough to sustain us both.

I mentioned my desire to start working again to the Brooks. Herb suggested he could call a friend, George Thompson, who was a hotel owner and operator and belonged to the Northern California Hotel

Association. He had some commercial work under way, including refurbishing the Sonoma Mission Inn. During the war, the Navy had claimed the inn as a place for rest and recreation for sailors and marines. Prior to my return, the military had returned the inn to Thompson. However, they had not taken good care of the fairly large grounds, so he needed help redesigning the landscape.

Right after dinner, Herb phoned George Thompson and recommended me as a fine landscape architect. We arranged to meet several days later in Sonoma, which made me feel both relieved and nervous.

Later, Margrit and I went for a walk through Sea Cliff. The evening out in San Francisco was even cooler than I remembered, maybe because the tropics had become my home for the last few years. There were large houses with beautiful gardens. I studied and admired them as we passed, hoping I could still design such landscapes. It had been four long years since I had my hand in design. We walked down to Baker Beach and watched the ships come in and out of the bay. A few carried returning soldiers, who, like me, would have to quickly adjust to a very different life of both external temperatures and internal temperament.

A couple days later, Margrit arranged for us to go to the opera, *Der Rosenkavalier* (The Knight of the Rose), a comic opera by Richard Strauss. The San Francisco Opera House is a lovely building on Van Ness Avenue. It was always quite an experience to go there with everyone dressed to the nines. Since I did not have any formal clothing I dressed in my uniform, my shirt freshly ironed, my shoes polished to a reflective shine. I felt proud, especially with Margrit on my arm. The opera was wonderful, but I think I stared at her delighted profile as much as at the action on stage.

The next day, using precious gas, I drove up to Sonoma and met with George Thompson. He showed me around the Sonoma Mission Inn grounds, and I suggested changes and improvements. There were a number of lovely old specimen trees that needed pruning to make them more presentable. The swimming pool needed a new coat of plaster. We could create new sitting areas with garden furniture and increase the available parking. I guess I still knew a few things, I thought with satisfaction.

But at the same time, I was bitterly disappointed in myself. I could recognize most plants by sight, but I could not recall their names. This was very stressful since I had always prided myself on my knowledge of plants. It would require a lot of study to relearn all the names. Thompson, nonetheless, engaged my services to prepare drawings illustrating the much-needed improvements. It felt like my first day at *Gartenbauschule*, exhilarating and overwhelming.

Since I was still on Army pay, I wore my uniform while working those first few weeks, waiting until I could buy a proper wardrobe. We had enough coupons for gas to drive down to Los Angeles the following weekend to pick up my old drafting tools and our skis.

Mr. Thompson found some old site plans, giving me a base from which to work, but I also needed to take additional measurements. On my next visit, Margrit came with me, and we had great fun doing this work together. Despite my anxieties of our long separation and reentering society, Margrit and I enjoyed each other from the first moment of my return.

Mr. Thompson was pleased with my preliminary ideas and asked me to find a landscape contractor and supervise the construction. There was so much to do, I figured the design and construction work would last about six months. Despite the commute back and forth to Sonoma, this was a great development. I had a job in my field that would provide some income while giving me the time I needed to reacquaint myself with the newest in landscape architecture and the vast encyclopedia of horticulture.

With the G.I. Bill, also known as the Servicemen's Readjustment Act of 1944, I knew I could attend college classes for free so I made an appointment with Professor H. Leland Vaughan, chair of the Department of Landscape Architecture at UC Berkeley. I asked if I could audit some horticulture classes. Vaughan refused, insisting that I enroll in the entire degree program in landscape architecture.

This was terribly disappointing and a real setback. There was no way I would start all over again, even though it would be at no cost to me. I had already graduated as a landscape architect. I had a wife to support and needed to quickly build my business, so I embarked on my own study by going to nurseries and arboretums, where the plants were labeled for the public. Once again, I had to create my own path through the landscape.

I studied landscape plans and read voraciously. I attended a meeting of the California Horticultural Society (CHS). It had been a long time since I had done so. There were a few old faces and many new ones, and though I was conscious of being behind in my knowledge, it was also terrific to be surrounded by other garden and plant enthusiasts. Fortunately, I was welcomed back into the fold by some of leaders — the real movers and shakers — in the organization: Roy Hudson, head of Golden Gate Park; Eric Walther, director of Strybing Arboretum; Jack Spring, head of the Golden Gate Park Nursery; and Victor Reiter, my old friend.

In order to learn the many microclimates of the San Francisco Bay Area, I visited nurseries in a variety of local communities throughout the region. This knowledge was necessary because the plant palette could change dramatically from one neighborhood to the next. I found plants like fuchsia, geranium, and bougainvillea grew well in San Francisco, but they could freeze if planted further east in Lafayette or Livermore, north in San Rafael or Santa Rosa, or south on the San Francisco Peninsula in San Mateo or Woodside. I knew one garden where tree ferns could not survive because in the winter the temperatures dropped below freezing; yet, only a mile away at a nursery, the ferns thrived.

Thanks to a number of nurserymen, I got up to speed rather quickly. I already knew some of them, especially on the Peninsula, because they had previously been estate managers when I took care of Mrs. Stern's estate in 1939. In the wake of the Depression, the Second World War, and a flood of returning veterans, the old, large estates were dying out. People could neither afford the high property taxes nor the needed maintenance on the stately Victorian and turn-of-the-century mansions as the paint began to peel and the gardens became overgrown. Moderately priced housing was in demand. Some of the old grand estates sat empty, waiting for new wealthy owners, while others were broken up and subdivided. Some of the most experienced and savvy estate managers turned in to nurserymen.

Several remembered me and were happy to help in my self-guided studies. I was very grateful. It turned out that visiting nursery after nursery created long-term friendships. In the following years, I was perhaps one of the few landscape architects respected by the nursery industry in our region.

I made it known I was willing to do any work in landscape architecture, which was developing into a large and varied field, somewhat like the field of medicine with all its specialties. Whether called on to design golf courses, river or ocean front properties, residential properties, commercial properties, roof gardens, botanical gardens, or even ski areas, I wanted to be ready.

There was the question of the best place to restart my business. Margrit and I discussed the possibility of returning to Los Angeles. We also considered settling in Santa Barbara or Carmel. After much discussion, we decided to stay in San Francisco. I was already starting to make new business contacts around the Bay Area, and we both preferred it there. I also felt the city was a good location for my main office address. A calling card from a well-known city, such as San Francisco, was a bolder statement than an address in a lesser-known suburb, such as Orinda, Palo Alto, or San Rafael. I did, however, use Margrit's mother's address as a second location for my business to attract my old contacts in Southern California.

Within just a few weeks of my arrival home, the Brooks said goodbye as they departed for the mountains, so Margrit and I had the place to ourselves. I set up my office in one of the bedrooms looking out toward the Golden Gate Bridge. This was a most inspiring view. When my twenty-sixth birthday rolled around that December, Margrit presented me with a drafting table. It was a beautiful gift, and I cherished it for many years. Decades later, I passed it down to our grandson, Brian.

Not just in work but also in every facet of life, it took a surprising amount of time to adjust to being a civilian again. It is not as simple as one might think. War changes people. Besides reacquainting myself with my wife after her two years of independence, I also had to rediscover myself out of uniform. There were simple routines civilians take for granted that I needed to become comfortable with again: shopping, cooking, driving, and arranging one's schedule, social life, and future. I no longer had responsibility for other men. I slept next to my wife and not next to my gun, although I would sometimes hear noises at night and instinctively reach for my phantom rifle. I often dreamt I was still in combat and would awaken sweaty, startled, and frightened. It became apparent these memories were not going to disappear overnight. I was reminded of my nightmares during my first years in the United States, hauntingly real visions of my experiences in Germany. Those horrible dreams faded in time, so I had to have faith these war dreams would, too.

Perhaps it helped that I had stopped drinking completely. I was never a big drinker, always needing to save money and usually wanting to keep my wits about me. But what I witnessed during war made me never want to touch another drop. Young soldiers at Fort Sill went to town to get drunk as soon as their paychecks arrived, and I saw terrible things happen to them under the influence of alcohol. Worse in Manila, men would mix together whatever they could find to numb their senses. Some even drank wood alcohol and went blind. It was terrifying. Alcohol, I decided, was something I could do without even though the post-war era was a time when it was standard to make business agreements over drinks.

As years passed, I became ever more grateful I made this decision. One friend drank himself to death. He had been a war prisoner in Bataan and Japan. He suffered greatly from these memories and drinking was the only way he could numb himself and forget them.

In January 1946, Margrit and I went skiing at Strawberry Lodge, reawakening our thrill of the winter sport and launching new friendships and work opportunities. We have made more friends on the ski slopes than almost anywhere else. I always enjoyed meeting people, but at the time, while still transitioning from soldier to civilian, the socializing took terrific emotional effort.

Among the new friends we met that weekend were the wonderful Dr. Lovell Langstroh and his wife, who would later ask me to design their garden. I believe the magnolia tree and dawn redwood we planted — two very special trees — increased their appreciation of plants. I first admired the *Magnolia x veitchii* (magnolia tree) at the Strybing Arboretum on January 30, 1939, my first day in San Francisco. It is one of the deciduous magnolias, a larger tree, unlike most magnolias, which grow as large shrubs.

We also planted a *Metasequoia glyptostroboides* (dawn redwood), a wondrous tree. This redwood was thought to be extinct when first found as a fossil, unearthed in China in 1941. But just three years later in 1944, Chinese horticulturalists discovered a small stand. It is the only redwood species that shows fall colors and drops its needles in wintertime. The needles are very soft to the touch, which is rather different from the other two species of redwood. At the time I started using it in design, it was very new to the United States and most of the world. Today, the dawn redwood can be found in gardens all over the globe.

A couple months after establishing the business — and our home — in San Francisco, it was time to send out a brochure announcing the reopening of my offices in both San Francisco and Los Angeles. I needed professional photographs of the gardens I had designed. Our friend Kurt Cristof, who had a photo studio in downtown San Francisco, knew a photographer who specialized in landscapes and nature photography, and Kurt arranged for me to meet him — Ansel Adams.

Adams had not yet achieved the degree of fame he would in the years to come, but he was already well known and greatly respected. I visited him in his home, a block from the Presidio. He was a bearded fellow with a wide smile, playful manner, and dreamy look in his eyes — very much an artist. Adams was very independent, and I practically begged him to do the job for me. He only agreed after we drove to Berkeley to look at the garden I wanted to feature on the brochure. It was designed and constructed for Mrs. Walton in 1940 using ample rocks and lush plants. Adams accepted the commission and visited the house several times to capture the scenery in the best light. I handed out that brochure to everyone I knew and to everyone I didn't know.

ANSEL ADAMS

The front of my 1946 brochure featuring the photo
of Mrs. Walton's garden by Ansel Adams

Ansel Adams, as he looked when I knew him

The Sonoma Mission Inn job went well, and I continued to supervise the landscape maintenance for a number of years. It turned out to be the beginning of a long business relationship with George Thompson. My work in that region continued, including a garden for General Henry "Hap" Arnold. Arnold was the Commanding General of the U.S. Army Air Forces during the Second World War. He learned to fly at the Wright Brothers Flying School, Orville Wright was his instructor. When I met him, the general surprisingly knew my name. He had heard of my discovery of the intelligence officers' airplane in the Owen Stanley Mountain Range in Papua New Guinea. It was strange to have my war years and my new civilian life intersect in such a coincidental manner. It would also be more than sixty years before I would speak of some of my activities in the war again.

Margrit and I were happy living a simple life together. Whenever there was snow in the mountains, we took whatever weekends we could to go skiing. After all, it was part of my wedding vow. I had already missed two years since the U.S. Army did not think I had to live up to my marriage contract.

The Brooks let us work for our keep, which sometimes added a free day or two to our stay, a real gift on our tight budget. Margrit waited tables, and I worked in the kitchen. From 1946 to 2011, Margrit and I skied together every year without exception. I guess this has made me at least a decent husband.

We enjoyed living in our modest house in a first class San Francisco neighborhood, but with housing at a shortage after the war, the owners decided to sell. They wanted twenty thousand dollars. Margrit wanted to buy it, but I could not see us going into so much debt. My upbringing and personal conviction had been to pay for everything outright. Besides, in my mind a house without a garage was not a good purchase. Today that house is worth well over a million dollars. I should have listened to Margrit. The new owners raised the house and cleverly created a two-car garage. Instead, we moved to a new, rental home on California Street between 25th and 26th Avenues, just two blocks up the street in the Richmond District.

I had really begun to separate myself from the trauma of the war, when I received a call in February 1946 from my old friend Toichi Domoto. Toichi was a Japanese-American nurseryman in Hayward, whom I had met before the war at meetings of the California Horticultural Society.

"Ernest, I understand you're back," said Toichi over the phone. "I managed to save my nursery, even though I was interned during the war. I need your help to design the garden for my church. Will you come and meet me on the site?"

I agreed.

Toichi smiled joyously when he met me on the steps of the First Congregational Church in Hayward. I returned the smile, but I was greatly dismayed by my initial reaction. As I looked at him, I saw the face of the enemy. Toichi was a fine gentleman and a respected friend. I had admired his beautiful bonsai collection, and he raised the best tree peonies in the area. Toichi was an American citizen and a Stanford University graduate so I was disturbed by my reaction. As we toured the land around the church, I hid my feelings — I hoped completely — and listened, focusing on the job at hand.

My friend Toichi Domoto, 1983

On the way home, I pondered my reaction. Before I reached our street in San Francisco, I came to an important conclusion. I recognized the feelings I had toward the Japanese in wartime needed to be forgotten. Those feelings didn't belong on the shores of the United States. Toichi had been interned, and he had forgiven his government and was moving on. I needed to move on, too.

It was a valuable insight I was reacquainted with that day. People's perceptions of others can be shaped and manipulated into hatred and fear by teaching or experience. It can become so ingrained to become unconscious and unquestioned. I was painfully reminded of the hatred I saw in the eyes of the brown shirts in Hitler's Germany as they destroyed Oma's temple and beat unarmed people in the street during *Kristallnacht*. With my coming of age as a Jew in Nazi Germany, I would have thought I should be immune to adopting prejudice.

As for Toichi and me, our friendship went on to last a lifetime. I often used his beautiful *Acer palmatum* (Japanese maple), in my landscape designs, as well as his multi-trunk *Acer truncatum* (Shantung maple), which he grew specifically for me. This variety can take heat and wind, but the problem is it usually becomes a large tree. Toichi discovered he could prune the tree at an early stage, creating multiple trunks and stunting the tree's height to about twelve feet. When pruned properly this creates a wonderful sculptural effect and a beautiful framed view of the surrounding area.

Many times over the years, Toichi and I visited the Filoli Mansion and estate, built in 1915, located in the small town of Woodside on the Peninsula. We helped Mrs. Lurline Roth, the owner of the estate, with flower shows in her gardens. Mrs. Roth, formerly Lurline Matson, was heiress to the Matson Navigation Company, which had built the SS Monterey, the ship that brought me home after the war. The "small world" department continued to find me in the most delightful ways. Mrs. Roth was a lovely woman and well versed in art and horticulture. As a result of these visits, Toichi and I felt there was a real need to preserve the Filoli estate for future generations. We were the first people to discuss the subject openly with Mrs. Roth. In 1975, she donated her 654-acre estate to the National Trust for Historic Preservation.

For many years, Toichi and I also served on the Board of Directors of the California Horticultural Society. In 1957, Toichi was elected president and I, vice president. Toichi's inauguration was the last time Margrit attended a formal CHS dinner, or any official dinner of that kind. At the beginning of the evening she had to stand for introductions. She hated it, but she did it for Toichi as much as for me.

In April 1946, fully ensconced in my renewed civilian life and struggling to build my business again, I received an unexpected letter. It was from a cousin of my father's, Dr. Wegener, who lived in Iceland. He wrote to tell me of my father's fate or at least most of it.

Before Pearl Harbor, in addition to the more regular correspondence from my mother, I also received a few awkwardly scribbled letters from my father. After his arrest on *Kristallnacht*, he was sent to a concentration camp. There, in the freezing cold of winter, he was forced to carry heavy steel beams without gloves. The resulting frostbite and nerve damage caused him to lose several fingers and limit the use of his right hand. He had to learn to write with his left hand. After a few months or so, he was sent back to Berlin as a street sweeper. I think he stayed with my mother when he came back, she had said as much, but it couldn't have been for very long with their divorce in 1940.

Sometime in 1941 or 1942, according to Dr. Wegener, my father remarried. To whom, I don't know. Whether this was for companionship, love, or some other reason remains a mystery to me. My cousin, Ilse Traube, the daughter of Uncle Alfred Traube, believed when my father left for Belgium and later Paris, he had an affair, I guess with his secretary. Ilse had no kind remarks about my father. In contrast, my mother never talked about him in any derogatory manner. I decided to leave that phase of my father's life with a question mark and not judge my father based on hearsay.

I do know, from a different source, that Father was still sweeping streets in the autumn of 1942. Between his release after *Kristallnacht* and until the latter part of 1942, he may have been in and out of labor or concentration camps again, but such facts are lost, along with all who would know these details. It was about the same time I received

Dr. Wegener's letter that my cousin, Elsa Wertheim Ziehm, Aunt Martha's daughter, forwarded me a letter my father had written to her in November 1942. At the time, Elsa and her husband still lived in the converted villa garage in Dahlem. Being adopted and not Jewish, she had not been persecuted. My father wrote in that letter, "Speaking for myself nothing has changed. I have much hard work sweeping the streets, which is better than what others have to endure."

In late 1942 or early 1943, Father was arrested once more and sent east on a freight train toward either Poland or Russia. Dr. Wegener was on the same train but escaped through an opening in the freight car's floor. Father did not follow. That was the last anyone knew of my father, Robert Wertheim.

As for Dr. Wegener, he somehow made his way to Sweden. He did not go into the details of his journey or how he ended up in Iceland.

When I received this letter I was already used to the idea that my father did not survive. We had inquired through the Red Cross several times, never generating any details. I suppose, if I kept trying, I might have discovered at which camp he was killed and how the Nazis had disposed of him, since they kept good records. But I think it is better not to know what happened.

Another casualty of the war: beautiful Wertheim
Department Store in ruins, 1946

Over the years, I learned about other family members and friends from Germany. In the same letter forwarded to me by Elsa, my father wrote, "Last week there was a letter through the Red Cross from Aunt Martha dated the end of August 1942. She wrote she was fine and that our son, George, was with her for a visit. George had found a family that is very good to him in Ackworth (West Yorkshire, England)." I know very little more of this situation since my brother does not wish to talk about it (nor do many others who went to England through the *Kindertransport*). I do know Aunt Martha somehow got to England and made a new home for herself in Bath, a lovely place with old Roman ruins. I don't know how well she got along — but she survived the war.

As I want to honor my brother's wishes about the war years and their aftermath, I will only say that we sponsored George to come to the United States in the early 1950s. I was thrilled to see him again. He studied the hotel and restaurant trade. Eventually, George became the respected general manager of a country club, married his wife, Catherine, with whom he adopted a lovely daughter. I have always treasured my visits with him over the years, and I am pleased we remained very close.

In 1946 my older brother, Werner, was still in Chile. We kept in touch through letters in those days, although later we would visit each other (more on that in another chapter).

Friedel Weiss, my first friend at Ahlem, made a quiet life for himself in Israel, although I do not recall the details. We corresponded a couple times before losing touch. Friedal helped soothe the nerves of a fourteen-year old entering college, and I will never forget his unassuming gift. It was instrumental that first year as I was gaining the educational foundation on which I built my life.

I never saw Dr. Levy or his wife, Flora, again after our parting at the Philadelphia Greyhound station. We did communicate for a while by mail, but this stopped when the war broke out. Nonetheless, their kindness is always with me. How different my life would be without their purchase of my bus ticket to San Francisco in January 1939.

I kept in touch with my friend, George Salomon, who co-founded a fund for refugee students while a student at Swarthmore College.

We continued to correspond after the war, and he and his wife came to visit us in San Francisco. Later on, I would visit him in New York, while I was there on business. George had a varied career. He worked in New York's printing industry and became a graphic designer in 1947. Among his works, he designed the first diagram-card for the New York City's subway system, while he was working for New York City's transit authority in the late 1950s. George was a journalist for the National Association for the Advancement of Colored People (NAACP), and he became an editor for the Association of Jewish Community Relations Workers and the Leo Baeck Institute, a New York City-based research library devoted to German-Jewish History. He wrote several books, including *The Many Faces of Anti-Semitism* and *Ethnic Lobbying*, and authored many articles, including a series on the Eichmann Trial, before dying from cancer in 1981 at his home in Great Neck, Long Island.

Uncle Ernst Hellinger in Chicago was promoted to professor at Northwestern University in 1945 and became professor emeritus upon his retirement in 1949. He died shortly thereafter the following March. Before leaving Germany, Uncle Ernst profoundly influenced mathematical analysis with his introduction of the Hellinger integral and the Hilbert-Hellinger theory of forms. His sister, Hanna, my first sponsor and to whom I owe so much, continued to teach at Purdue until her retirement in 1965. She was widowed in 1959 and lived until 1989.

Aunt Hilde and Uncle Alfred Traube continued to work very hard in Queens, New York. After my aunt and uncle's immigration in 1939, their daughters and my cousins, Ilse and Annemarie, would also make it to the United States. They had both escaped Germany on a *Kindertransport*, after my brother, George, but I know nothing of their time in England or exactly when they arrived in the United States. Years later in the 1950s, Alfred actively worked to recoup some of the property taken away from our family by the Nazis. I was not very interested in this pursuit, because it opened wounds I tried to forget. Nonetheless, I am grateful to my uncle for his efforts. His success led to a distribution of money among my brothers and myself, which helped to pay for our dream house in Alpine Meadows in the 1960s.

My old friend, Lore Kingsley, and her husband called me to design their garden in Pacific Palisades near Los Angeles, around 1948. They were neighbors of our friends the Strakosches. Lore and I had stayed in touch by cordial letters during the war, but I hadn't seen her since her visit to Oma Guttman's apartment in Berlin in 1938.

The reunion was very polite. Margrit was with me, and both Lore and her husband acknowledged us as friends. No one brought up Germany in this first meeting as adults. We discussed their garden and house and our mutual friends next door.

Seeing Lore again, I realized I was never truly in love with her. We only knew each other from that one short visit at Oma's house in 1938, along with some faded childhood memories. I was young, naïve, and quite alone when I first arrived, so I thought when a pretty girl wrote me letters signed "With Love," she must surely mean it. It almost makes me blush to think about it. Those unplanned weeks at Donner Lake, meeting so many new people, helped me move on and realize the whole thing had been a fanciful dream.

On a trip to Southern California, we spent time visiting with Margrit's brother, Fred. Though he had done his military training with the 10th Mountain Division in Colorado and skied on occasion during basic training, his ski days in uniform ended when he and the division were shipped to Texas and later overseas to Italy. There he went through hell, but he survived and was grateful to be back in California. Like me, it had taken him some time to readjust to civilian life. Fred married Doro Frankel, a German-Jewish schoolteacher from Berlin, just before Margrit and I did. Fred worked for many years at UCLA maintaining the campus's landscape before starting a successful piano tuning business.

I suppose it is tempting to ponder all the "what ifs" of my first quarter century. But I am not a person who lives in the past, even though I must remember, even though I cannot forget all I witnessed and lost. Maybe foremost, I am my mother's son who carries her optimistic torch ever onward. Or perhaps, I am kin to the first brave crocus of spring.

Fully a civilian again, 1948

When Margrit and I celebrated our fifth anniversary in June 1947, we received a card from my old client and friend, Mrs. Walton in Berkeley. Inside the card was a picture of a baby and underneath she wrote this message: "If you don't know how to do it, I'll be glad to tell you."

Margrit and I laughed and then seriously discussed having children. I did not want Margrit to have a child before I went overseas because I might never have returned. I feared if she were a widow with a child, it would be difficult for her to find another husband. When I returned, we needed time to adjust both to each other and to my new civilian life. Plus, I needed to know I could support a family. Now, however, after a tough couple of years, my business was going reasonably well. We decided it was time to expand our family. It took only one full moon before Margrit became pregnant.

Margrit loved her work and continued her photography during her pregnancy. In general, she was very active. For example, on a brilliant, sunny day in January, while Margrit was seven months pregnant, we walked on skis up Sugar Bowl and to ski down the mountain.

On March 12, 1948, I was in Orinda when the client's phone rang. It was Margrit. I had given her the number since she was nearing her due date. "I'm having contractions," she said, "You'd better come home and take me to the hospital."

I'm not sure what I said to my client as I rushed to my car and then drove — I am quite certain well over the speed limit — across the Bay Bridge towards our rental house. Margrit was ready and waiting. Gingerly, I moved her into the car and drove down California Street to Children's Hospital.

For six hours, I did what they show in movies from those times — I paced. I walked nervously from one end of the waiting room to the other, forgetting to eat, and not able to read a magazine. Finally, a nurse came and told me it was a boy. A half hour later, I was allowed to see Margrit. My first thought when I saw my wife propped up on pillows in a hospital bed was she looked so beautiful; she took my breath away. It was as if she was lit by golden light, the birth making her more lovely than I thought possible. The nurse brought the baby in for feeding and handed this tiny bundle to me. I was so nervous. I didn't know how to hold a baby. What if I dropped this delicate living creature? At the same time, it was amazing to hold our son.

Margrit was required to stay in the hospital to recover for three nights. When I got home and closed the door behind me that evening, I felt terribly lonely. I heard creaking in the floors I had never noticed before, and it was hard to sleep. The next day, I went to visit Margrit and our new son, George Andrew, who we called Andy. I shook hands with our doctor, Dr. Herz, a German immigrant, who believed youngsters should have plenty of fresh air. That was his recommendation to me and the only parental advice I received at first. Three days later, I took my family home.

We had to adjust to the sleeping schedule of our new son. Using a bottle, I would take turns with Margrit feeding him during the night. Since I had my office at home, I could take Andy for a ride in his new baby carriage during the day. We walked through Sea Cliff, by all the lovely residential gardens. There was so much to learn about being a parent, and there weren't many people to turn to when we needed advice. Andy had only one grandparent, Margrit's mother who lived in Hollywood. I often thought of my mother and how happy she would have been to hold her grandson.

With my son, Andy, 1948

It was a major event when his first tooth arrived. When Andy took his first steps, we were beyond ourselves. Since the bedrooms were on the second floor we purchased a gate, so Andy would not fall down the stairs. Andy was two years old when we took him skiing for the first time. There was a small saucer-like lift and gentle slopes at White Hills Ski Resort at Spooner Summit on the eastern side of Lake Tahoe. I would ski while he was standing between my legs.

In 1951, we bought our first house at 2378 39th Avenue in San Francisco's Sunset District with a thirty-year government loan, thanks to the G.I. bill. The newly constructed house had a one-car attached garage, one bedroom downstairs, two bedrooms upstairs, a kitchen with a breakfast nook, a living room, and one bath, just like all the other new houses in the neighborhood. The downstairs bedroom became my office where I prepared plans for jobs like the Trefethen Gardens.

I met Eugene and Catherine Trefethen, who lived in the Oakland hills, in 1948, through Jack Schneider of Orchard Nursery. I met Jack during my horticulture "re-education" when I had spent time at his nursery, in the small town of Lafayette located east of the Oakland-Berkeley hills. We became good friends, and he was an important figure in my life.

Jack and his business partner, Stewart Wade, grew up together near Santa Rosa, California, and were good friends all their lives. Both graduated from UC Berkeley. Jack became a chemist but soon realized he didn't like the corporate life. He and Stewart bought a pear orchard with a fruit stand in Lafayette, then built a store and started their retail nursery in 1946. For many years part of their income, came from selling their pears. I used them as a supplier for a couple small jobs, and they started to recommend me to some of their customers for garden designs and consultations. This is how I met the Trefethens. Catherine Trefethen stopped at Orchard Nursery to purchase some plants and mentioned to Jack she needed help with her garden. Jack recommended me.

IT TAKES A FIRM

Don't let Ernest fool you; the firm of Wertheim, van der Ploeg and Klemeyer is a full-sized, full-service architectural and landscape architectural firm. It takes much design, planning and hoop jumping to set the wheels in motion of the many garden centers they work on. Ernest and Jack, who has been with the firm since 1970, are the firm's partners (Jacob van der Ploeg has passed away), but it takes seven or eight supporting designers to develop all the architectural drawings, site details, floor plans and construction details of all the projects the firm undertakes. The devil—and your profit—is in the details, and they ensure the details of each project are covered.

Ernest, Jack Schneider, and Stuart Wade (one-time part owner of Orchard) circa 1953.

Ernest with Jack Schneider and Stewart Wade at Orchard Nursery, 1953

The Trefethens had a two story house and wanted a garden that would be interesting to look at from different angles. Designing their garden was very special because of their daughter, Carla, for whom I wanted to create a special place in the garden. Remembering the fun George Salomon and I had playing among the rhododendrons, I focused on a large English laurel shrub that provided nice shade and a place to hide because children love to play hide-n-seek. Near the shrub, I designed a playhouse for Carla. For her birthday, I gave her a yellow climbing rose called 'High Noon.' I dug the hole and then encouraged her to plant the rose bush with her grandfather's help.

The Trefethens were so pleased with the garden, they referred me to many of their friends and colleagues. Mr. Trefethen was an executive at Kaiser Industries, eventually becoming president and vice-chairman of Kaiser Industries, who worked very closely with Henry J. Kaiser and later with his son, Edgar, in building Hoover Dam, Shasta Dam, and many other Kaiser projects. In 1968, they purchased property in Napa Valley that would become Trefethen Family Vineyards. Over the years, I created three garden designs for the Trefethens.

Years later, after Carla was married and had a daughter of her own, she asked me to design a garden at her home in San Francisco. It included lawn and edge plantings as well as roses. She always remembered her High Noon. In addition, Carla wanted a fence placed partway across the back garden with a play area behind it. I asked if she was sure she wanted it there. Didn't she want to keep an eye on her daughter? She smiled at me and nodded, "I want a play area that is out of sight where my daughter can play. I want to recreate my experience as a child playing behind the big English laurel."

This has been a most treasured memory.

It's wonderful how referrals work. One thing leads to another and often doors open where you would least have expected. Jack and Stewart also recommended me to the Messerschmidt family. Mr. Messerschmidt was a contractor in San Francisco, who was adding onto his home in Orinda, just west of Lafayette, and needed the garden redesigned. I told the family I would like to work collaboratively with their architect, since I had previously learned the value of such a partnership. It is important the garden design and house design relate to one another and the client knows he has a unified team working together on something as personal and subjective as a private residence.

They arranged for me to meet their architect, Jacob van der Ploeg, a tall, quiet, creative fellow of Dutch ancestry. We liked each other right away. Soon after, I began a job for a family who wanted a swimming pool and bathhouse with a small kitchen, bar, and changing rooms. This was well beyond my training as a landscape architect, so I called on Jacob, who was working as the right hand man for a well-known Bauhaus architect, Erich Mendelsohn. Jacob began helping me during the evenings and weekends in my home office. He was in the midst of a divorce, so I invited him for dinner at our house several times while we worked. It was nice to work side-by-side with someone else. It was terrific to offer an architect and landscape architect together in the same office. In those days this was highly unusual.

In the meantime, it was time to move into a new house. Margrit was pregnant again, and it was a rough go. I asked the movers to load her bed on the truck last, so we could unload it first at the new location and have her relax in bed while we unpacked the rest of the truck. I was very hands-on managing the move.

On May 8, 1951, I was home working in my office when Margrit called out my name and told me it was time to go the hospital again. A neighbor came to look after Andy, and I loaded Margrit into the car. En route, when we reached 25th Avenue and California Street, I suggested we take a short sightseeing trip through Sea Cliff because so many trees and shrubs were in bloom. I do not think Margrit liked the detour.

She gave birth to another healthy boy, who we named Richard Robert or Rick for short. I was much less nervous waiting for Rick to arrive and even sat down in the waiting room.

We soon developed new routines with a baby and toddler in the house. They weren't the only additions to our home. Jacob continued working with me part-time in my office downstairs, and as my business grew, I often had one or two employees working there, too. It was very cozy, but the overhead costs were low. I do not know how Margrit put up with having so many people use our only bathroom, but we made it work.

Jacob and I had such success working together that in 1953 we formed a partnership: Wertheim & van der Ploeg. We presented quite an odd pair. In contrast to my diminutive five-foot-six, Jacob was a lanky six-foot-two. His quiet, calm nature complemented my talkative and enthusiastic constitution. He was pleased that I handled the business side of the office, the firm's administration and banking. And I welcomed his edits to my letters, which were sprinkled with second-language grammar. Jacob did much of the design and drafting work for both architectural as well as landscape projects — just excellent work. He shared his knowledge, and I learned a tremendous amount about architecture, how to read plans, and how to work with architects to create a successful environment for our clients. This helped me in both my professional and personal lives. Meanwhile, I was in charge of all contact with clients, which later included quite a lot of travel.

After forming our partnership, there were people coming and going from our 39th Street house all day long. Finally, it got to be too much, and we rented an office on the corner of 38th and Vicente. From there we moved to 2145 19th Avenue in the Sunset District, where the office still is today. My old home office became Andy's bedroom.

When the boys were young, Margrit began working with our friend Kurt Cristof. Kurt worked conventions, taking photos of exhibits and special affairs. These normally lasted three or four days with very long hours. Margrit helped retouch the photos and getting them printed and mailed. It was ideal since her job was not every day. Sometimes she accompanied Kurt on trips to help take photographs at special events in places like Palm Springs. She always managed to find time for some swimming on these whirlwind trips, a wonderful break from the full-time job of parenting.

On the weekends, Margrit and I enjoyed going to movies. Drive-ins were the easiest with the children. In the back of our Ford station wagon we placed short mattresses on which the boys slept. This was also the method we used on ski trips and longer drives to Los Angeles to visit Margrit's mother. Seatbelts did not exist then.

Andy and Rick with one of our many Wertheim station
wagons and the station wagon in Yosemite, circa 1955

Before the boys began school, we had a nanny who would care for them during Margrit's business travels. The nanny was the sister-in-law of my old friend Dieter Nassau, from my days at Ahlem and Berlin. Dieter had immigrated to Argentina, and we corresponded every so often. His brother and wife lived in San Francisco, not far from us, and she did a wonderful job taking care of our children when Margrit had to work. We would bring the boys to their house in the morning and pick them up before dinner. They were in touch with Dieter, too. I believe he made a good life for himself in South America, but the details are lost in my memory.

Later, as my boys got older, they would walk to and from school and had their own keys to the house. Margrit left instructions for Andy, who was the appointed cook. When dinner was ready the boys called me at the office, which was no longer the cramped room downstairs. I drove home, the boys served our meal, and I cleaned up the kitchen. This lasted for a number of years. Margrit would continue to work with Kurt Cristof until 1995. Kurt was also a skier, and for many years he would spend several days at our house in Alpine Meadows.

Jacob and I remained partners for more than forty years before he retired in 1996. In those forty-three years, we had only one argument — over concrete. Jacob insisted it was the nature of concrete to crack, but I did not like concrete paving with cracks and wanted to have every measure taken to prevent this on all of our projects. Technology eventually solved most of the issue. It still cracks, but not so frequently. My partnership and friendship with Jacob was solid, more than concrete. He passed away in 2008, and I still miss him.

In the early 1950s, my relationship with Jack Schneider became even stronger when he called on Jacob and me to work on his lovely house and garden on Spring Hill Road in Lafayette. He asked us to create a circular driveway, redesign his garden, and add a music room to the house — in which he would play his harmonicas, fine organ, and piano, often while his daughter sang. Margrit and I started to join the Schneiders at the theater. We really had great fun socializing, and in the years ahead, this would extend to family vacations together.

In 1952, Jack and Stewart of Orchard Nursery asked Jacob and me to design their exhibit for the California Spring Garden Show in Oakland. To the best of my knowledge, no nursery at that time had ever hired a landscape architectural firm for such a purpose. We all labored side-by-side to bring their exhibit to life, with a subcontractor doing the concrete and stonework.

What a success! The June 1952 issue of *Sunset Magazine* featured our patio design on its front cover. This great publicity scored us a number of jobs, although Jacob and I made it a point to explain the exhibit was due to the efforts of <u>all</u> those who participated.

In the summer of 1955, my brother, Werner, visited us in San Francisco. It was the first time I had seen him since he rolled his bike into my willing hands before leaving Germany for Chile in 1936. Then we were boys; now we were men. It wasn't as emotionally overwhelming as one might expect. We talked about old times and our parents and about the things we did as kids. It was peaceful and comfortable.

Margrit welcomed him. He was good with the boys, and Andy and Rick called him uncle. He liked to travel and see new things. We spent a lot of time showing him California and drove all the way up to Vancouver and Victoria, in British Columbia, Canada, as well as down to Los Angeles, where he met Margrit's mother. Werner was interested in my work, and I took him with me on job sites. We had a good time together. When he returned to Chile we kept in touch, mostly through letters. It was a few years later that he returned to live in Hamburg.

I learned a lot from every project, but one in particular reinforced a lesson that has tracked the arc of my life, from Germany to the Pacific and back again. At the end of the 1950s, as part of a redevelopment project, we won the contract to redesign the landscape around the Hunters Point neighborhood in San Francisco. Hunters Point had gone through huge growth and transition during World War II when there was a large influx of blue-collar workers in the neighborhood, many of whom were African American, who came to work in the ship building industry. As a result a great deal of housing was hastily built and now the area was badly in need of repair and beautification.

I asked the landscape contractor to preserve any existing landscaping, but sometimes this was difficult, especially when replanting, repairing, or installing irrigation pipes. One day, I heard a resident shouting at the crew and hurried over. A woman in a housedress was shaking a finger at the men. She was most upset about the loss of her marigolds, which she had planted at the base of a tree. A crowd of onlookers had formed and our crew looked extremely nervous.

I approached the woman and apologized for the damage, explaining it was impossible to install new irrigation pipes and sprinkler heads without first removing the flowers. I told her we would replace the marigolds with primroses, which were just coming into bloom. She looked me straight in the eye and said, "You white people always make promises and never keep them!" Her look was penetrating and accusing. I asked her to tell me when I had personally failed to live up to a promise I had made. Prior to starting the work, I had made it a point to talk to the residents — including this woman — informing them of our intentions and getting their input.

We discussed her concerns, which were not favorable towards the contractor's crew. I defended them, while keeping my patience. I told her I would go to the nursery myself and buy the primroses for her garden. I asked what colors she preferred. Still very upset, she just walked away muttering, "No, never seen a white man keep a promise."

Early the next morning, I arrived with a flat of primroses in full bloom and planted them myself. Having more than needed, I placed the extra plants on the doormat in front of her second-floor apartment with a note that said I hoped they would fit into her window boxes. She called that afternoon and was very sweet on the telephone. The next day, she made a chocolate cake for the crew.

Several weeks later the contractor laid out a large area of sod. The following morning, the sod was gone. It had been stolen. The residents were very upset because this was the only sizable lawn in the neighborhood. We replaced it, and the redevelopment agency hired a guard, but this was not a permanent solution, and the sight of a uniformed guard pacing the lawn's perimeter made people in the neighborhood unhappy.

I asked my marigold friend to bring a group of young children to meet me near the new sod. I asked one girl, "What would you feel if I were to lift you up by your hair?"

"It would hurt!" she replied, looking somewhat fearful.

I picked up a piece of sod and showed the children the many new white roots developing and explained how picking the sod up this way hurt it in the same way. Then I asked them to help protect it. They took on the job like overprotective parents, making certain no one destroyed the lawn. A guard was no longer necessary.

The project began with a great deal of uncertainty and uneasiness. Will these residents accept or reject us? It was similar to going to *Oberrealschule* as a young Jewish boy in Hitler's Germany or visiting a tribe in New Guinea, representing the U.S. Army. Each time I had to create trust and cooperation.

It had been almost fifteen years since I was a soldier and twenty-one years since I had escaped Nazi Germany. The many close calls now seemed far behind me. I had a beautiful wife and two healthy children. I had a successful business moving in a direction that promised new adventures and greater financial stability. And yet here, at Hunters Point, were perhaps the themes that had shaped my life more than any other: Why do people quickly judge others based on assumptions? How can you change people's perceptions? How do people resolve their differences? I had witnessed so much loss and so much nobility on this eternal battlefield. At Hunters Point, I was humbly reminded that making acquaintances with patience, listening, and respect could, indeed, defeat fear and ignorance.

One weekend during the Hunters Point project I was driving toward the mountains with my boys, our skis and bags piled behind them. During the drive, I explained to the boys they should never judge other people by their appearance, religion, or nationality.

A few years later when Andy came home from college with very long hair, a fashion of the 1960s, both Margrit and I encouraged him to cut it.

"But Dad, you taught us never to judge a person by his appearance."

It was the last time I brought up the subject of hair cutting. It seemed I was still learning, still in need of reminders, despite all my life had tried to teach me.

Part II

CHAPTER 12

Becoming a Garden Center Guru

Al's Garden Center in Sherwood, Oregon

The deepening relationship with Jack Schneider and Stewart Wade of Orchard Nursery led to a serendipitous event the following year, which steered my career in an entirely new, unexpected and wonderful direction. One that would forever change the course of my professional life.

After a long day at work, I arrived home quite hungry to be greeted by the savory smell of vegetable soup Margrit had warming for me on the stove. Before I had a chance to take off my jacket, the phone rang. It was Jack Schneider. Oh dear, I thought; Jack was usually longwinded, and I feared Margrit's soup would overcook. That would not be well received on the home front.

Jack anxiously explained the California Department of Transportation just informed him a new freeway, California State Route 24, was going to be built and it would go through Lafayette. He and Stewart were going to lose half their leased property on which Orchard Nursery was located.

"Ernest, we need you to design a new retail nursery for us where the pear orchard is now."

I told Jack I had never designed a nursery — the term "garden center" didn't exist yet — and they would have to find someone else. Jack asked for the name of an architectural firm which had the necessary experience. There was no answer to this request. No one used architects to design nurseries.

"Well look," said Jack, "Why should I go to an unfamiliar architectural firm? You and Jacob have done great work on our house, you've redesigned our front garden, and we even go to the theater together. We're friends, we trust each other. I think you have to do it! And anyway," he added, "Who else comes to the nursery telling me how to do things differently?"

"Jack," I replied, "Margrit's soup is boiling over!"

He simply waited on the line for an answer. Finally, I laughed and said, "Okay, I'll do it. Goodbye."

By Jack's estimate, I had about a year before the land deal would be settled and the nursery had to be relocated. I started touring nurseries in both Northern and Southern California, as I had done for so many years, but this time with an eye for design. I quickly learned most retail nurseries were not planned. They just happened incrementally. Few of them had any security. Usually a cigar box held the extra cash. Sometimes I just couldn't help myself, and I would point out such issues to the owners. Very few of the nursery owners could explain to me how their spaces developed. The longer I looked at retail nurseries the more I concluded we needed a brand new approach.

A friend of mine arranged for me to meet with the president of the Safeway, Inc., the supermarket chain. I also met with the architect, the display manager, and the merchandise expert. It was very fascinating, and I translated many of their design and marketing principals to the design of the nursery. For example, I started treating bedding plants like the grocery staples of milk and meat: everyday items that everyone buys and which are displayed in refrigerators at the rear of the store. Shoppers had to walk through the aisles, past everything else, to get to them. Nurseries in the 1950s usually had the bedding plants in the front, sometimes on a porch, so customers often could get their bedding plants without entering the nursery. They wouldn't even see the other plant varieties for sale. I also visited with the head display people at both Macy's and The Emporium in San Francisco, learning similar principles to those used at Safeway and other strategies such as how to effectively use multilevel displays.

It also occurred to me I could learn from Orchard Nursery's customers. Since Jacob and I did a great deal of work in the residential neighborhoods near Orchard, we knew some of the customers personally. I met with as many of them as possible, spending time in their houses and gardens, to discuss Orchard Nursery — what they liked and what improvements they would like to see in the new set-up. I found people would be honest and direct with me, sharing constructive feedback they would never express directly to Jack and Stewart out of fear of hurting their feelings. During these visits, I always left time to share my thoughts about maintaining their home gardens or slight changes they may wish to make. For every visit, I brought a blooming plant from Orchard Nursery as a thank you.

I assembled valuable information this way. For example, I learned on Sunday mornings there was very little business at the nursery. Catholic and Protestant families would pass by the nursery on their way to and from Sunday services, but they never thought to stop. Many mothers told me they wouldn't dream of entering the nursery with children all dressed up for church because the sprinklers turned the walkways to muddy goo. Once home and changed, the families explained they would eat lunch, after which they did not wish to go out again. They rested and maybe listened to a football or baseball game on the radio.

With all of our new knowledge, Jacob and I made a plan in which the parking lot and all walkways within the nursery were paved and graded properly. The irrigation system was designed so customers would never get wet unless there were unusually strong winds, and even then, most irrigation was scheduled for nighttime. All trees and shrub beds were placed over drain tiles so surplus water drained off quickly.

In the middle of the nursery, we created a picturesque patio surrounded by plants. There were a dozen or so comfortable chairs around tables that invited customers to sit, relax, converse, and take in the lovely flowers around them. It could also be used for special events. Jack and Stewart hosted fashion shows, parties, and occasions of all sorts on this patio. The most rewarding change came on Sundays when people stopped by after church, still in their "church" clothes. They came to look at the plants and socialize and have their children admired by others. Sundays at Orchard Nursery became a routine, a weekly social event enjoyed by the whole neighborhood.

Jack and Stewart were ecstatic. Business at Orchard increased, and the nursery looked beautiful. Orchard Nursery set off a fruitful venture into the brand new field of retail nursery design, later recognized as garden center architecture. We added this specialty to our regular business portfolio.

Shortly after Orchard was completed, several other local nursery owners had come to us for advice. Initially this was very limited in scope, but Jacob and I realized we had something to offer this growing industry, and it was worthwhile to do some promotion. As a result, I was asked to speak to various nursery chapters in the San Francisco Bay Area. Then the invitations spread to central California, including a California Nurserymen's Association convention in Yosemite and horticulture students at California Polytechnic State University (Cal Poly) in San Luis Obispo.

In 1958, I was invited to speak to the American Association of Nurserymen (AAN) at their 1958 convention in Dallas, because of our work for Orchard Nursery. This talk would provide Wertheim and van der Ploeg with our first national exposure, offering us the possibility to work beyond the state and tremendous growth for our firm. Jack Schneider asked me to be his traveling companion, and I spent hours preparing my comments and writing notes for this presentation.

In front of the hundreds of people attending the AAN convention, I learned a lesson about truth and how I have no choice but to live it and tell it, no matter the reaction.

"May I introduce to the lectern — landscape architect, Ernest Wertheim."

There was reserved applause as I made my way to the front of the room, and for a brief moment I thought about meeting the stoic and fierce headhunters in New Guinea.

I had been excited to give this talk, but events of the previous twenty-four hours had caused me much trepidation. That's because all of my clothes were stolen.

Jack and I had stopped-over in Denver to visit garden stores run by the W.W. Wilmore brothers. One brother ran a regular retail store with a large garden furniture department and many garden goods and tools, but not much plant material. The other brother's store combined a retail nursery and a landscape design/build business.

Afterwards, Jack and I checked into a downtown hotel. The rental car agency was across the street so we parked our rental in the agency's garage, went to dinner and then a movie, *Bridge Over the River Kwai*. It was the first war film I had seen since returning home many years earlier, and I was not prepared for it. It brought back some unpleasant memories as well as unexpected anger. General MacArthur had been correct, there had not been enough support from Washington for this theater of the war.

After the movie, I returned with Jack to collect our bags from the trunk of the car only to discover my suitcase had been stolen. We had the car keys with us so how they had opened the trunk was a puzzle. An inexperienced attendant simply told us the garage was not responsible.

Luckily, I had kept my briefcase with me, because it contained the notes and slides for my lecture. But I did not sleep well that night, pondering the expense of a new suit and suitcase. We didn't have credit cards then; everything would be bought with cash.

Arriving in Dallas the next morning in my wrinkled clothes, the first thing we had to do was go shopping. But it was Sunday and not many stores were open. My anxiety seemed to increase by the minute. Fortunately the hotel had a men's wear store with, of course, traditional hotel boutique prices. But what choice did I have?

At midday, newly suited up, we arrived at the convention headquarters where we started introducing ourselves to other AAN members. They were almost all growers and one of their first questions was, "How many acres do you have?"

Of course, I did not have any acres. I did not have a nursery or growing area. Jack had only his three-acre retail facility. These people had hundreds of acres. They had purchased their land for twenty-five dollars an acre, while Jack Schneider was sitting on a piece of land worth twenty-five thousand dollars an acre (1958 value), but that didn't seem to matter. While the handshakes were polite, I could see a few of them dismissed us right away. In their eyes we were nobody. This made me apprehensive about the day's lecture.

Finally at the lectern, I greeted everyone and predicted that in a few years all plants would be sold in containers rather than bare root or B&B (balled and burlapped). The audience just laughed. So much for future work, I thought. It was a revolutionary idea at the time, but I was confident about my prediction. My cheeks grew red, but I continued on with my explanation.

Even prior to World War II some nurseries had started placing plants in containers. This allowed customers to plant them any time of the year. I noticed plants endured fewer traumas and transplanted far better if they remained in their containers until they were ready to be planted. I conceded that, so far, the practice applied only to mild climates such as those in southern and northern coastal California. Shipping was becoming easier and more common, so companies like Monrovia, founded in 1926 by Harry Rosedale, in Azusa, California, started shipping to the East Coast. Plants in containers shipped much better than their B&B counterparts, not to mention the relative ease of handling and watering. Monrovia is now known as one of the early "container" pioneers.

In contrast, I knew very few of the growers at the AAN conference — if any at all — grew shrubs and trees in containers. They kept perennials in the ground and dug them up when the customer wanted them. This, I argued to the quiet audience, took precious time since the roots also needed to be wrapped in moist newspapers to prevent them from drying out, making each customer transaction longer. It also limited the experience that followed since the purchase had to be planted quickly.

My own experience showed the demands of the public were changing. People wanted to take their time to choose the locations of their plantings, and plants in containers gave them this flexibility. They also wanted "exotic" plants, not just those available in their area. Our firm was designing retail nurseries based on the premise that plants would be grown in containers. Orchard Nursery was still a hybrid, providing a small area for bare root and B&B, but most of the plants were sold in containers.

I thanked the audience and to a tepid applause took my seat beside Jack, who patted me on the shoulder encouragingly.

Containers did indeed become the future of plant sales, although it took longer than I expected. Starting on the West Coast, it eventually became standard on the East Coast as well. But this is the nature of change, especially when it involves a large group of people. The adoption of drip irrigation was similarly slow to catch on. This practice came from Israel many years ago, but it took a long time to be accepted in the United States.

The container idea in 1958 may have been unpopular, but I had to give my opinion. Just like when General MacArthur inquired about the morale of the troops. It was and still is my job to carefully observe and absorb what is happening in the industry. I then use those ideas in our designs and share my findings with colleagues. I do this with my clients, too. Not everyone takes it well, but it's essential both in creating realistic expectations for the project and because I have no choice. It's who I am.

Maybe this came from my mother. My brothers and I were trained to be on time and have people depend on what you tell them. A handshake was a contract. I always felt if I was paid for my advice then it should be straightforward. Honesty makes you dependable. Maybe it is not always the best way, but it is my way.

Despite the room's dubious reaction to my prediction, we didn't have to wait for very long to land our first job east of the Rocky Mountains. Hugh Steavenson of Forrest Keeling Nursery in Elsberry, Missouri, a big grower with several hundred acres for tree and shrub production, wanted to start a small retail space. Hugh gave me a ride to Forest Keeling from Dallas. After two days of consulting, we got the job to design the retail center.

Most of Hugh's trees were sold bare root, which meant they were dug up in the fall and wintered in underground caves where the temperature was cool but steady. He covered the trees with sawdust, moss and pea gravel, which they had in abundance. Though the caves were effective for storage, they didn't lend themselves to a stellar customer experience. We were able to help Hugh bring his business above ground with a simple new garden center, selling plants primarily in containers. The garden center is still in operation over half a century later, serving the local community with a new emphasis on native and environmentally sound plant materials.

After our work together, Hugh took me to Chicago for another nursery meeting where I met more retailers. I had to make due the whole time with the clothes I had bought in Dallas before flying home from Chicago.

I secured two other leads from the AAN convention. As part of the event all the attendees visited local retail nurseries as well as Lamberts, hailed as the city's first landscape architectural firm and responsible for the first azaleas in Dallas. They also sold plants, large specimen trees, and garden art. The owner asked me to look at a retail facility that needed remodeling in Shreveport, Louisiana.

Just weeks later I flew to Louisiana, arriving on a Saturday afternoon, and was a guest in the Lambert home. On Sunday, I expected to get right to work. Instead, we had breakfast — eggs and tomato — and there was hardly any talk about the project all day. The suggestion of working received only patient smiles. Not until Monday did we discuss the remodel. By the end of Tuesday, it was clear that remodeling the existing facility would involve too much money and was not a good investment for the Lamberts. While we didn't end up remodeling the garden center, I learned a lot about southern culture, which was very important in my education. As is often the case, the greatest value is in the process and not the project itself.

For example, when we first started our firm, Jacob and I entered competitive design competitions, like the one to landscape the Stanford Shopping Center. We invested hundreds of dollars and worked day and night, but we came in second and didn't get the job. Our efforts did, however, get our firm's name out in front of people. It was also good for office dynamics because we developed a team spirit with everyone working so hard together.

We also had to balance jobs that paid properly with the ones that made no short-term financial sense. A series of architectural projects for a builder in San Rafael, north of San Francisco, made us an average of twenty-five cents per hour. But the experience — which included a model home design by Jacob — built our portfolio and eventually led to profitable work.

In 1964, W.W. Wilmore in Denver, which I'd visited on the way to that first AAN conference in Dallas back in 1958, commissioned a design for a new retail facility. This really began my travels around the country to work with garden centers. The young general manager, Steve Driftmeyer, told us he understood the value of having one provider accommodate both his architectural and landscaping needs. We completely remodeled the facility to create a retail shop.

It was fortunate for us that the next AAN convention met in Denver shortly after we completed our work for the Wilmore Garden Center. The garden center was featured on the convention's tour, and this exposure to the members of AAN led to new projects. This was very exciting for the firm of Wertheim and van der Ploeg. I enjoyed seeing new places, and I particularly liked meeting new people and making their nurseries more successful. But it took a toll on the office and my family. At work, since I took care of administration, my desk piled up with papers and tasks while I was away. At home, at first my family was anxious to hear about my travel experiences. After a while, though, they stopped asking as many questions, as they became busy in their own pursuits and accustomed to my departures and arrivals. Margrit spent as much time as possible in Alpine Meadows, hosting friends on weekends. I missed her and the boys.

Before building, rebuilding

By Ernest Wertheim

You've decided to build a new garden center or remodel your present place. But now what? There are some obvious concerns like building codes and site location. But what about the loss of business you may suffer when closed for remodeling or the

Ernest Wertheim

cost of an environmental impact study?

This is a checklist compiled by an expert garden center consultant-designer. These aspects should be considered in the planning stages of garden center construction. Study them before you lift a measuring tape or hammer.

This outline on garden center design does not attempt to be all-inclusive. It should serve only as a guideline, such that each garden center operator will be able to prepare his own building program in accordance with his specific requirements.

1. Why do you want to build a new garden center or remodel the existing one?

A. Do you want to modernize to keep in step with other businesses in your area?

B. Are you forced into it because of your competitor's new or remodelled garden center?

C. Are you just progressive and want to be the leader in your field?

Editor's note: Ernest Wertheim is a leading garden consultant and is a partner in Wertheim, van der Ploeg & Klemeyer, a San Francisco architecture, landscape architecture and planning firm. The company has had the opportunity to be involved in the preliminary planning of a score of garden centers throughout the country and the actual drawings of several. Wertheim is a well-known lecturer on garden center design.

An excerpt from a long article I wrote for the *Home and Garden Supply Merchandising Handbook*, published circa 1970

We became so busy as the 1970s began, we had to tell many potential clients it would be three months or more before we could begin their project. This was a wonderful problem to have. To solve it, Jacob and I decided we needed another full-time architect on the payroll. I knew Bull, Field, Volkmann and Stockwell, the respected San Francisco architectural firm, had been interviewing for an architect. Dan Volkmann and Sherwood "Woody" Stockwell served with me on the Bear Creek Planning Committee (more about this to come). I called them and learned they had hired someone, so I asked who their number-two candidate had been.

We invited the young man, Jack Klemeyer, a graduate of Cornell University, to our office for an interview and were very impressed. Jacob and I had a rule when interviewing: never give the candidate the job right away. We would wait until the next day, so we would have time to discuss our impressions. I excused myself from our meeting with Jack, beckoning Jacob to join me.

"I understand the reasons for our rule, but I want to break it." Jacob agreed. Jack accepted the job and started with us in August 1970.

Jack was a wonderful addition to our company. After only two years, though, he was offered the opportunity to teach design and construction at the Swiss Federal Institute of Technology in Zurich. Jacob and I agreed he should go with the offer of a partnership upon his return. Jack worked with us until December 1972, after which he and his wife, Carolyn, left for Zurich. He returned after three years, and our new partnership was formed in January 1976. Our firm officially became Wertheim, van der Ploeg, and Klemeyer (WVK).

Like Jacob, Jack provided a great contrast to my outspokenness. Always wearing a bow tie and keeping a small trimmed beard, Jack had a pleasant smile, calm countenance, and would never intend to insult or hurt anyone. He provided a good balance to my direct approach.

Jack is a great host and a wonderful cook. His daughter is the light of his life, and he appreciates his home in West Portal, San Francisco, just a few minutes from our office. Since Jacob's retirement in 1996, Jack and I have shared the responsibilities of office management. It is a wonderful partnership that has lasted almost forty years.

CHAPTER 13

Risk and Happiness Amongst the Pines

Trunk of the *Pinus jeffreyi* (Jeffrey pine)

One Saturday in 1958, I had an experience which challenged my deeply held conviction to never go into debt. As usual in the winter, when I wasn't working on weekends, I was skiing with Margrit and our boys. While at Squaw Valley we stopped at the small mountaintop restaurant on KT-22 for a hamburger. Peter Klaussen, who knew us well as regulars, came to our table and said, "I have someone you have to meet."

He introduced a fellow customer, John Reilly, who promptly told us his dream to develop a ski resort in the valley on the south side of KT-22. Margrit and I looked at each other with excitement. It was a beautiful side of the mountain. John and his partner, Fred Smith, who lived in San Francisco, were forming a company to finance the new ski area. He was looking for charter investors. We definitely wanted to learn more.

We attended a meeting at Fred Smith's San Francisco house in the upper Geary Street district. I liked Fred. He was passionate about preserving the natural environment by using native plants and not overdeveloping the area. Most of the attendees were enthusiastic about the project and Fred offered to take those of us interested on a tour of the proposed site, to be called Alpine Meadows Ski Resort.

On a cloudless winter day with fresh powder on the ground, Margrit, our two boys, and I were part of a small group who assembled in front of the River Ranch Hotel on Highway 89. We rode in a snowcat up a forest road to an open area designated as a future parking lot. Here, we put on our skis and skins to ascend to the first knob, which would later become the beginning of the Ladies Slalom Run. It offered a breathtaking view of the whole valley, and we fell in love with the place. Of course, the beautiful day and the virgin snow contributed to our reaction.

We really wanted to become a part of the proposed Alpine Meadows corporation, but we needed to invest at least a thousand dollars, which was a large sum for us. I watched as Margrit's eyes lit up at the thought of our own mountain, allowing us to ski all winter long. I thought of my wedding vow, which I renewed annually, to take her skiing, and I certainly wanted to be a good husband.

We decided to invest. I didn't know it then, but this would turn out to be the best investment I ever made. It also redirected my home life. During the next five years, the design and building of the Wertheim cabin at Alpine Meadows became a major theme in our lives. It would also bring my firm fascinating and challenging projects in the Lake Tahoe area.

Some investors from San Francisco offered additional capital if John Reilly would turn over part of his lease from the Southern Pacific Railroad to a new organization that would be called the Bear Creek Association (BCA). It consisted of eighty-five acres, located in the western portion of the valley, which could generate one hundred and ten lots. Running through the center of the acreage was Bear Creek, providing drainage for the valley and emptying into the Truckee River. Each five thousand dollar investor was promised the right to choose a lot. We took most of the money from our savings and signed on the dotted line to become charter members of BCA. Of course, I also needed to shake hands on the deal.

When Alpine Meadows Ski Area opened on December 28, 1961, most of the people skiing on the mountain knew each other, because we were all stockholders. There was no grooming equipment, so in the morning, members of the ski corporation assembled at the top of the lift and ski-packed the slope. We all wanted to create a good experience for our customers. It was a very friendly gathering, culminating that evening in a celebratory dinner in the comfortable new lodge.

From then on I played a professional role in our new mountain neighborhood as well as a personal one. The BCA board contracted me to oversee the tree removal necessary for the association's road construction, with the goal to extract as little original vegetation as possible. It's a rare contractor who cares about such things, and on my watch the contractor did not get away with anything.

After the lots were staked out according to the subdivision plan, members could send in their first three choices for a lot. We drove up during summer vacation, walked the entire subdivision, and chose lot #84 on what would become Cub Lane. It was on a corner, bordered by three streets, which meant we would not have close neighbors, and we could probably reach our lot by shoveling even if no snow plowing had been done within the subdivision. We did not want to worry about being snowbound.

One summer's day, while the whole family was looking around our chosen site, Larry Metcalf, the president of the Bear Creek Association, walked up waving enthusiastically. He proposed that I should be on the Bear Creek Planning Committee (BCPC), the committee responsible for reviewing all building plans for the Alpine Meadows valley. I raised my eyebrows and grinned at him. I was deeply involved already in volunteer work in San Francisco, having just completed my fourth year as president of the California Horticultural Society, as well as ongoing activity in the American Society of Landscape Architects. I was tempted since this place meant so much to my family, but I told him I did not want to get involved. I just didn't have the time.

Larry said to call him if I changed my mind, and I returned to where my family was setting up a picnic lunch on a blanket laid on a cushion of pine needles. When they heard what Larry wanted, the boys — teenagers at the time — encouraged me to join because they felt that volunteer activities in this small community could accomplish more than in a large city like San Francisco. I would serve on the Bear Creek Planning Committee for the next twenty-seven years! The boys were right, and my many years on the committee were very rewarding. But between trying to do my best and dealing with the inevitable complexities, such as a lawsuit that dragged on for over ten years, the commitment too often consumed the hours of a full-time job. This took me away from my family, especially on weekends, which I regret to say was not the best thing.

The first task of the Bear Creek Planning Committee was to formulate building restrictions, but there were no previously written guidelines to consult. On principle, we agreed we would only approve houses that architecturally "disappeared" into the forest. Just as with the building of the roads, we wanted to minimize the impact on nature while constructing homes, driveways, and parking areas. It was our intention for the houses to become a part of the forest.

In the mid 1960s, when it came to landscaping, the committee tried to follow the recommendations of Robert Royston, a well-known landscape architect who wrote about landscaping in the mountains through the use of native plants. The problem was people who lived in their mountain homes year-round wanted colorful gardens like the typical residential plantings of petunias, marigolds, or geraniums. In addition, local nurseries carried very few native High Sierra Nevada plants since there was barely a market for them.

I spoke to the nursery owners, and they didn't even know how to propagate plants of the area such as *Arctostaphylos nevadensis* (pinemat manzanita) and *Arctostaphylos patula* (green leaf manzanita) — the two most common forms of manzanita in the valley) — or Ceanothus prostrate (Squaw carpet). My two major objectives for the committee were to find a plant palette that would create color with native plants and encourage local nurseries to grow such plants.

The Bear Creek Planning Committee issued a list of High Sierra native plants expected to do well in the valley. That was the relatively easy part. Now we had to find the right solution for the propagation and use of these plants.

I set out to figure out how to acquire plants native to the Lake Tahoe for landscaping Alpine Meadows as soon as possible. This meant finding someone with the time and interest to devote to this pursuit. That's when I thought of my friend Dr. Andrew (Andy) Leiser, a horticulture professor at UC Davis and fellow member of the California Horticultural Society. I told Andy the situation and encouraged him and his students to work on the propagation of native plants around Lake Tahoe. "Wouldn't it make a great project?" I asked him.

He took it on, and he and his students studied and learned how to raise such plants as Squaw carpet, with its delicate violet or white clusters of blossoms, and the two native manzanitas. They tried various propagating methods in the greenhouses at UC Davis with lovely, colorful Sierra Nevada species like *Aquilegia formosa* (western or red columbine), *Eriogonum latifolium* (wild buckwheat) and *Lupinus breweri* (Brewer's lupine). The students ended up teaching the nurseries in the Lake Tahoe region the propagation techniques. I was very grateful. This helped me encourage property owners in Alpine Meadows and many other Lake Tahoe communities to use such native plants in their gardens.

With this innovation, I was ready for the next Placer County Planning Commission meeting in Auburn, California. Their standard approach was to re-vegetate along highways or road banks with certain species of grass. I protested this longtime practice. While the grasses did provide erosion control, when they went to seed they would blow into undisturbed areas becoming an invasive species, overgrowing smaller flowering plants and native low growing plants. The Planning Commission was growing tired of me trying to convince them not to approve these grasses. That afternoon, I brought it up again. The chairman of the commission looked at me with frustration.

"Mr. Wertheim," he said, "you know we cannot specify native shrubs because they are not available."

At this point, I retrieved two flats of Squaw carpet in four-inch pots I had hidden in the back of the room waiting for this moment to come as I knew it would. I carried the flats to the front table and told the chairman and the board members that nurseries could now propagate them, thanks to the work of Dr. Andrew Leiser and his students. Today, just as you reach the top of Donner Summit on Interstate 80, the center strip between the east and west bound lanes is covered in spring with bright flowers of the native *Penstemon Newberryi* (Mountain Pride), pink to lavender in spectrum.

It is still not simple to propagate these native plants, and we have a long way to go. Fortunately, people are becoming more aware of the need to use natives, and I think their use will continue to grow.

While Dr. Leiser conducted the Sierra Nevada native plant project for a number of years, he and his students also studied and created wattling, a method of erosion control on steep banks achieved by digging shallow trenches and inserting bundles of native willow branches that are held in place by stakes. The students conducted several trials, including on the banks along Highway 89 between Tahoe City and Meyers (on the south end of Lake Tahoe). Since these traits were very successful, I followed Dr. Leiser's methods and used the wattling in Alpine Meadows.

After graduation, two of Andy Leiser's students opened a nursery specializing in High Sierra, high-desert plants near Medford, Oregon, which they aptly named Forest Farm. They supplied the plants for one of my most challenging jobs, re-vegetating the fourteen-mile Tahoe City-Truckee sewer line in 1974.

The building of the Wertheim cabin in Alpine Meadows was a family affair that drew us all closer together. My partner Jacob van der Ploeg designed our house, a simple ski cabin with three bedrooms and two bathrooms, a real luxury for us. No more single-bath homes for Margrit!

In designing a house in snow country, one must calculate the snow load the roof must be able to bear. I told Jacob he should figure on beams that would hold eight feet of wet snow, which came to about two-hundred and twenty pounds per square foot. We would remove snow from our roof when it rose above eight feet. The contractor saw the beams specified and thought we were crazy; but when the first roofs in Alpine collapsed during an unusually heavy winter, the building inspector came to our house wondering why we did not have any damage. He later influenced Placer County's decision to revise their building codes so the snow load calculations related to elevation. In heavy snow years, we have walked directly onto our roof to shovel it off, and we have dug a tunnel to find the front door.

We were distraught when the bid for constructing our house came in well over a price that we could afford. But my distant aunt, Hanna Hellinger Meissner, who had been one of my two sponsors allowing me to come to the United States, came to the rescue again by generously offering us a ten thousand dollar loan. I planned to pay back Hanna with interest, but later she surprised us by making it a gift. We also took all of our stocks and savings and asked Wells Fargo for a loan so we could not only build the house but pay our dues to the Bear Creek Association.

We were over our heads in debt. And yet, I was banking on this investment to create a lot of happiness for our family. It did and continues today.

After the sewer and water contracts were set, groundbreaking for the Wertheim mountain cabin took place on August 23, 1963. Andy and Rick, then fifteen and twelve, worked hard to dig the foundation trenches. Our family did as much of the work as we could to save money. We traveled up to Alpine Meadows almost every weekend, camping in tents. Some of our skiing friends helped, too. Their payment was staying with us on weekends once it was completed. A contractor poured the foundation and installed the joists for the first floor. Margrit, Andy, and I nailed down the plywood flooring, and the contractor then returned to frame the walls and put up the roof beams. The six inch by sixteen inch Douglas Fir beams came from a Cazadero mill owned by Jack Schneider's brother.

By late fall, weather in the mountains grew too cold for sleeping in tents. Under the living room the contractor poured a concrete floor, making a four-foot high crawl space. This space became our temporary bedroom with Army cots for beds and flashlights for lighting. It was awkward; but, since we are not very tall, we managed. It was much warmer than outside, and the mice came to the same conclusion. One morning we woke up to an early October storm, and everything had turned white with snow. The low ceiling was definitely better than a tent!

After several weeks, we were able to run a cable to a temporary electrical connection so we could have better light in our cozy basement bedroom. I had come a long way from being a "city kid" from Hamburg.

Jacob designed a lovely large fireplace for the living room under a ceiling that was thirteen feet high. We chose light gray, Sonoma River washed stones for the fireplace's facade. Bob Ellis, a landscape contractor who did a great deal of work for our firm, came up for two weeks and built the façade, with Andy and Rick carrying the stones from the driveway so he could work on a continuous basis. The boys and I placed the insulation in the walls, a relatively easy job, but much harder in the ceiling and in the basement. The contractor put up the sheet rock, and the family masked it.

We decided to have electric heat in the ceiling, and Andy and I installed the wires for the system between two layers of sheet rock. We had to stand on a ladder and use a staple gun. The wires were spaced three inches apart and each wire ran the length of the ceiling, about twenty feet. The work reminded us of installing the track for a small-gauge toy train. We had to use great care when installing the second sheet rock — no nail could interfere with the wires. This system has operated well for fifty years, and we love it. Although the operating cost is high in the winter, we have never had to replace a furnace which many neighbors did after twenty years. It is so peaceful at night without the sound of a furnace. The only downside is when the electricity goes out: no lights, no oven, and no heat. But, we have learned to cook in the fireplace in such situations. We also have a camping stove we can use and a radio that operates without electricity. It is always good to have a lot of candles as well as spare batteries for the flashlights. Of course, we did not have cell phones at the beginning, but now they are most helpful when the power is down.

A friend did the electrical wiring, but unfortunately, the building inspector did not approve it because he did not have a license. We had to hire an electrical contractor who knew less about wiring than our friend. We simply needed his license, which this was another blow to our finances.

When Thanksgiving came around, the interior was far from finished with the wall studs still exposed and a hard Masonite floor instead of soft carpet, but we had a roof over our heads. The kitchen stove and refrigerator were working, and friends wanted to come and stay with us. Our friends helped us put the bunk beds together, and they made up the guest beds for the first time.

The Wertheim cabin in Alpine Meadows

We had a big celebration with Margrit cooking. While the turkey was in the oven, we had to turn off the central heat because we did not have enough electricity yet for both cooking and heating. The water and sewer lines were not installed, so we took turns carrying buckets of water up to the house from the creek. Because of this, we served dinner on paper plates. With winter surrounding us, our chilly outhouse was over a hundred feet up the hill. Not eager to face that snowy uphill walk in pajamas with a shovel and flashlight, people learned to cut down on drinking liquids in the evening. Finally, one of our friends installed a flood light on a tree near the front door, so the need for flashlights was eliminated. We didn't take down this light until forty years later when we built a garage

But none of these obstacles mattered. Twelve people gathered for Thanksgiving dinner around a ping-pong table covered with a lovely tablecloth given to Margrit by her grandmother. We ate delicious warm turkey and shared many stories and laughter. The next day everyone was on the ski slopes.

Just before Christmas, we finally received word we could connect to the new water and sewer systems. A contractor dug a trench for the pipe installation. The area was very rocky, which involved a great amount of blasting at the cost of an additional thousand dollars. I hadn't finished sweating the costs yet.

The final inspection was completed on Christmas Eve day, December 24, 1963. When we had visitors during the holiday week, Margrit proudly showed off her two bathrooms, flushing the toilets with a great smile. "Look," she said, "they flush! Two of them!"

Margrit was also very happy with her six-foot long bathtub. She could stretch out her whole length and relax under the water.

We put up our first Christmas tree and many friends including members of the Bear Creek Association came to visit. Our house was the first in the development to break ground, so it was a celebration for everyone — our family and friends as well as those anticipating their own new mountain homes.

Our first years in the quiet snow at Alpine Meadows in the mid to late 1960s were quite a contrast to the tensions in our changing nation with civil rights and anti-war protests. Andy graduated from high school and attended junior college in San Francisco, which meant the entire family could still drive together up to the cabin on weekends. In the summer the boys stayed at the Bear Creek house full-time, and Rick worked as a cook in a Squaw Valley restaurant. When Rick attended UC Berkeley, he took the winter quarter off to work as a ski instructor at Alpine Meadows Ski Area. Because he was an excellent teacher, he often had requests for private lessons. With the money from this annual routine, he worked his way through college. We were (and are) very proud of his achievements.

We had a steady stream of friends coming to stay with us in winter and summer. Two families, the Mixers and the Newmans, came on a regular basis. At the time, Frank Newman was dean of the law school at UC Berkeley, and Joe Mixer was in the university's fundraising department. Much of the great controversies during that time were amplified on the Berkeley campus with the Free Speech Movement. I fondly remember the evenings around the dining table when we would hear about the issues from both the student and administration vantage points. Sometimes we sat for hours in heated discussion, allowing all of us to hear the various viewpoints. Despite the prevalence of drugs during these turbulent times — one of the topics of conversation — both our boys steered clear of them, for which Margrit and I were very grateful.

Andy transferred to the University of Arizona to study architecture. However, with half a year to go before graduation he decided to return and marry his girlfriend, Carol Nye, whom he had met at Squaw Valley. Andy and Carol lived at our house in Alpine. Margrit and I came up on the weekends. During the week, I worked out of my San Francisco office as usual, and Margrit continued her photography work part-time. Then in the summer of 1970, we welcomed a wonderful addition to our family with the birth of our grandson, Brian.

Alpine Meadows in 2014

During one Christmas week in the early years of the community there was an unusually heavy snowfall. The Bear Creek Association only had a pickup truck for plowing, with a small blade that did not work well in wet snow. This was before people had four-wheel drive car, so we were all stuck in our homes.

I called the local dairy, and they agreed to drop off food at our upper parking lot while delivering food to the restaurant at Alpine Meadows Ski Resort. The dairy said the order could be for multiple families as long as they could deal with only one person for payment. Margrit and I called all our neighbors and asked what they needed. Margrit made individual lists for each family and tallied the cost. Sales tax complicated things, but we figured it out.

The driver could only get part way up the street and placed all the food into the snow bank. Margrit and I carried it all back to our house. The food was arranged by type, not by family, so we did our best to separate the various orders. Sometimes our neighbors took the wrong food, which created havoc with the ice cream orders and resulted in some surprising disharmony. But mostly, the blizzard was an experience that created new friendships.

A huge four-day storm at the end of March 1982 dumped nearly seven-and-a-half feet of new snow, doubling the base at Alpine Meadows. Winds gusted up to 120 mph, and the ski area issued an extreme avalanche hazard warning and was closed to the public.

With new snow or changes in weather conditions, there is frequently a chance of avalanches in the Alpine Meadows valley. To mitigate this risk, the ski patrol tries to get the snow to release, or slide, before people are in harm's way. To do this, the ski patrol used explosives. They also used a Howitzer cannon, until the U.S. Army requested it back at the beginning of the Gulf War.

Our home on Cub Lane is about a mile from the ski lodge. The ski patrol had moved its cannon to our upper parking area and was shooting high on the mountain hoping to decompress the snow's accumulation. They were unable to bring any avalanches down and finally gave up. That afternoon, a monstrous avalanche hit chairlifts, the main ski lodge, small buildings, and part of the parking lots. It created a huge debris field extending about a quarter of a mile.

Even with the avalanche warning some people were caught off-guard. No one expected the damage to be so severe. Our son, Andy, was the manager for a group of condominiums, and he helped search for several people who were buried in the parking lot. Our son, Rick, hunted for people buried in the remains of the Summit Chairlift building where the ski school was located.

In all, seven people died. One woman survived after being buried for almost five days. The phone at the Wertheim cabin was one of the few still working in the valley. I had been in San Francisco when I heard of the catastrophe. I quickly phoned home, relieved to hear Margrit's voice. After a few days, the authorities were using helicopters to drop explosives onto the mountains, hoping to trigger avalanches above Alpine Meadows Road to make it safe for travel. Our cabin was in the possible avalanche area; one avalanche, which buried Alpine Meadows Road under twenty-five feet of snow, came uncomfortably close to our house. Margrit evacuated with Andy and girlfriend, Irene, to the bottom of the valley for two days.

Skiing with my son, Andy, in Alpine Meadows, 1980s

I invested in Alpine Meadows for my family. Yet my involvement in the valley has been good for me professionally, too. It generated several good projects including the landscaping of two ski areas, Homewood and the Tahoe Ski Bowl, as well as the creation of a master plan for the Sherwood area of Alpine Meadows in Ward Valley. My work with Placer County would benefit me later when I would go with clients before their planning commissions to talk about their construction/re-model plans. Sometimes, being true to oneself in one aspect of life can bring rewards in another.

CHAPTER 14
Teaching and Healing Through Horticulture

Rosa "Madame A. Meilland" ('Peace rose')

In 1971, I was invited to teach a six-week summer class on plant materials for the Department of Landscape Architecture at UC Berkeley. Since education is important to me and a regular element of what I do with clients, I agreed. I just had no grasp of how much preparation it requires to create meaningful and effective classes.

Students were expected to learn about three hundred plants in six weeks. I worried over the class content, because I knew a lot more than three hundred plants. I concluded it was most important to choose plants commonly used in landscape design while introducing some special plants in each lecture. I also wanted the students to know some basic botany so they could look at a plant and understand the makeup of foliage and blossoms.

Prior to my first class, I fretted about learning my students' names. I never was very good at remembering names. During the first lecture I took notes on what students were wearing and the color of their hair. Back at the office my secretary, Carole Haan, looked at my notes and asked, "Ernest, what will you do when they arrive in different shirts and jackets for the next lecture? Or if the girls dye their hair?"

My notes obviously did not solve my problem, but I felt if I expected the students to learn the names of so many plants in six weeks, I certainly should learn twenty-five names. The next lecture I had them wear nametags and worked hard to remember each name with the face.

I focused the first two lectures mostly on botany to teach some basic facts about leaf, flower, and fruit structures. I did not believe there was value in rote memorization. It was important for the students to not only know how to identify the plants but also how to use them in a landscape, what their climactic requirements were, and how best to combine them with other plants. In my lectures, I told stories connected to the plants because the stories, in most cases, made the plants easier to remember. The university required four meetings per week — which meant the students needed to learn about thirteen plants per class.

To aid their learning, I took the class on many field trips. We went to a new residential development with model homes that were all landscaped. I identified the plants used and why. For example, many new subdivisions used fast growing shade trees in their landscaping because they were developed on barren land and people want shade. I also pointed out errors in judgment — poorly chosen plants or plants poorly placed. I took them to some of our landscape projects under construction and also explored some of my favorite gardens our office created. The UC Berkeley campus itself has many mature plants I made a part of our classroom. We also visited the Strybing Arboretum in San Francisco, Sunset Gardens in Menlo Park, and nearby nurseries, such as the Berkeley Horticultural Nursery and East Bay Nursery.

Out in the field, I had students list all the plants in groups such as:
1. Low growing plants or groundcovers
2. Medium height shrubs against the house
3. Screening plants to hide the neighbor next door
4. Shade Trees
5. Flowering trees such as cherries, crab apples, plums, and peaches
6. Fruit trees, berry bushes, and grapevines
7. Fragrant plants
8. Perennials such as peonies, ferns, and daylilies
9. Annuals such as petunias, marigolds, and begonias

At the end of each week, I gave a test. When I noticed some students were falling behind, I went to campus on Saturdays and Sundays to spend extra time with them. For their last project, I took the students to the Pacific Nursery in Colma, a distribution center used by contractors rather than a retail center. At the nursery, I divided them into three groups and each group received a set of plants to find. They had to tag the plants on their list and select what they thought were correct and healthy specimens; I then evaluated all of their selections. This was a wonderful and fun experience for the students. It reinforced their identification skills, while also teaching the students what to look for when selecting plants for a project to ensure the highest quality product.

This teaching job was also a great experience for me. I believe every landscape architect should go through such an exercise because everything we do should involve teaching in some way.

I was delighted when every student passed the final exam. The university invited me to teach another class. I declined, however, because I decided teaching was too stressful when combined with my responsibilities at the office, my duties on the Bear Creek Planning Committee, and my other volunteer commitments not to mention my family. However, I mentored several talented, young people interested in becoming landscape architects.

Will Jung was the president of the Jung Seed Company, which did a great deal of mail order business and had a small retail outlet in Randolph, Wisconsin. I would see Will at the annual conventions of the American Association of Nurserymen. For years he told me he needed help with the garden center, but he could not convince his father to engage the services of a consultant. Then in October 1975, I received a call from Will asking me to come for a two-day consultation.

Will picked me up at the Madison Airport, and we drove to Randolph, where he had a lovely contemporary house on a large wooded lot. On the way to his house, he asked if I would mind spending the evening with his daughter, Sunny, who was interested in studying landscape architecture. She was a high school senior and wanted to know more about the profession. Apparently, no local landscape architect was available. We started talking that evening and ended up chatting into the early morning hours about the profession, clients, and the great variety of projects in the field. She had lots of thoughtful and insightful questions.

Her father passed away a few years later, and our work for the company ended. Yet, I kept in touch with Sunny, including continuing our correspondence while she attended college. I advised her on her first job, cheered for her when she entered a successful partnership in Washington D.C., and later I toured some of her major projects. I saw her through relationships and marriage. And I congratulated her when she retired, something I have yet to do. She was my guest when I received the Paul Ecke Award from the American Horticultural Society in 2011. It has been an enchanting friendship.

In 1981, an architect, David Tucker, living in Alpine Meadows recommended me to his client, John Robinson, who owned a house on the shore of Lake Tahoe in the Dollar Point subdivision and wanted a new design for his rear garden. After our initial meeting, we agreed to work together. As I was leaving, Mr. Robinson's daughter, Suzanne, and her best friend, Peggy, arrived. He introduced us and told me they were staying at Lake Tahoe for the summer. I discovered they were both studying landscape architecture in college, so I suggested, "We should involve the girls and use this project as a learning experience." Everyone agreed, and I started the project by bringing survey equipment to teach them how to take elevations and prepare a contour map. They also had to take detailed measurements of the outside of the house and the property line as well as existing locations of trees, patios, decks, stairs, and any other items that would be in the landscape.

Next, they decided what they wanted in the garden. They had to consult with their family and allow for the family's frequent entertaining. They also had to consider the subdivision's restrictions. After they created their design, I took the drawing and had the office create a good looking presentation, which we showed to the Robinson family.

The next step was to teach the girls to do a construction drawing, which included a dimensioned layout plan, a planting plan, an irrigation plan, garden lighting, and details of structural elements such as fences, stairs, benches, and paving. They decided to be their own contractor and engaged outside help only when they were unable to do the work themselves. One day, Suzanne called me in tears. One of the subcontractors had been less than honest and professional. I asked her to put the man on the phone, and we had a one-way conversation.

The project turned out well, and the family was very happy with the garden. When Suzanne graduated, positions in landscape architecture were scarce. I gave her a job at our firm to broaden her experience. Before too long she found another job. When she got married, the ceremony took place in the garden she designed at Lake Tahoe. It was lovely to be a part of it all. She went on to have a successful career, marriage, and children. We continue to keep in touch.

For almost two decades, one of our largest engagements was with the College of Marin, a community college. Our firm was the college's official landscape architect until the passage of Proposition 13 in 1978. The effect of this was to take away local tax monies from the college budget, which meant that college could no longer afford a landscape architect.

In 1964, along with Bill Davis of the UC Davis Extension, we designed a lawn for both the baseball and football fields, which had bases of imported soil — a combination of sand, redwood sawdust, and nutrients. The fields were the only ones in California with this soil mixture. We watered the area using an injection system with nutrients, the same principal being used in nurseries. Periodically, the formula was adjusted in accordance with monthly soil tests. We were the first landscape architecture firm in Northern California to use this injector system. What we did decades ago is now common practice, but it took many years to have the industry adopt new principles about soil amending.

During the 1960s and early 1970s there were numerous student demonstrations that played out on the landscapes of our country's universities and colleges. For example, in order to build the new library building at the College of Marin, we had to remove several trees. One was a beautiful *Ginkgo biloba* (ginkgo or maidenhair tree), a unique species, native to China with no living relatives. It is considered a living fossil, dating back two hundred seventy million years. During autumn the leaves turn a bright yellow and are known to fall very quickly, sometimes over just a couple of days.

Our plans called for the ginkgo to be relocated. But when the contractor starting digging, he found there was a large electrical conduit right below the center of the tree. It was not shown on any drawings. My suggestion was to use a fire hose and completely bare root the tree, which meant we would save a lot more of the roots than if we created a root ball.

I knew Bill Evans, the landscape architect who worked with Walt Disney to create his theme parks, had used this method. Over the phone I asked my longtime friend, if I should consider this option. Even though he had not moved a ginkgo bare root he encouraged me to try, but stressed the importance of minimizing the time between extraction and relocation.

I contacted the student body committee to explain the situation and tell them I could not guarantee the tree would live. The students agreed and many of them skipped classes to watch the operation. It involved cranes, a lot of water, and all of my attention, but it was successful in the end.

Alas, a lot of our lovely landscapes suffered after Proposition 13, and this was very sad to see. We also had contracts with Cal Poly in San Luis Obispo, as well as the Lafayette, Orinda, and Diablo public school districts that similarly met untimely ends with changing budget constraints. But as our California academic institution business began to wither, new opportunities started to unfold.

One December morning in 1979, I headed out for the office after breakfast. I got out my car keys to unlock the door and just as I reached for the lock I slipped on the wet lawn, fell backwards like a felled tree, and hit the ground with my legs sliding under the car. My left knee hit the underside of the car, and suddenly I felt stabbing pain. Straining against the intense throb, it took a few minutes before I was able to scoot my body back onto the grass. I tried but was unable to stand up.

Fortunately, a neighbor saw me stretched out on the lawn and ran over to help. It was a Saturday morning when few doctors have office hours. Margrit thought of a client and skiing friend, Dr. Tom Lewis, in Hillsborough, and was able to reach him at his office. The neighbor helped Margrit move me into the car and for the forty-five minute drive, I took deep breaths to try to manage the pain.

After a short examination, Tom told me I had to go to Mills Hospital across the street because I tore a tendon in my knee and it had be repaired immediately. Checking into a civilian hospital was a brand new experience for me. I was not used to the surrendering of my clothing, as wallet, and even my partial false teeth. But most of all, I did not want to give up my watch because it was the same one I had worn when the submarine took me to Luzon, and it had allowed my safe return. I did give it up, but I would ask for it the moment I got out of surgery.

When I woke up in the recovery room, my left leg was in a large cast. During the next several days I walked with crutches until I was released. Margrit brought the station wagon and the nurses helped me lie down on the old mattress we had used for the boys to keep them content during the drive to Alpine Meadows. It was December 23, and I was eager to be in the mountains, where our family always spent Christmas Eve together.

Upon our arrival, Andy and a friend used a toboggan to move me downhill from the parking lot to the house. Then the two young men carried me on the toboggan into the living room and transferred me onto the couch. Despite my situation everything went as well as could be expected, and I was happy to be with the family. I moved around the house on my crutches and felt very confident I would soon walk without them.

On the day after Christmas, however, I suddenly had great difficulty walking and renewed pain in my knee. A doctor friend in Alpine Meadows advised me to have a blood test. Another friend, a nurse, came to the house to take the blood sample. When the test results suggested an infection our friend contacted Dr. Lewis, who wanted me to return to Mills Hospital immediately. This was not so simple. When Margrit was taking the blood sample to Tahoe City, a gravel truck had rammed the back of the station wagon, doing considerable damage. She was unhurt and could still drive the car, but the back door could not be opened, so I had no access to the mattress.

We called our friend, Bob Quatman, who had a house in Dollar Point. His wife was also my travel agent. Bob had told me several times if I wanted to change my station wagon to a newer model, he could help because, in his business, he frequently bought vehicles.

Luckily, his family was up for a week of skiing. Bob contacted the car dealer with whom he normally worked, and about an hour later, he called us saying he had a brand new Ford station wagon waiting for me in Oakland. He would take a flight out of South Lake Tahoe to Oakland that afternoon, get the car, and drive it back up. This was an amazing offer, especially given the holiday week when he was supposed to be with family.

That evening his wife, Polly, had dinner with us. When Bob returned he joined us around the table. I was so impressed. Only a real friend would have done this.

The next morning, Margrit drove me back to Mills Hospital in San Mateo, about two hundred miles from Alpine Meadows. When we stopped for gas at the Nut Tree, we decided to wash the salty residue off our new car. Lying on the mattress as the car went through the automated wash, I suddenly felt moisture. I had left the rear window open for some fresh air. I called out to Margrit, who quickly turned on the engine to close the window but not before my cast also got a good washing.

Dr. Lewis was waiting for us and told me I had a staph infection. This pronouncement was the beginning of a four-week stay at Mills. I had to lie on my back, which resulted in barely any rest since I usually slept on my stomach or side. They gave me antibiotics and put a valve on my knee, which I manipulated to keep it drained. The mechanics of the valve were similar to those on sprinkler systems, so I was very comfortable with this part of the process.

Frequent blood tests showed the antibiotic was not helping. One Sunday morning, Dr. Lewis's partner came into my room and told me they needed to change to another antibiotic. It was brand new, so they could not guarantee it would help or what it might do to my kidneys. I asked what would happen if I did not agree to the new medication. His answer was I would most likely die within two or three days. "Doctor," I said, "I am in a master planning profession, but I didn't plan to end my life so soon."

Margrit found another doctor, a woman at the hospital, to give us a second opinion. She told us Dr. Lewis's partner had done a great deal of research on the drug he suggested. They would watch the results very carefully in regard to my kidney function. Her advice was to go ahead with the new antibiotic.

One time Dr. Lewis's partner came in the room and noticed that the IV was not working properly. He called the nurse into my room and reprimanded her. I did not like the way he spoke to my nurse and told him he should apologize. He looked at me stone-faced, turned, apologized to the nurse, and then left the room. The news that I had spoken up to this doctor seemed to travel through the hospital very quickly. The new medicine also worked quickly, and I soon started to improve.

I made friends with all the nurses on the ward. I asked Margrit to bring my Polaroid camera, and I gave it to one nurse and then another to take home and snap photos of their gardens. When they returned with their pictures, I suggested design ideas or replied to their questions about how to care for certain plants. Most of these conversations happened at night when they were not as busy. They loved it, and nurses in other wards asked if they could do the same. For me, hardly one to be idle, this was excellent therapy, keeping me busy at something I enjoyed. I think it really helped my recovery as did the attention from the younger women.

During the third week, I was delighted to be able to get out of bed and walk down the hallway. I saw a lady exiting the elevator with an armful of *Rosa "Madame A. Meilland"* ('Peace roses'), and I remarked how lovely they were. This is a very special flower; its petals are a creamy pale yellow, slightly flushed and tinged around the edges with crimson pink. The 'Peace rose' is one of the most popular garden roses in the world. It is also special for what it has come to represent: peace. It was developed by French horticulturist Francis Meilland during WWII, who wanted to name it after Field Marshal Alan Brooke to thank him for his part in the liberation of France. Brooke, though honored, said his name would soon be forgotten and suggested the more enduring name 'Peace.'

Later, the lady asked one of the nurses for the name of the gentleman who had admired her roses and knew the variety by name. The nurse told her I was a landscape architect, and that I had advised some of the nurses about their gardens. She asked if she could visit with me the next day.

She came into my room with a shy smile, and I encouraged her to sit down and be comfortable. She told me her husband had been an ardent gardener, but he had been in bed for a long time and had hardly spoken or even moved.

"I wonder," she asked hopefully, "if you wouldn't mind visiting him and just talking about his rose garden." She gave me some photographs.

The following day, I hobbled into the man's room where his wife smiled at me and waved me into a chair beside the bed. He was lying listlessly on his back under his blanket when I explained who I was. I then admired his bouquet of roses and asked about his rose garden. He didn't answer so I talked about the garden with his wife. While we discussed roses, we glanced over to involve her husband in the conversation, and to our amazement we noticed his eyes were moving. It was obvious we had stimulated something in his brain.

I arranged to have some vegetable seeds and a seed flat with special soil brought to the hospital. I placed the flat on the dining tray right in front of him. We moved the hospital bed so he could sit up, and then we both prepared the soil mix in the flat. Although at first I did all the work, he soon moved his fingers and tried to participate. We seeded lettuce, which germinates rather quickly. When the lettuce came up, he was so delighted he started to speak, even though he had not spoken for the previous three weeks.

It was truly inspiring. The introduction of gardening seemed to create a desire to live, and he ultimately made an almost complete recovery. After I was released from the hospital, I visited him several times. It's hard to explain, but it happened. There are books about therapy through gardening, but this was my first experience with such a power, despite my long love affair with all things that spring from the earth.

I had all kinds of visitors while I was in the hospital. Since I was the president of the Bear Creek Association, the members arranged to have a meeting in the hospital around my bed. That was very nice and also quite practical.

I also had an unexpected visitor from Germany, the editor and publisher of a garden center magazine, Gerhard Klette, who wanted to interview me. I knew Herr Klette from his visit to New York in the mid 1960s when he invited me to give a lecture to German garden center owners on designs for garden centers. This interview concentrated on

WVK's garden center design work and on what was happening in the United States. By that time, I was fairly well known in the domestic industry and was able to give him a lot of information about what was taking place in our country.

Much of my recuperation took place in Alpine Meadows. Margrit placed me on old-fashioned snowshoes and gave me ski poles to use as I took my first steps on our snow-covered deck. This was apparently an excellent exercise because I was able to walk much earlier than the doctor expected, and he wrote an article about this in a medical journal.

When I was more or less fully recovered, I drove down to Mills Hospital with a large bunch of roses for all the nurses who had taken such good care of me. I only wish I had brought the Polaroid to capture the reunion.

CHAPTER 15
Blossoming Internationally

Sequoiadendron giganteum (giant redwood), the world's largest tree
Photo by Jim Lopes © 123RF.com

The work of WVK gradually extended into Canada and overseas. I credit Jack Schneider of Orchard Nursery with the first international outreach for the U.S. nursery industry, when he attended the 1973 International Garden Center Association (IGCA) Congress in England. To the best of my knowledge, this was the first time an American attended a retail association meeting outside of North America. At the time, Jack was the president of the Garden Centers of America (GCA) and the chairman of its board of directors. Jack and I were involved in the formation of the GCA just a year earlier.

A few days before Jack planned to leave, he received a request to give a talk about U.S. garden centers at the Congress. On very short notice, I assembled slides from our collection and put together a lecture for Jack. The presentation was such a great success, he was interviewed on BBC television. Several garden center people from around the world came to California to visit him over the years, staying with Jack at his lovely home in Lafayette. This was a great start to a meaningful relationship between European and American garden centers.

In 1981, Jack Schneider and I convinced other U.S. garden center owners to sponsor the first meeting of the IGCA in the United States. American businesses wanted to learn what the IGCA was about and many in the global community wanted to see what was happening in the United States. Jack and I volunteered to be responsible for the planning and execution of the 1981 Congress, which included the challenge of communicating with people in many different languages.

The first half of the meeting took place in San Francisco and the second half in San Diego, making this also the first time a Congress would visit two cities. This required transportation via two chartered planes. In San Francisco, we arranged for seven buses with docents (and translators), who could talk knowledgeably about each area — the plants, horticultural history, and local garden centers. We planned a tour and picnic lunch for three hundred people at the Strybing Arboretum, spreading out plastic blankets and serving box lunches from either McDonalds or Kentucky Fried Chicken, which were both a novelty for foreigners at the time. People loved the picnic and networked more than if we had been in a restaurant. The group visited the San Francisco Japanese Tea Garden across the street and then boarded the buses to tour Golden Gate Park all the way to the Pacific Ocean.

Over the following days, the group saw many other sites of interest, including the *Sunset Magazine* gardens designed by Thomas Church, the well-known American landscape architect. Elsa Knoll, the magazine's editor, gave a very thoughtful talk. On the way back to the San Francisco Hilton Hotel, I arranged for my bus to visit the Moorman family's garden in Atherton, which my company designed. We had planned their first garden in San Mateo and were asked to design the garden when they built a new house in Atherton. This was a truly special garden including a natural swimming pool and a Japanese structure that served as a teahouse. This was a treat for my bus, which they talked about the rest of the Congress.

I greeted the entire group each morning, which felt natural given my outgoing nature. I often started with a joke before announcing the day's activities and introducing each of the Garden Center hosts. I also made sure we arrived and departed on time at each destination. Such timeliness is part of my make-up, perhaps an inborn German attention to precision. All this meant everyone on the tour knew Ernest Wertheim.

From then on I attended both International Garden Center Association and American Association of Nurserymen meetings every year, as well as the American Nursery and Landscape Association (ANLA) Retail Road Show for Garden Centers, and the Independent Garden Center show in Chicago. I have been to the ANLA Management Clinic more than thirty-five times. I also regularly attend the bi-annual garden center tours sponsored by the Garden Centers of America.

With Victor Reiter at a California Horticulture Society field trip to Domoto Nursery in 1983, many years after he first invited me to join CHS

My good friend Jacquie Williams-Courtright says, "He is basically everywhere doing everything. That's what has kept him so young."

I think she's right. At the end of the day, it's not because of the business, but rather the opportunity to learn and meet people, old friends and new contacts alike. It's now eighty years since I went away to college in Ahlem. I can't spade rhubarb all day long or compete in track races anymore; but my interest and joy in plants and landscapes and the people who nurture them has never diminished.

I've been lucky to have two loves to sustain me, Margrit and our beautiful world, which beckons me to step outside and explore.

In 1982, I went to my first International Garden Center Congress overseas. I thought it would be good for our office to further relationships with all the garden center owners I had met the previous year. The Congress was in of all places Germany.

The Congress was to begin in Cologne and end in Munich. Since we celebrated our fortieth wedding anniversary that summer, Margrit decided to join me on the trip to mark this special occasion. It was our first visit to our former homeland since we had immigrated to the United States, Margrit in 1937 and me in December 1938.

Margrit's presence makes any event special, but this trip was particularly big for us. We had never taken a trip together that wasn't within driving distance or a military train ride. It was our first time flying across the Atlantic Ocean, and, as it turned out, it would be the first time since 1939 that I spoke so much German. We didn't know what to expect when we got to Germany. Neither Margrit nor I had spent time in this part of the country, several hundred miles from Berlin and Hamburg, where I grew up, and Emmendingen, where Margrit grew up.

As we took the train from Frankfurt to Cologne, we enjoyed the pastoral scenery dotted with castles. There was nothing about the landscape to jog our memories. It hardly felt like we were in the Germany of our childhoods. We were simply tourists.

Margrit had no interest in attending industry sessions. While I participated in the meetings, she rented a bicycle and had a great time riding through the city along the Rhine River. In the evenings she joined me for the lovely IGCA dinners. For us, it was very much like a second honeymoon.

While we were in Cologne, the whole group visited Dinger's Garden Center. I, however, had a special purpose for our time there outside of the tour. I had met Gunter Dinger the year before in San Francisco, and he had asked me to give him my impression of his garden center. After the organized tour, I returned to the entrance and retraced our steps, recording my observations in my dictating machine. That night during cocktails and prior to the gala dinner, Herr Dinger, dressed in his tuxedo, came looking for me.

"What do you think? What did you see?"

Though his eagerness was apparent, I knew he was the master of ceremonies for the evening, so I convinced him to wait until the next day when we were to sail up the Rhine River.

When Margrit and I arrived at the dock, Herr Dinger was waiting for us at the top of the gangplank.

"Herr Dinger, I have reserved a table for us in the coffee room." He had also arranged for friends to entertain Margrit while we talked business. He kidnapped me! I missed all the beautiful scenery along the river, stunning vistas of castles perched above steep vine-covered slopes I later saw in Margrit's photographs.

Gunter Dinger, his wife, Carla, and their general manager, Herr Buchholz, were all in the coffee room. Before we began, I told them I did not wish for them to defend their garden center when I shared my impressions; I was not going to recommend changes. They agreed. "I'm just going to tell you what I saw," I reiterated.

After five minutes, Herr Dinger started defending. Luckily his wife stopped him, "Remember what Herr Wertheim said?"

For many of our clients, the beginning of our relationship is often difficult. In some cases they are doing a lot of things wrong. Nobody likes to be told such things. On this occasion, the longer we talked, the more obvious it became that Herr Dinger would have to make some major changes to his garden center. Just before we docked in Rüdesheim, Herr Dinger said, "This was the most expensive cup of coffee I have ever had because now we have to remodel our garden center."

The Dingers asked me to return to Cologne in November 1982 to commence with the redesign of their center. Herr Dinger liked the covered walkways he had seen at Springdale Garden Center in San Jose, California. Springdale was one of WVK's favorite garden center designs. Our business relationship with the Dingers started in 1982. We are still friends today; in fact, I visited with them in March 2012. I saw the garden center again, which is now run by their son, Christian, and his wife.

The next day the group boarded buses for the trip to Munich along the Romantic Road. It is called this not because of any love story, but because of its ancient walled towns and the natural beauty along the Tauber River. We stopped at *Rothenburg ob der Tauber*, a well-preserved medieval town, where we visited a wonderful year-round Christmas shop. It was so popular among our group, it was hard to persuade people to leave. This was a situation when a good tour leader had to remember the caution: "Count your chickens before they go in and when they come out."

One of the problems with the garden center business is the slow period in the winter. Having a Christmas display and sale is a good idea to create business during that time of year, so garden center owners were eager to see the Christmas store to get ideas for their businesses back home. When WVK designed Orchard Nursery in 1954, we decided Orchard should develop a Christmas business. Orchard did a first class job with its Christmas displays and people came from forty miles away just to see the decorated trees and holiday setting, as they still do today.

In Munich, we stopped to see the Dehner Garden Center. At the time their shop was nothing special. They had a lot to learn, but they were determined. In fact a few years later, they made a special trip to the United States. Jacob and I welcomed them to San Francisco, and we visited many local garden centers. Today, under the leadership of Herr Weber, Dehner's is one of Europe's largest Garden Center Groups. Operating in Germany and Austria, they employ over five thousand people at more than one hundred branches.

The final stop of the tour was Munich, where we attended the prestigious German Flower Show. This annual event, which continues today, takes place in various German cities. This brought back memories of driving to Essen in the spring of 1937 for my first German Flower Show, packed into my old Hanomag with Dieter and other friends from Ahlem. At that time, we focused on the exotic plants at the show.

The flower show was as stimulating as it had been in my youth. Because of this, I was one of the few in our English-speaking group who knew what to expect. I became a bit of a translator and tour guide for members from the U.K. since the signage was in German.

Bob Lederer, the executive director of the AAN (later ANLA), presented the director of the flower show with a *Sequoiadendron gigantean* (giant sequoia), a tree native to the western slopes of the Sierra Nevada that was already eight feet tall but still young. A plant pit was dug for us, and I was elected along with Bob to plant the tree. I was truly honored and proud to share this unique American species with plant lovers in Germany. The ceremony spoke to my identity as an American first and foremost. Forty-five years after my first German Flower Show, I was reminded my dream had come true.

After the tour was over, Margrit and I rented a car and drove to Austria, where we stayed at a small resort owned by our client, Mr. Robinson, Suzanne's father. In exchange for the consultation about his Lake Tahoe house and garden, we stayed free of charge. We met nice people at the resort and savored delicious pastry with lots of *schlag* (whipped cream). I had never seen the Alps before and was awed by their grand scale and rugged beauty.

The IGCA trip helped me and WVK become better known in Europe. Later that same year, I returned to start work with three new clients: two in Germany and one in the United Kingdom. I consulted with Herr Dinger, as well as the Nordharz Garden Center in Goslar, Germany, and Warren Haskins in the UK. This was the beginning of my frequent travel to Europe.

While working on garden centers in Germany, the topic of being Jewish was never brought up. In fact the discussion of Hitler, the war, and what happened was kind of taboo, which suited me just fine.

On my third or fourth trip to Germany, I managed to find some personal time to visit my older brother, Werner, who had returned from Chile many years earlier. He and his wife had a modest but quite adequate apartment in a suburb of Hamburg. It had a small garden, which I took pleasure in redesigning for them. It was the first time I met his Chilean wife, Jovita, who was a gracious hostess, along with their children who were married with children of their own.

All Werner's children and grandchildren lived in Hamburg and each evening we had dinner with someone else. It was nice to meet everyone, but I did not become well acquainted with my brother's children. The exception was his oldest son, Gunther, because he came to see us in San Francisco a couple of times. This visit to Hamburg was the only time I ever spent with Werner's other children. We did not warm up to each other. Perhaps there just wasn't enough time. They were very "German-oriented," and this made me cautious. Werner's youngest son was openly anti-American. For these reasons and others I don't really understand, I never took on the role of being their uncle. I guess, many years later, there can still be casualties of war.

Werner drove me to our old street, the Parkallee in Hamburg. This district, in general, had suffered minimal damage during the war. The apartment house we grew up in was still there as was the market across the street. There were the chestnuts trees, much larger than I remembered them, lining the sidewalks. I remembered the activities Werner and I did together, but that was it. My life in America was my reality. I felt great affection and emotion for my brother, but seeing all of this was not very much different than being on vacation and seeing a new city.

The same was true when my brother drove us to Berlin. We started at Bendlerstrasse. The street had been renamed Staufferbergstrasse and a new building had replaced my grandparents' apartment house, which had been bombed. I wondered what happened to Gladys Wells. I never saw her or communicated with her again after leaving Germany.

Then we drove to Dahlem in West Berlin, which had been a very popular place to live for U.S. high ranking military officers stationed in Germany. At the estate our cousin, Elsa Ziehm, the daughter of Great Aunt Martha, greeted us warmly. Werner had been to visit her many times and had grown close with her adult children. Elsa and her husband, Hans Juergen, still lived in what had been the garage of the estate, but they had enlarged it some time ago. They had another apartment which was occupied by their children. Hans Juergen had been a deserter. He would not join the Nazi military, and Elsa had to flee Berlin with the children. Her friends would not help her or were too afraid to do so. I do not know the whole story, but my cousin says she went to Riesengebirge, the same mountains where I skied refugees to safety. She ended up in Prague when the Russians arrived. She had a very difficult time, having to steal food to feed the children. But eventually she made her way back to Berlin. She did receive some reparation after the war, which allowed her to create the addition on her home.

The smaller house at Aunt Martha's, for which I had designed the gardens, was still standing. It was occupied by others, and I presume it was taken during the war. The large villa had also been confiscated, and Werner told me it had been used by a high ranking Nazi for what was officially a "dance school." In reality, it had been a place to host and entertain important Nazis.

Toward the end of the war, the Allies dropped bombs on the grand old mansion. I do not know why they would have bombed this area of lovely homes and gardens if not to target the estate. All traces of the villa were gone. Herr Glaubitz was killed during one of the bombings. This made me very sad as I remembered his kindness to and loyal support of my aunt. He was an honorable man when such figures were in short supply, and he was a good friend and driving instructor. Elsa reported that Mrs. Glaubitz was still alive and doing well. Elsa visited with her as late as 2005.

Aunt Martha's orchard had survived, and the trees I had planted had grown to full size. The asparagus was still there. I leaned down to feel one of the green stalks between my fingers and touch the soil. I was most interested in seeing how the landscape had matured and changed over the years.

It was in getting to the Leipziger Platz when my emotions finally took over. At the border crossing into East Berlin and the German Democratic Republic (GDR or East Germany), the Berlin Wall severed the city into two halves when it was constructed in 1961, to prevent emigration and defection from East Germany. Guard towers loomed over the concrete wall, an unnerving sight. Handing over my passport to the stoic border guards in their uniforms, I suddenly began to sweat. I vividly recalled the cabinet of nails and the German-Dutch border guards. I remembered the forbidding gates and walls of the Sachsenhausen camp. I felt very uneasy long after we had left the checkpoint. Werner, who hadn't experienced what I did, and who now lived in Germany, was used to this passing. It had been a long time since I had felt such emotions.

The Wertheim Department Store, the pride of the family, was gone. An Allied bombing attack in late November 1943 had damaged the building beyond repair. The demolition of the ruins was completed in 1956. Of course right across the street from the rear of the store had been the Reich Chancellery building, the *Vorbunker* and *Führerbunker*. I told Werner about watching from Great Uncle's office window as construction materials arrived and how I had shared this with commanders of the U.S. military. My Opa's face came to mind. I could see him complimenting one of the flower stall merchants and handing me a rose to take home to Oma.

Rather than cross back into West Germany, I made arrangements to fly out of Berlin — no more border crossings for me. Perhaps I overreacted, but I did not want to experience that again.

Over the years we saw Werner and Jovita a number of times. Margrit and I brought our grandson, Brian, with us to visit them in Hamburg a couple of years later, and afterwards we took Jovita with us to Copenhagen for a few days as part of my business trip there.

Werner worked for many years in Hamburg. When he reached the age to receive his pension the money exchange was such that he and Jovita discovered they could live better in Chile, so they moved back to Santiago. During their retirement they traveled to Germany once a year to spend time with their children and grandchildren. Normally they stopped on their way there or back in the States, spending time with us in Alpine Meadows. We always enjoyed these visits. Margrit and I, along with our son, Rick, and his wife, Lin, visited them once in Santiago. Werner and Jovita also welcomed other good friends of ours — Fred Hicks and his wife and another friend, Peter Turner, and his wife — when they, too, visited Santiago. Werner died in Santiago in 2006, and Jovita moved back to Germany to live with their daughter. Although I have tried, we have never really been in touch since then.

In 1985, the AAN convention was in Miami Beach at the Fontainebleau Hotel. A friend of Jack Schneider's convinced Jack that he and I should return to California, for no extra cost, by going via

Havana, Cuba, to Mexico City to Los Angeles. I was concerned because neither of us had our passports, but we checked with the consulate in Miami and were told there would be no problems. The friend also gave us the name of a limousine service to take us sightseeing in Havana. It seemed like a once-in-a-lifetime opportunity given the U.S. embargos limiting travel to Cuba.

We enjoyed Havana, managing to see tourist sites as well as some wealthy neighborhoods with beautiful gardens. Continuing on to Mexico City, we stayed in a downtown hotel across from the new Hilton. We planned to stay for three days. On the first day we toured the city as well as suburbs and visited several garden centers.

Early the next morning we were jarred awake. The entire hotel was swaying back and forth. An earthquake had struck, a big one. We were on the ninth floor. I held on tight to my mattress, thinking that if the building collapsed I would fall on something soft. The TV fell on to the floor, along with lamps and books, but when the shaking subsided we were still on the ninth floor.

Jack and I went out into the hallway to discover the elevators did not work and the doors to the stairways were locked. We tried the phone in our room, which had fallen on the floor, and managed to get in touch with the front desk. They said they were sending someone up to unlock the doors.

We dressed and packed quickly.

"Jack, I need to shave before leaving," I told him.

"What?!" he asked. He thought this was crazy, and perhaps it was, but I was trained not to leave my room without brushing my teeth and shaving. So he waited like a good friend.

In the hallway, I went to task. Our self-appointed job was to make certain all people were ready to go down and to keep people from panicking. My military training for emergencies came in handy. Floor by floor, we made our way down until we were in the lobby. The staff, trying to remain calm in the chaos, helped us make arrangements to fly out of the city. Before we took a taxi to the airport, we went across the street to see the Hilton Hotel basement where concrete columns had moved several inches off their foundation.

We managed to get the first flight out of the country and arrived safely in Los Angeles. Before we even got out of the gate area after disembarking, we were mobbed by reporters, who were anxious for any information. It was a mad house. We were some of the first witnesses to have contact with the outside world. We shared with the reporters what we saw and felt. After answering what questions we could, we got to a payphone. I called Margrit to tell her I had arrived safely, and Jack called his wife. We were most concerned about getting our luggage and making our connecting flight. It was not until I arrived home that I learned we had endured a magnitude 8.1 earthquake, and many hundreds of buildings had collapsed, and at least ten thousand people were declared dead.

CHAPTER 16

Design Is About People

Children playing in the Stone family garden

In my experience, most people think they know more than they really do about what they want in their house or garden. I'm always trying to prompt and gage reactions. I give them books in which they are to tag pictures they like. "What do you love about this?" I'll then ask. In this way I can gently force them to analyze their own reactions so we can determine the right plants for their garden. I have also found most people don't know enough about plants, flowers, or design. Very few understand the interplay of soil and water, climate and seasons, shading and light. It has always been our job at WVK to educate our clients about all this and expose people to a variety of garden situations in order to find a solution they will enjoy well into the future.

By getting to know my clients, I can design a garden reflecting their values and lifestyle, which they will truly love and enjoy for a long time. An example is the Stone family garden. I spent time with the adults listening to them talk about not just what they wanted in their garden but also how they live their lives and what they enjoy. I watched the children play and got to know them, too.

As a result of our time with the family, Jacob and I included several unusual elements in their garden design, including a bridge over a make-believe "river," a dry bed of pebbles which the kids loved, and a cement "road" that wrapped around a sand area and on which the children could drive replica power cars. The family loved it.

Dr. and Mrs. Upton lived in San Francisco's Pacific Heights. The house was three stories high with a dining room that looked out over an undeveloped area with the Golden Gate Bridge in the distance. The idea was to create something that made an architectural impact because you probably couldn't tell a rose from a geranium at that distance. As Dr. Upton told me, they wanted the garden to make a grand impression on their guests as seen from above because most would likely never venture out into the garden itself. I listened to their ideas and finally Dr. Upton said to me, "I want you to make my wife happy."

"Oh no," I replied, "This is a family affair. You have to be a part of it. You have to be equally happy."

Dr. Upton thought this over and said, "Well, I love roses. I would like a rose garden."

During the spring when roses were in bloom, we went to the San Francisco rose garden, and they picked the colors they wanted. I like to plant no less than three roses of each variety so garden owners can cut enough to create a nice display/bouquet in the house. Our final design had roses surrounded by English boxwood, which was very bold and created an architectural pattern when seen from above. We also put in a custom-designed fountain backed by a simple, white stucco wall, and this created a wonderful contrast with the boxwood and roses.

When the garden was complete, I suggested to Dr. Upton that he learn how to prune his own roses. Over the years I have tried to turn as many people as possible into enthusiastic gardeners. He was hesitant about this at first, but he listened carefully to my instructions and gradually reached the point where he would not allow anyone else to prune his roses.

Near the end of his life, he became very ill. Up until just a week before his death, Dr. Upton, carrying shears on his lap, would ask his caretaker to push him in his wheelchair along the path through his rose garden. These are the stories that fuel my passion.

The Morgans of Atherton loved color in their garden so I wanted to provide a year-round palette. There was sun on the swimming pool area, but the property also included several large California live oak trees that provided ample shade. This was an opportunity to use a large selection of azaleas and rhododendrons.

We created a special soil and a watering system to accommodate both the native oaks and a whole assortment of new plants. Next I chose Fielder's white azaleas with rhododendron 'Blue Peter' and 'Pink Ruby Bowman', which in combination bloom from October through June. We planted the edge of the bed with coral bells azalea, which normally blooms in coral pink from early winter to spring. The pink macrantha azalea we planted is a late spring bloomer, perhaps the latest bloomer in the azalea family. Between the rhododendrons we planted ferns and hostas, the latter a perennial that blooms a waxy white in late summer earning it the nickname of 'August Lily.' Hydrangeas provided more summer color — a splash of delicate blue, pink, lavender, and white. We used the oak leaf hydrangea, which blooms even later and produces good fall color with leaves turning a rich orange and burgundy. Through this combination of plants we created a dynamic, watercolor setting through every season.

Dr. Morgan loved orchids and hired us later for a special project. Jacob designed a small greenhouse as an add-on to the master bedroom to house the doctor's extensive orchid collection. The greenhouse was half the size of a bedroom. It had sliding doors so he could step into it without going outside. The care for the orchids was almost completely automated, with irrigation and ventilation perfectly balanced, a necessity since the doctor was a very busy person.

Landscaping can change as the priorities and lifestyles of a family change. Eventually, I designed garden weddings for both the children. Years after the children had grown up and moved out, the Morgans decided to move to a warmer climate. They invited me to design the garden for their new house overlooking the ocean in Freeport, Bahamas. I stayed as their houseguest at least four different times to get to know the property and the plant palette in that area. Because the plants could not be obtained there, we imported them from Florida. I designed the garden, and we hired local contractors to create it.

I have a deep gratitude for the warmth in which this family welcomed me through all the seasons of their life. Doing work on someone's home and garden is, by its very nature, a personal, sometimes intimate affair. As a priceless benefit, so many clients have become lifelong friends and have further enriched my life.

The Coynes are among the many clients that are multi-generational friends. I first met Susie Coyne's mother and father when we were skiing at Sun Valley in 1950 or 1951. He was an eye doctor and a rose lover with a beautiful garden. He passed away just prior to the printing of the first edition of this book. Susie and her husband, Kevin Coyne, had their first home in Belvedere, and they called me in October 1988 for help with the landscaping. They were very young and didn't know much about gardening. The site had a number of large trees, some of them native trees. In one of these trees, a beautiful *Clematis armandii* (climbing white clematis) grew. It has prolific blooms in March but needs to be pruned properly. This was the first plant I taught Susie to prune, and it was the beginning of making her a gardener. And of course, she had to have roses to remind her of her father's garden.

When the Coynes moved to Woodside, WVK worked on another garden for them and replaced an old swimming pool. When they moved to Atherton, we designed a garden that remains one of my personal favorites. I still keep two panels of the design on the wall in my office and the garden is on our website. It has been truly delightful to watch their five children grow up and to become friends with them all.

Since creating a landscape for a home can take months or years, you never know what kind of life events will take place during the process — birth, death, marriage, divorce — and I have found it best to be ready for anything. This attitude was helpful when, in the mid-1960s, we had the opportunity to create the largest private garden in our company's history on a fifty-acre lot.

Our first meeting with Dr. Henry Fee was at the hospital, where he performed heart transplants. Dr. Fee was well traveled in Europe, specifically in France, where he had fallen in love with the traditional architecture. He wanted a home built in the style of a French chateau. Jacob's architectural background was very significant to Dr. Fee because Jacob had gone to school in the Netherlands as well as in Michigan. He was very familiar with this type of architectural. Dr. Fee also liked that our office offered both architectural and landscape architectural services.

Two weeks later, we met again on a property in Los Altos that Dr. Fee considered buying for his chateau, but we quickly realized the property did not lend itself to Dr. Fee's requirements. We stopped for lunch in downtown Los Altos and thumbed through some books illustrating different chateaus in France.

It was only a few days later another meeting was planned in Los Altos on a fifty-acre site. Given the size of the lot, we suggested to Dr. Fee that we allow for several hours to inspect the property; we would bring some lunch along. It did not take us very long on the hilly site to determine where the house should be, but it would involve a lot of grading for the main house and swimming pool. Henry wanted to have a vineyard, an orchard, and a vegetable garden in addition to gardens around the house. We ended up spending five hours there. The anticipation of painting a landscape on such a wide canvas was very exciting!

The property was located in Santa Clara County outside of Los Gatos. However the city of Los Gatos had an arrangement requiring the applicant to get city approval for construction prior to submitting plans to Santa Clara County. This created many unforeseen problems to overcome.

We suggested taking some very rough sketches to the Los Altos Planning Committee to determine what they would approve and what they would not. It took a three-hour meeting with the planning directors of both Los Gatos and Santa Clara County, but it resulted in an agreement that both agencies would remain flexible as we progressed with the design. This meant Henry Fee could purchase the property. Despite the success of this meeting, we had to meet with the government agencies many more times with varying results, but it worked out in the end.

First we needed to complete a survey and a full topography. Then we got to work. Jacob designed the beautiful French-Californian chateau. I designed the landscape from the driveway to the hillside vineyard with all of its angles and areas and features and colors. We worked on the project for four years. It helped that Dr. Fee was very capable of reading drawings. There was much discussion about the swimming pool, the dressing room, the tennis court, the stables, the vineyard, the orchard, and the driveway.

During this time Mrs. Fee filed for divorce. Understandably, this delayed the project for a number of months. The Fees had two children who stayed primarily with their mother but also had regular times with Henry. Our design was supposed to provide a room for each child plus rooms for two additional children. At this time there was no other woman in Dr. Fee's life, but he wanted to provide for future children plus a governess. The house was to be his domicile for the rest of his life, and I suppose he thought he wouldn't be alone forever. There was a lot of discussion about the arrangement of the various bedrooms.

After a couple years a young woman did enter Henry's life. As the future Mrs. Fee, she came to a meeting with us. Jacob and I were considerably older than she, and as a result, I felt she was not comfortable in our meeting. So I suggested that Carole Haan, our talented administrator, join us. Carole is thirty years younger than Jacob and I and her presence was most helpful in putting the young woman at ease. Over many years, Carole has been the secret weapon in our success. Nothing seems beyond her.

The discussion about the landscaping was turned over to the future Mrs. Fee. This meant spending a lot of time teaching her about plants. At the beginning she told me she did not want any conifers at all. I wondered what made her so opposed to conifers but agreed to this condition. She did not like plants like rosemary either, which reminded her of a conifer.

By then the building drawings were well along, so I suggested to both Henry and his fiancé spend the good part of a day with me walking the San Francisco Botanical Gardens. I chose a Sunday and brought lunch for all of us. There were so many plants to see, but our visit was most valuable because they could react to such a wide range of plants. I kept careful notes and was surprised to find out that Henry did not like large leaves as we see on English laurels, camellias, and hollies, but they both liked azaleas and rhododendrons and many other flowering plants.

Toward the very end of our tour I walked them past a *Metasequoia glyptostroboides* (dawn redwood tree) and touched the foliage, encouraging them to do the same. She was taken by surprise at how soft the needles felt and said she wanted this tree even though it was a conifer. We planted dawn redwoods on both sides of the long driveway creating a lovely, dramatic approach to the chateau.

NORTHEAST ELEVATION

Fee Residence

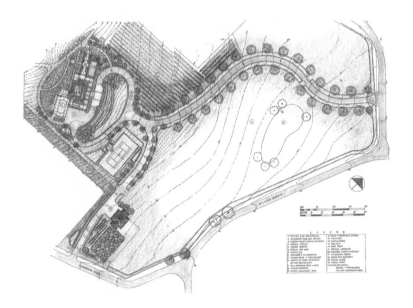

While I made many friends of my clients when landscaping their homes, I developed even more friendships by designing garden centers around the world. I am grateful to have had so many people give me the opportunity of helping them with their businesses. Often times, my consulting extended well beyond the initial design project. This was true with the LeBoutilliers, owners of Waterloo Garden Center in Exton, Pennsylvania.

In February of 1979, I consulted for the first time with Dennis Burd of Country Market Garden Center in Mechanicsburg, PA. Our company would work with him for many years until he sold to another company. Dennis appreciated WVK's service and encouraged his good friends, Bo and Linda LeBoutillier, to engage our services, but Bo was hesitant. Bo then attended a lecture I gave to a Pennsylvania nursery group; afterwards he asked Dennis to bring me over for dinner before we returned to Mechanicsburg.

When we arrived, Bo invited me to see his large nursery. While viewing the nursery, most of the discussion was about plants. We quickly made a strong connection when we realized the other was a knowledgeable plantsman. Linda was a great cook, and we had a delicious dinner. From the start, there was a lovely sense of comfort and trust among us.

When Dennis and I thanked them for the evening, Bo asked when I could return to help them redo their garden center. My first consultation was January 19, 1980. For several years we made minor changes in various parts of the garden center until we converted one existing warehouse to a gift shop and furniture department. This change resulted in a new entrance and a new checkout station allowing for better traffic flow throughout the store. We also made changes to the large outdoor sales area and developed a department for landscape contractor sales. I stayed with Bo and Linda several times during this work.

We also made improvements to their garden center in Devon. The property was very small, so we had to be creative with the space. We designed a greenhouse with a basement below, which became their warehouse. We used an upstairs attic to create a gift shop and offices. It is not simple to have customers walk upstairs or even use an elevator — another useful lesson — so it took several years before customers started to really use the gift shop. Waterloo was also one of our first garden centers to incorporate computers thanks to Bo's son Bobby. This was another learning experience for everyone.

When Bo contracted ALS (Lou Gehrig's Disease) and his time was getting short, he asked me to come for a "consultation." When I arrived, I realized he had actually invited me to say goodbye. Our last meeting was very touching. He discussed what he wanted done after he passed on and asked me to help his wife, who was very capable, to continue. Bo died just a few days later. I assisted Linda as she became the leader of Waterloo, and I hope I was a help as she grieved for her husband. I have been blessed in working with some very wonderful people.

In the early 1980s, Warren Haskins became our first British garden centre (as they spell it across the pond) and one of our youngest garden center clients ever. We met at the 1981 IGCA Congress in San Francisco, when he was only in his early twenties. His father died when Warren was twenty years old, leaving him to take control of the family business started by his grandfather in 1882. He had bundles of energy and a big vision for the business. However, being young and an inexperienced leader, he had a lot to learn.

I saw Warren the following year in Cologne and agreed a stopover in the UK the next time I traveled to Germany. At my request, Warren took me on a tour of the area. When I begin work on a new garden center, I always research local garden centers as well as the residential communities that provide the likely customer base, so I can observe the local landscaping trends. I was not very complimentary about the design of the gardens we visited, particularly some young gardens in a new subdivision.

This sparked an idea for Warren. He asked if I would be willing to be interviewed on the radio about garden design and plant selection. I agreed. By the next day, Warren had arranged a live interview with a local radio station in the gardens of that new subdivision. I explained what I felt needed improvement and offered a call-in audience a number of ideas based on my experience. Haskins sponsored the interview, of course.

It was a marketing and educational success. Many people called in and asked the radio station to replicate the program but to include other gardens in the next show. The next morning, we did a similar show from a different location. The show generated both increased good will and clientele at Haskins.

Warren's goal for our initial meeting was to discuss his main store south of Southampton. Over the next two years, we concentrated on improving the existing facilities. When Warren was presented with the opportunity to purchase additional land, WVK worked on the design to increase the space within the store as well as the parking lot. We also redesigned three more garden centers Warren bought to make part of Haskins.

While the original Haskins Garden Centre location was extremely successful, Warren was offered an incredible price for the property he couldn't refuse. He intends to reinvest the money in a new, very large property that would meet and hopefully exceeded his vision for growth. He wanted it to be a center with a real "wow" factor. Warren retained WVK to work on this new project.

When one of the IGCA Congresses was in the Netherlands, I became acquainted with the greenhouse firm called Thermoflor. Their greenhouses had overhead doors allowing the ceiling and walls to open up over a large expanse, much like a garage door, which was very unique at the time. Their design created a light, bright, expansive, clean space — an impressive sight. After watching a different garden center install some of these greenhouses in the UK, we realized this might be perfect for Haskins, so we invited Thermoflor to furnish a bid. Warren accepted it, and the finished Haskins Garden Centre provided a fresh and inviting environment for an extended range of plants and accessories. The new garden center also included a two hundred sixty seat restaurant, one of the largest privately owned restaurants in the south of England. It definitely had the "wow" factor Warren was after.

The new facility was an instant success. This was good for both Haskins Garden Centre and WVK. With our assistance, Warren replicated this design on a property in Southampton, making it into a grand garden center. We used a similar design on Haskins' Roundstone site, with some modifications, which included a five hundred seat restaurant. This new facility opened in 2012. The success of Haskins Garden Centres and Warren's testimonials also helped promote WVK in Europe, particularly in the United Kingdom.

Making the news with Warren Haskins, 1991

I was (and am) always watching and listening to see if there are innovative ways garden centers attract customers during the slow winter months. During the 1990 IGCA pre-tour in the United States, I introduced Warren to Franks' Nursery and Crafts in Detroit. The Franks had more than one hundred stores combining plant sales, which did best in spring and summer, with craft sales, which did best in fall and winter. This was a further extension of the Christmas décor idea.

As a result, Warren established the first real hobby shop in the UK as part of his new garden center in Ferndown. Then in 1995, Warren started stand-alone stores called Hobbycraft. Over a period of nearly twenty years, it became a fifty-store operation before Warren sold it. He now is Chairman of the Board of Haskins Garden Centres and is still active as the visionary of what the British press has called his "garden centre empire."

Haskins Garden Centre, a WVK design

The main entrance is designed only for pedestrians

The first view a customer sees upon entering the store

I have always enjoyed spending time with Warren, whether for work or play. While visiting us in Alpine Meadows, Margrit and I took him skiing. I think this started his passion for the sport. Warren and Margrit both share an enjoyment for gambling at the casinos, which they do whenever he comes to visit. Given my fiscally conservative nature, I am not prone to indulge in games of chance.

In 1984, at the AAN meeting in Louisville, Kentucky, I was checking my coat when Fred Hicks approached me and said, "Ernest, I need more office space at my nursery. Do you think you could help me out?" That was how he greeted me: no "hello" or small talk, just right to the point. Fred and I hit it off immediately.

Fred was already well known in the nursery circle on the East Coast and was very active in the industry on Long Island and in the state of New York. When Fred first took over the nursery as a very young man, the place was in financial trouble. With a shoestring budget, Fred did most of the work — construction, repairs, finances, everything — rather than contracting it out. This habit didn't change even as his business became successful. Once, when I was there consulting, there was a leak in the copper pipe that fed the heating boilers, and I found Fred flat on his stomach in a ditch, trying to locate the leak.

"Fred," I said, "you are paying me one hundred dollars per hour, and here you are in a trench while I watch you. This is not the most efficient way to run a garden center."

At my first dinner at the Hicks' house, the entire family sat around the dining room table, with me included. I virtually became a member of the family, like a favorite uncle. Their teenage daughter, Karen, told me about her work as a cashier in the garden center on weekends, describing all she saw and experienced. This information helped inform my recommendations to her father.

Fred was with me when I helped get the master plan for his garden center accepted by the local planning board. (Because of my volunteer work with the Bear Creek Planning Committee, I was comfortable addressing the county planning committee.) We reappeared before the board four different times over a period of twenty-eight years to do remodels and additions.

The respect we held for each other only deepened as we worked together professionally and as volunteers. We served as co-chairmen of the 1990 IGCA Congress in New York and spent time together at every IGCA conference. It was always a pleasure to host Fred and his wife, Marilyn, when they visited us in Alpine Meadows over the years.

One of the most significant features of my work with Hicks Garden Center was the use of Thermoflor greenhouses, which I had used in Haskins Garden Centres in the United Kingdom. In fact, I took Fred to visit with Warren and see Haskins during our planning process. In 1996, after two years of planning, the existing Hicks greenhouses and buildings were all torn down, except for the 1928 barn. A new Hicks Nursery with the first ever Thermoflor construction in the U.S. was built to the design of WVK. Its entrance featured an indoor plant house full of color. Customers were (and continue to be) greeted with the sight of flourishing, flowering plants and a wonderful smell in a spacious setting. The total roofed-over greenhouse area is forty-two thousand square feet. In addition, there is an eleven thousand square foot shade house for perennials.

I can't explain it or truly understand it, but I developed an intuitive connection with Fred. One day I had a feeling something was wrong. I called his home and shared my uneasiness. "Who told you about what happened today at the East Coast Garden Centers (ECGC) meeting?"

I told him no one had said anything. It turned out Fred had a major disagreement with a fellow member of the ECGC board about what the group was doing. As a result of the meeting, Fred had angrily written a letter of resignation. I told him to fax it to me.

"You should let some time pass before resigning," I told him, "You're very upset now." He took my advice.

Another time I called and Marilyn answered. Again, I had a feeling.

"What's going on with Fred?" I asked.

"How did you know, Ernest? He's in the hospital. I'm talking to you from there." Fred was asleep, and Marilyn explained his blood condition, I believe it was Polycythemia Vera, had worsened. Later that day I talked to Fred on the hospital phone, and he said goodbye to me. He died not long after our conversation.

There is not enough space in this book to share the many wonderful experiences I've had with Fred and his family. I still keep in touch with Marilyn on a regular basis, and I will always miss my good friend.

With Fred's death, their son, Stephen, became president of Hick's Nurseries and continued the relationship with WVK. In 2008, we worked with Stephen on the design of a landscape distribution center for Hicks Nurseries. I am delighted I have developed a good rapport with Stephen. Margrit and I attended his wedding, and I have stayed with him and his wife, Sabrina, at their home. I enjoy a close relationship with the entire family. Their oldest son, Haydon, asked me if I would help him when he had to write something about World War II. As these last words are being typed, Sabrina has been one of my guides in the development of this book. I consider it a real privilege when the sons or daughters of my clients choose to continue working with me and also become friends.

The first time I visited with Ron and Wendy Bent was in the spring of 1988. I arrived in Manchester, England, and they picked me up at the airport and took me to a hotel in Warrington outside of Manchester. During dinner, Ron explained he and his brother, John, had inherited the nursery from their father, who had been primarily interested in growing roses. Ron and John added shrubs and trees to the inventory, as well as annuals, and had built a retail store. I looked forward to seeing it in the morning.

Their entrance was through a small door, creating a rather negative first impression in comparison to what my training and experience had taught me. They needed a larger, better-designed entrance to create a customer friendly appearance.

As we entered the outdoor sales area, I saw the ground was covered with dozens and dozens of flats, eleven inches by twenty-one inches in size, several rows deep, stretching perhaps fifty feet long. They were filled with wonderful looking annuals in bloom. Although the color made a fantastic impression, the customers could only pick plants along the edge of this great display. I suggested we create some walkways so customers could reach all the flats. Otherwise, if the customer wanted a flat that was deeper in, it meant a sales person had to remove some flats to get to the one the customer desired. This was very labor intensive and awkward.

I also recommended that such flats should be on tables to make it easier for people to pick them up. I think Ron was taken aback by all my criticisms and recommendations. He didn't seem too pleased with me, and I thought my consultation might end right then. Nevertheless, he asked his staff to create those walkways right then and there. By the end of the day most of the flats had been sold, and I was invited to stay.

I suggested the Bents visit other garden centers in the UK and participate in the UK garden center organization. I told them about the International Garden Center Congress and encouraged them to attend the 1990 Congress in New York and participate in the pre-tour I was conducting. They agreed to attend.

My office arranged everything for the 1990, four-city IGCA pre-tour. I chose the locations and visited all the cities ahead of time, speaking to the garden center owners and managers so they would be prepared. I arranged for hotels and restaurants at each location, hired the buses and figured out the times and distances to create an accurate itinerary.

We started at Bachman's Floral Gift and Garden Centers in Minneapolis. Dale and Ruth, who knew me well by then, just smiled as I announced to the group, "I run a tight ship. It's important to be on time because we have a lot of great things planned." The group found out I was serious when one person went back to sleep after his wakeup call and, that evening, had to buy a drink for the entire group.

We flew from Minneapolis to Detroit, so I needed to arrange the flight. The rest of the travel was by bus. I also had to handle all the money, contact each participant, give instructions where to meet, let them know about the weather and what to wear, and arrange for special food when required.

When we visited Longwood Gardens outside of Philadelphia, I arranged for a recital on its famous organ for just our small party. We viewed chrysanthemums that were trained into baskets and Longwood's great selection of espalier fruit trees, accompanied by a wonderful lecture about their training and pruning. It had been so long since my first visit to Longwood in 1939 when I was searching for work. This time I was a well-established landscape architect, doing what I loved, and surrounded by wonderful colleagues and friends.

In Detroit John Darin, owner of English Gardens there in the Detroit area, wanted to include a certain well known restaurant in downtown where he knew the owner. I suggested they serve *Kirschsuppe*, the cold cherry soup my mother made us in summer. I thought it would be refreshing at the end of a hot day. I contacted my aunt Hilde Traube in New York to obtain the recipe and furnished it to the restaurant.

When the tour group arrived at the restaurant, the cook came out to see me.

"You know Mr. Wertheim, we have had the recipe for three weeks and have gotten very good at it." For a long time after that the soup was a popular dish on their summer menu. I thought it was delicious, and it brought back pleasant memories of my dear mother.

The IGCA tour offered the Bents the opportunity to see what could be done to create an exemplary and highly successful garden center, and, from then on, the Bents participated in the annual garden center tours. They started to make major changes to their garden centre. We have worked with them for a number of years, and during that time, the Bents and their two daughters have visited us in Alpine Meadows, which allowed us to develop a wonderful friendship. In 2007, we covered part of the outdoor sales area with a large Thermoflor greenhouse called Open Sky. The roof opens up almost completely so that the sky comes inside when the weather is good. This is quite dramatic and makes for an enjoyable experience. In 2013, they created a new parking lot, and in 2014, they will build a two-story addition with a checkout area boasting fourteen registers.

I think there are good merits to the "apprenticeship" method of learning a skill or trade, including in the garden center business. For this reason, I arranged for Ron and Wendy's son, Matthew, to spend a year working in the U.S. for Fred Hicks of Hicks Nurseries in Long Island, Tom Courtright of Orchard Nursery in Lafayette, and the Darins and Vespas of English Gardens in Detroit. This was a great experience for Matthew. Today, he is president of Bents Garden Centre. His three sisters are also involved in the business. Ron Bent and Wendy, their children, and their staff have made a major contribution to the industry in the United Kingdom. Several times Bents Garden Centre has won the title of "Best Garden Centre in the UK," a very special honor.

I was tremendously honored Ron and Wendy (as well as Warren Haskins) came all the way from England to attend my 90th surprise birthday party in San Francisco, hosted by my partner, Jack Klemeyer, and our assistant, Carole Haan. That's a long way to travel for sourdough bread.

Bents Garden Centre, United Kingdom

In February 1990, I gave an unusual presentation that turned out to be very meaningful for my audience, but it happened quite by accident.

David Rabenold of Colonial Tree Maintenance invited me for a two-day visit to Allentown, Pennsylvania, to give him advice about a possible new garden center. About two weeks before our planned meeting, he called again, asking me to give a talk on garden center design to his local nursery group. I agreed and requested two projectors and two screens for my "usual" presentation.

When I inspected the room I found only one projector was working. I did not have time to reorganize my slides for one projector. Many more people showed up than expected because someone had sent announcements out to the Penn State Nurseryman Association. I recognized many people in the audience: colleagues, clients and friends. I took a deep breath and chose a completely new topic.

After greeting everyone I asked, "Are we as good as we think we are?"

The answer to this question, I told them, was "no." They laughed, and then I told them why. The talk, completely off the cuff, went over very well. Many people there had heard my slide lectures before, and though it got good reviews, this talk evidently really made everyone think. Afterward, the founders of the East Coast Garden Centers (ECGC) Distributers approached me and asked if I would give the same talk to their group.

The ECGC was an important boundary-breaking group. East Coast retailers regularly flew to Oregon to spend several days visiting the growers and placing orders. Many growers of nursery stock are based in Oregon, especially near Portland, where the climate supports a great variety of plants. Until the 1990s, each retailer was doing this independently when several retailers decided they could make better use of their time and knowledge if they combined their efforts. Three Pennsylvania garden center owners, Bo and Linda LeBoutillier of Waterloo, Dennis Burd of Country Market Nursery, and Brad Snipes of Snipes Farm and Nursery in Morrisville, were the first to organize themselves into one informal buying group, traveling from one grower to the next to combine their purchases and to arrange for one delivery. This meant they could fill one semi-truck, rather than several smaller trucks, creating significant savings in delivery costs. Later, Don Riddle of Homestead Gardens in Davidson, Maryland and Eddie Anderson of McDonald Garden Center in Hampton, Virginia, joined them. They incorporated ECGC in 1996 and met a few times a year. Each meeting was at one of their garden centers, and they critiqued each operation during the visit as a way to help each other.

I agreed to conduct a seminar based on my talk on "Are we as good as we think we are?" and asked them to send me a list of the owners, managers, and assistant managers. I sent them all the same questionnaire, keeping the answers confidential. It was interesting that the assistant managers made the same complaints about the managers as the managers made of the owners — they were not listening to each other.

At the end of this successful seminar, ECGC asked me to coordinate their quarterly programs. I accepted the position and continued with it for a number of years until the group became so large it would have been a full-time job. But it was a great learning experience providing me with a deeper understanding of garden center operations, which was invaluable experience for designing garden centers.

I would be remiss not to include my relationship with the Bachmans of Bachman's Floral Gift and Garden Centers in Minnesota's Twin Cities, and this friendship emerged without our ever forming a contractual business relationship.

In 1958, Larry Bachman was one of a handful of people, including Jack Schneider, invited to form a retail group within the AAN. I was asked to serve on the committee as well, even though I was not a member since I did not own a nursery. I worked on this committee until 1972. Our frequent meetings resulted in a long friendship with Larry. He had been a pilot in a bomber squadron in Europe and kept up with yearly veteran's meetings. He told stories of his adventures in the war, and while I did not really share mine at the time, his honesty has inspired me to share this journey of my life in which we are now all bound together.

Since my brother, George, managed a country club in Minneapolis, I was periodically in the area. Larry and his wife, Louise, often joined us when we went out for dinner, as did their son, Dale, and his wife, Ruth. When Larry retired, Dale became the fourth generation to run the business, tracing a lineage back to 1885. Through challenges in health and circumstances, I've been very fortunate to also share in Dale and Ruth's lives. In keeping with the family tradition that Larry started, they've both given me great inspiration.

Larry passed away some months before this book came to fruition. He was very interested in it and read early chapters, and both he and Ruth encouraged me to see it through to the end.

With Larry Bachman and Susie Usrey in Washington DC to receive the Paul Ecke Award by the American Horticulture Society, 2011

In 1998, to add more acreage to Sycamore Grove Park, the city of Livermore, California, annexed part of Alden Lane Nursery, owned by my friend, Jacquie Williams-Courtright. As part of this process, nine acres of the walnut orchard planted by Jacquie's father were demolished for new housing. The city also eliminated all the nursery's parking as well as the main customer entrance on Alden Lane.

I had already done some minor consulting work for Jacquie, who incidentally is married to Tom Courtright, the current owner of Orchard Nursery and Florist in Lafayette. They make a wonderful couple. When this major challenge to her business occurred, Jacquie engaged WVK to help her.

Inspired by a country village in Burgundy, France, my partner Jack Klemeyer designed a two-story building and a new entrance for the nursery. Seventeen ancient valley oaks create a major attraction at Alden Lane Nursery, providing shade and graceful beauty. The biggest challenge was to design the buildings in such a way they would be woven through the trees and not interfere with the health of the oaks. The project took several years to develop. WVK prepared an estimate of what it would cost to build a new store, parking area, entrance, and outdoor sales area. The city of Livermore did not intend to compensate Jacquie properly, so she had to engage the services of attorney Ron Lopez to help find a solution. When we appeared before the planning commission, Jacquie drew great comfort from the many homeowners who supported the project. For years, Jacquie had been involved in city events and people loved her nursery.

Near the end of the design process, Jacquie's neighbor offered her two big horse barns. The barns were rolled across empty farmland onto Jacquie's property, where they became picturesque storage buildings for the nursery, after meeting the city's building department required upgrades.

It was a great ordeal, but Alden Lane Nursery is beautiful and functional, bringing in a growing stream of loyal customers as well as industry people from around the world. Jacquie is a friend, protector, and confidant. I can't imagine where I would be without her at this stage of my life.

PROFIT

august 2010
Ideas for a
profitable garden center

18
Bill McCurry on why you need
a Policy Book

24
Judy Sharpton quotes Five Man
Electrical Band's "Signs"

30
Holiday Discount Dos and Don'ts
with Sid Raisch

THE IMPORTANCE OF *Ernest*
How landscape architect
Ernest Wertheim created the
modern garden center
P. 26

TO SEE
ERNEST'S WORK
AT ALDEN LANE NURSERY
IN CALIFORNIA,
SNAP THIS TAG.

My career as a garden center designer was featured in *Green Profit*

Jacquie, her husband, Tom, and I were once stuck at the Salt Lake City airport because of a flight cancellation. During the four-hour delay, I told them part of my life's story. They were fascinated and the hours passed quickly. Ever since then, Jacquie has asked to hear the stories of my life and encouraged me to tell them to others.

In 2007, when she was president of her local Rotary Club, Jacquie asked me to speak at the Veteran's Day program. When I agreed, she casually mentioned I would have to give the four-hour spiel in thirty-five minutes. The brief talk went over very well and was quoted in three Bay Area newspapers. Jacquie arranged more talks including one in Redding, California, through a connection with mutual friends, the Hansens. Here I became acquainted with Dr. Steve Zlotowski, president of the Jewish Temple. In February 2012, he invited me to the temple and one of the local high schools to share my stories.

Dr. Zlotowski suggested he interview me, something I had tried a couple times when speaking to nursery groups at the ANLA management clinic in Louisville. As it turned out, Steve and I hit it off very well and were told that our chemistry created an excellent performance. With the support of Simpson University, I returned to Redding two more times, and we did a couple interviews during each visit. One evening we entertained a community audience of one thousand people for over two hours. On another occasion, about seven hundred students from several schools attended as part of a local "field trip."

Since my first military talks about mail censorship, most of my presentations have been about landscape and garden center design. In these interviews about my life, I have enjoyed sharing my experiences, but I always worry about the audience. Each group is different because they come from different backgrounds.

I also wonder about the four generations in the audience that I'm trying to reach: *Does this youngest generation wish to hear stories about a concentration camp or about* Kristallnacht? *What do I include, what would be most significant to this audience in the limited time that I have?* And this is where Steve and I have trusted one another, to both lead and follow, as the interview unfolds.

I am often told that today's youth doesn't know much about the history I have lived through, and it is important to share my first hand experiences with them. If I can assist in educating them about the discrimination and inhumanity that have shaped my time, maybe it will be less likely such savagery will find willing accomplices in the future. When I am no longer here to be interviewed, hopefully this book will continue to share my story and the events of my era. I hope people will take away that they should not generalize and stereotype a group based on the actions of one or two individuals; it is important to develop personal relationships with people. Also, if people pay more attention to the plants and landscapes around them, then the world can truly be a more beautiful place.

CHAPTER 17

A Senior Plantsman and Statesman

Orchid X Doritaenopsis 'Dorado' (orchid)

In 1996, Margrit and I traveled to South Africa for that year's International Garden Center Association Congress. We were excited and expected this to be a once-in-a-lifetime experience, so we allowed for an extra week in Cape Town afterwards. I was especially interested in the horticulture since many of the plants in California gardens come from South Africa, such as *Gerbera jamesonii* (Transvaal daisies) in the sunflower family, or *Clivia miniata* (Natal lily or bush lily). Many bulb plants come from South Africa as well.

The first leg of our trip took us to New York, where we stayed with Fred and Marilyn Hicks on Long Island. Marilyn and Margrit took a long morning walk along the Long Island beaches overlooking the

Atlantic Ocean, while Fred and I had a consultation. That evening we took the Hicks out for dinner and to *River Dance* at Radio City Music Hall. It was Margrit's first visit to New York City since we had been there together right after I became an Army officer in 1943.

We arrived in Johannesburg a couple days before the conference was to begin. Local nursery owners met us at the airport and were very kind. They were quite protective, vowing to look after us during our entire stay. It seemed a bit much, but they assured us it was necessary. On the way from the airport, we could easily see expansive collections of oddly angled corrugated tin roofs, the slums around the city.

We were told not to go to certain places and only to engage one particular taxi company. Warren Haskins' cell phone was taken right out of his hands in the Johannesburg airport. We did not feel afraid, but the extent of the poverty was beyond our naïve view of the world. I had seen some tough goings in my life, but this was new to me. It was two years after the end of Apartheid and Nelson Mandela's election as president. There was a lot of hope in the air among our hosts.

In contrast to the crowded and dusty tin houses, our Holiday Inn and the nearby shopping center were just as modern as any in San Francisco. Everyone in the shops was very friendly, although guards stood at the entrances. Our hotel restaurant had many more waiters than required, but we discovered this was to meet the country's goal to employ as many people as possible. Even if they did not make much money, something was better than nothing. The waiters were very anxious to keep busy. They would take your glass of orange juice or plate of food away from you if you stopped drinking or eating, even if you were far from done.

On our first full day we went to a great museum that depicted the country's history. Our tour bus leader was Mike Gibbons of Life Style Family Garden Center in Johannesburg. He was very knowledgeable, and during the next few days, we had one very memorable, private conversation that fostered a close friendship. That evening we met in the home of one of the organizers, where they had set up a big tent in their back garden in which we had dinner and enjoyed performances by traditional South African singers. A speaker briefed us about Mr.

Mandela and his vision for the country. It was a most impressive evening, and we learned a lot.

The tour included a trip to the capital, Pretoria, which had many Jacaranda trees in full bloom, frosting the sidewalks with periwinkle blue from the fallen petals creating a lovely sight. At the same time, the Jacaranda, a native of South America, is regarded as an invasive species in parts of South Africa.

Jacaranda mimosifolia (Blue Jacaranda trees) in Pretoria

Our first stop in Cape Town was the famous Kirstenbosch National Botanical Garden, acclaimed as one of the greatest botanical gardens in the world. For the first time ever, I saw a clear yellow Clivia. It was a beautiful plant with its clumps of buttery, yellow flowers and waxy petals on stems above long, arched leaves. I put the person in charge of the Kirstenbosch hybridizing program in touch with Joe Solomon, director of the Saratoga Research Foundation. Joe worked for years on breeding of Clivias in his nursery called Plant Horizon. He created a beautiful yellow form and many others, which are being distributed by Monterey Bay Nursery.

Our group had flown to Cape Town from Johannesburg on three different flights, all departing at different times. A group of Germans were on the last flight scheduled to depart, which was delayed. By the time they arrived the scheduled tour of the botanical garden was over, and they were, understandably, very disappointed. I was able to negotiate the language barrier, and everyone agreed we would add an hour to our visit. This allowed them to see at least part of the botanical garden.

After the IGCA Congress ended, Margrit and I stayed at a quaint bed and breakfast in Capetown. The whole trip I had been hampered by back pain stemming from a mad dash through an airport just prior to our big adventure. Flying half way around the world and sitting in buses hadn't helped. The host saw me wince in pain, and I told her about my back. She introduced me to a therapist, who gave me a massage that worked miracles. While there, we visited my partner Jacob's sister, who lived in a very nice retirement community. We also toured the beautiful wine country. Our B&B was a completely private place with a small garden on a residential road and an automatic gate and two guard dogs at the entrance. Life was not simple in South Africa.

After our trip, I spoke with Mike Gibbons from Life Style Family Garden Center again at some international events. Eventually, he invited me to do work for his garden center, and I made several trips to Johannesburg. The last time was in 2008 when I was eighty-nine years old. While I was in South Africa the IGCA, during its Independent Garden Center trade show in London, awarded me a Lifetime Achievement Award. My partner Jack Klemeyer accepted it in my absence. I was very touched by this honor.

In 1984, the year I turned sixty-five, I had a good team in the office. I loved my work, and there were many interesting projects on our drafting tables. I had no reason to retire even if Social Security along with our personal savings would have been enough. We had just begun our work in Europe and our work with Fred Hicks on Long Island. Things looked good, and I was healthy. By this time, Margrit was enjoying regular trips to Austria to hike with her friend from Lake Tahoe, Shirley Allen. Traveling to Europe and building up our international business were exciting and proving financially advantageous. Garden center projects were rewarding, both in the design work and the satisfaction of helping people strengthen their businesses. Some of our clients had done extremely well following our work with them.

Margrit's favorite village in Gargellen, Austria, circa 2008

When I think about it now, I just enjoy working for and with people. Maybe work has become a part of me. Like any other activity it has its shortcomings and not every day is wonderful. In general, though, I love what I do. I guess that's the best answer for why I still work so much at ninety-four years young.

When I arrived in this country, working and earning an income was the difference between living and dying. My first job with Mrs. Stern in 1939 paid ninety dollars a month. I learned to live with few creature comforts. Buying a hot plate was a big deal, because it allowed me to prepare my own food. Buying a second hand bike was an even more important, providing me with newly won independence. While trying to secure an affidavit for my mother, I saved every penny I could. In those days earning money was always on my mind and working long hours was just what I did. My life was very simple: work, eat, and sleep, with my one outlet being meetings of the California Horticultural Society.

When Margrit and I were courting, we drove to the beach and went to movies and drive-in restaurants, all inexpensive dates. We always watched our pennies, but we had fun anyway. Then came army life, which was rough until I became an officer. Most of the first checks went to pay back what I owed to the nurseries and people who helped me get the Cuban visa for my mother, a visa she never used.

For much of my life, money was a worry for me, but somehow we managed. The fact that Margrit worked helped a lot. We lived a modest life, saved, and bought our first house. The cabin in Alpine Meadows was a huge financial commitment, and that's why we did so much of the work ourselves. Our youngest son paid his own tuition to attend UC Berkeley and also built his own house in Alpine Meadows. Our oldest son made his earning by selling houses. I think they both have enough to live on. Money is important, but being happy with your wife and children and spending time with them is much more important.

I am grateful to be active and relatively healthy at the age of ninety-four, but one of the consequences of a long life is I have lost many people so dear to me. In 2008, it was my friend of almost sixty years, Jack Schneider. It was Jack who launched my foray into garden center design and fundamentally changed my professional life. It was his friendship that I valued more. Who else but Jack would have tolerated my personal hygiene habits on the ninth floor of a tottering building in Mexico City?

Back in 1972, Jack and Stewart Wade sold Orchard Nursery to Tom Courtright. Stewart moved to Hawaii, but Jack agreed to hang around for a year to make the transition easy. Tom and Jack soon discovered their philosophies were different and amicably ended this arrangement. I got along swimmingly with both men so my world just got bigger. (Stewart took up real estate in Hawaii and at ninety-nine years old had no plans for retirement in 2014.)

In 1987, I was given the Jack F. Schneider Award by the Garden Centers of America, which Jack had helped form in 1972. It is the highest award given by the GCA to "an individual who shows tireless energy, imagination, creativity, generosity, and dedication to the betterment of the garden center industry." I was very honored by what the award said about my contribution to the industry, but it meant even more that it bore Jack's name.

Jack's friendship remained dear to me, and it did not end once he sold the nursery. Jack had taken a Cordon Bleu cooking class in France in the 1960s. When he opened a small shop in Orinda to sell cooking supplies and offer cooking classes, WVK helped remodel the store.

After three years he sold the shop and started a cooking school at his home in the redwoods in Timber Cove. He advertised well, and people came from all over the United States for a three-day weekend of culinary education and delights. I helped in the beginning with some of the housing arrangements and whatever else Jack needed to support his school. For one session, he invited Julia Child, and I was assigned to pick her up at the airport. Even my mother could never have predicted I would chauffeur a pioneering celebrity chef. Julia was a delightful person. By now, you might be expecting that after our chance meeting I would design a garden for her, but that never happened.

For so many years friends enjoyed visiting Jack in Timber Cove, savoring his specialties: abalone sandwiches and huckleberry pie, always served on his beautiful blue dishes. How I wish we could have just one more meal together. I miss him very much, but I am comforted because I often feel like he's still with me.

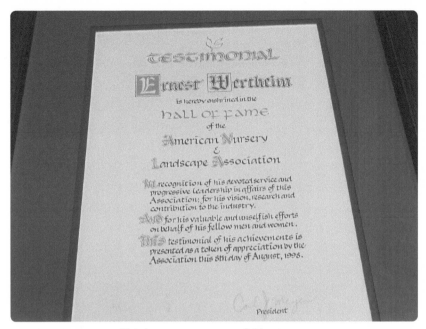

This honor means an awful lot to me.
I cherish it more than any other I have received.

Awards are very humbling, and I have been grateful to receive many over my long career. One of the most recent honors came in June 2011. The American Horticultural Society (AHS) had a special ceremony and banquet at their beautiful headquarters at River Farm along the Potomac River in Alexandria, Virginia. I received the Paul Ecke Jr. Commercial Award, given to an individual or company whose commitment to the highest standards of excellence in the field of commercial horticulture contributes to the betterment of gardening practices everywhere. Paul Ecke Jr. is often called the poinsettia king, having hybridized the plant in Southern California and eventually transforming it into the country's best selling potted plant. The AHS names all its awards for renowned horticulturists. Accompanying me was Sunny Scully Alsup, my protégée from so many years ago when I consulted with her father, owner of the Jung Seed Company. She was a teenager back then, and on the eve of this ceremony she was a successful, retired, landscape architect.

A number of other friends also attended. One of them was Katy Moss Warner, who was in charge of all horticulture at Disney World and is now an emeritus retired executive of the American Horticultural Society. Dale and Ruth Bachman brought Dale's father, Larry, who wanted to be there despite his failing health. That meant a lot to me. I am blessed to have such good friends of many different ages.

As the final pages of this book draw near, it is now over eighty years since I went away to Ahlem to begin my college studies. I guess the awards remind me how true the landscape architecture star has steered my course and how faithful I have been in my journey.

In 2012, I returned to the *Gartenbauschule* in Ahlem. The local government in Hannover, in which Ahlem is located, decided to create a museum inside one of the original *Israelitische Gartenbauschule* buildings to commemorate the school and inform people of the atrocities committed by the Hannover Nazi government against the Jewish people. I was invited to fly to Hannover and visit with the staff for two days. A group took me through the old buildings and also through the greenhouses. I felt quite a nostalgic tug. My time there had been fairly happy, full of learning and hope for my goal of coming to America. But things changed after I left in 1937. The school became a private school for Jewish boys and girls in the Hannover region when it was illegal for them to attend public school. Then I learned how the Nazis closed the school and converted it to Jewish prison camp to hold and transport the Jewish men, women and children of Hanover and Hildesheim to concentration and extermination camps near Riga, Latvia. It also held people from Lodz, Poland in transit to other concentration camps. The Gestapo took over Herr Rosenblatt's office, and in 1943, Leo Rosenblatt, his wife, Margaret, and his children, Ruth and Gerhard, were deported to Theresienstadt concentration camp. In 1944, Leo was transported to Auschwitz and killed.

I didn't like to think of the college, a place so dear to me, being used in this terrible way. Inside the main building, they had assembled all kinds of photographs and newspaper clippings. Hearing about Herr Rosenblatt was terribly difficult, but my hosts were wonderful and helped me get my mind out of the past. It also helped that a horticultural school is once again in operation, but on much smaller acreage.

They interviewed me for nine hours and took me out for lunch and dinner and to meet some government officials. Everyone was very kind to me and most pleased, because I added a lot of information that they did not know. I was invited to participate in the opening of the museum in 2014, at which I presented the first edition of this book.

For my remarks, I did not elaborate on the details of what Hitler did. Others who spoke during the ceremony and the museum itself gave voice to those horrible truths. The people listening were not responsible for what happened, but they do need to know about it and learn from it. Rather, I wanted to encourage the younger generations to have a positive outlook. The *Gartenbauschule* gave me the skills and training to be successful, for which I am eternally grateful. However, I could not have done it without the deepest kindness of many people, including a great many strangers. I wanted (and want) people to know how important it is to recognize that everyone is a human being who needs our understanding, respect and sometimes, our help.

Afterword

Primula suffrutescens (Sierra primrose)

I love my country. I believe there is always a chance to succeed in the United States, both for the people born here and for its immigrants. Education is highly important, but it does not have to be a university education. We need trained people in various fields, so many of which include the skilled use of our hands: aquatics, carpentry, plumbing, painting, landscaping, floristry, concrete work, welding, and stone masonry. In any endeavor, I believe it's important to work beyond expectations and always be on time.

If I was asked to give advice to new immigrants I would say learn the English language and the American culture. Learn to take responsibility, work hard, and become a leader. Give more than you take. I admire what I see as an important American ethic: being willing to help others. I saw this often in Alpine Meadows in the aftermath of storms and the big avalanche. People banded together and helped. People were not selfish. I feel this is the real American way.

Some people say the close personal connections I make with people don't occur anymore. Perhaps this is true, but one must make an effort. Relationships are always there to be made. At conventions and other large meetings, I always choose an empty table at breakfast even though it would be easier to sit with friends. I want to give others the opportunity to ask me questions, seek my advice, and direct our breakfast conversation. Much of our quality of life is making new friends and making connections so that the work we do is more fulfilling.

To this day I love to teach, to influence young people to make good choices, to make people into gardeners, and to help garden center owners succeed. At ninety-four years old, my role today is primarily as an elder statesman of the nursery industry. There are always young people who want my advice, and I enjoy getting to know them and helping if I can. This is the reason why I participate in the American Society of Landscape Architects mentoring program, supporting young landscape architects who are looking for work or who have a job but need to learn more about the profession. I have attended all the meetings for the past two years and have hosted individual sessions in my office.

I have a dream to create a lovely garden of native plants in Bear Creek adjacent to the pond, a place where residents and members of the Bear Creek Association can learn to identify the High Sierra plants growing in the valley. Wertheim Glen exists, but it is not yet really developed. If I ever retire, I'll probably realize my dream with more wild flowers and other native plants, leaving behind a garden legacy in our beautiful mountains. Both of our sons live in Alpine Meadows and our grandson lives in Truckee. The garden will be there for them as well as anyone else who cares to wander down the path.

With my bride, Alpine Meadows, 2006

On the upper part of the mountain in Alpine Meadows there is a steep slope that is covered with striking *Primula suffrutescens* (Sierra primroses). The perennials, endemic to California, come out after the snow has melted, which, depending on the season, is in mid-July or early August. Margrit, our two sons, and I for many years enjoyed walking up the mountain and looking at the native flowers, whose names we all learned, that would change from spring through summer and into fall. These family hikes brought us great pleasure, and we looked forward from year to year to admire nature in Alpine Meadows.

It is on the mountain, among the primroses, where both Margrit and I would like to be put to rest. We hope our ashes will provide some nutrients for these beautiful plants, just as my relationship with plants has nourished me. But it is the love and joy of my family — particularly for Margrit, our sons, and grandson — along with the gift of good friends and the many lessons I've learned that have humbled me and hopefully made me a better person. How lucky I have been.

Ernest Wertheim is a licensed landscape architect with seventy-five years of experience and principle of the firm Wertheim, Van der Ploeg and Klemeyer, based in San Francisco. He attended the Horticultural College Ahlem, Germany, and took classes at Dahlem Botanical Garden in Berlin and University of California, Berkeley Extension.

Ernest's experience as a landscape architect and horticulturalist is well known throughout the industry worldwide, he has been honored with numerous awards, and served many community and professional organizations throughout his life.

Ernest splits his time between San Francisco and Alpine Meadows, California, with his wife, Margrit. He finally gave up skiing at ninety-three years old, but still plans gardens, tells his stories, and has a good laugh with friends at ninety-four. He lectures on landscape architecture and designing garden centers and tells his stories all around the world. This is his first book.

Linda Parker Hamilton is the author of numerous books, including *A Century of Service and Friendship: The Story of the Rotary Club of Oakland,* and the centennial story of Diablo Country Club and many privately published histories, memoirs and biographies (StoriestoLast. com). She has also authored several Falcon guidebooks for hiking and camping (Globe Pequot Press) and features in the *San Francisco Chronicle, American Heritage of Invention and Technology, The California Magazine* and other publications. She lives with her husband, Doug, and her children, Ben and Max, in Oakland, California.